VIRTUALBOX MADE EASY

Virtualize Your Environment With Ease

By James Bernstein

Copyright © 2023 by James Bernstein. All rights reserved.

All rights reserved. This book or any portion thereof
may not be reproduced or used in any manner whatsoever
without the express written permission of the publisher
except for the use of brief quotations in a book review.

Printed in the United States of America

Bernstein, James
VirtualBox Made Easy
Part of the Computers Made Easy series

For more information on reproducing sections of this book or sales of this book,
go to **www.madeeasybookseries.com**

Contents

Introduction 5

Chapter 1 – What is Virtualization and VirtualBox? 6
    Virtualization Explained 6
    Virtualization Benefits 9

Chapter 2 - Installing VirtualBox 12
    System Requirements 12
    The Installation Process 13
    Installing the VirtualBox Extension Pack 18

Chapter 3 – The VirtualBox Interface 18
    VirtualBox Manager Interface 20
    Menu Items 21

Chapter 4 - Creating a Virtual Machine (VM) 28
    ISO Files 28
    VM Storage Location 28
    Creating a Windows VM 30
    Installing a Linux VM 54
    Installing the Guest Additions Software 63

Chapter 5 – Virtual Machine Settings 70
    Virtual Machine Status Icons 70
    Virtual Machine Console Menu Items 72
    General Settings 85
    System\Hardware Settings 86
    Display Settings 88
    Storage Settings 92

Audio Settings 93

Serial & USB Ports 94

Shared Folders 97

User Interface 99

Chapter 6 – Networking.. 100

Virtual Machine Network Settings 100

What is an IP Address? 106

Finding Your IP Address 107

DHCP 109

Host Network Manager 111

Chapter 7 – Preferences and Additional Features 115

VirtualBox Manager Preferences 115

Snapshots 119

Cloning a Virtual Machine 126

Adding an Additional Storage Controller or Hard Disk to a VM 131

Adding Other Hardware to Your VMs 142

VirtualBox Manager Tools 148

Exporting and Importing Virtual Machines 157

What's Next? 165

About the Author 167

Introduction

The world of IT (Information Technology) has come a long way in the past 5-10 years and one of the greatest advancements in this field has to be that of virtualizing computers and servers in order to save IT administrators a lot of time and their companies a lot of money when it comes to building their backend systems. And now we can even go beyond virtualizing computers and virtualize our networks as well.

Since virtualization allows us to run multiple computers (machines) on one piece of hardware it makes it's easy to set up multiple systems quickly and also allows a way for us to set up "test" systems that we can use for our labs to test out new software and operating systems. Then when we are done, we simply wipe out that test system and it was like it was never there.

Since virtualization is so common within organizations, it was just a matter of time before it was implemented on a smaller scale so we could use it on our desktops. Now we have software like VirtualBox and VMware Workstation that allow us to create multiple virtual machines within one physical machine (your desktop computer) and even let them communicate with each other via their virtual networks.

The goal of this book is to get you comfortable using Oracle VirtualBox without confusing and irritating you at the same time. I find that if you explain things like someone is a total beginner, even if they are not, it makes that topic much easier to understand, and that is the way this book was written—so that *anyone* can make sense of the content without feeling lost.

This book will cover a wide variety of topics such as creating virtual machines, sharing storage, setting up your network and so on. There is not a whole lot to using VirtualBox so it should be pretty easy for most people to get to or near to the expert level with the software. The examples I use will be based on version 6 of the software, so if you have a different version, things might not look exactly the same, but you should still be able to follow along pretty easily. Or you can simply upgrade since VirtualBox is completely free to use!

So, on that note, let's start making some VMs and virtualizing our environment!

Chapter 1 – What is Virtualization and VirtualBox?

Oracle is a company based out of Redwood Shores, CA that produces database software, cloud management systems and other enterprise level software products. They have been in business since 1977 and are most well known for their relational database management system. If you are familiar with Microsoft's SQL Server software then you should have a better idea of the main software that Oracle produces.

Even if you have never worked on a database and don't ever care to, you can still enjoy using Oracle's VirtualBox virtualization software to create your own virtualized environments with multiple computers that behave as if they were each their own physical machine sitting at your desk or in your server rack. It's also a great stepping stone to get you a leg up if you plan on working on a VMware vSphere or Hyper-V system in a work environment.

Virtualization Explained
Since you have decided to read a book on Oracle's VirtualBox software, then you must be at least somewhat interested in the concept of virtualization. But you might be wondering what exactly virtualization is.

Virtualization, in the IT world, is when you take something that would normally be a physical object such as a computer, server, network switch, storage array etc. and create a virtual or software based version of that object. That way you can take that virtual object and run it on multiple types of hardware and even transfer it between hardware. And when I say hardware, I mean a physical device like a server that supplies the virtual device its resources such as CPU\processor power, memory (RAM) and storage for its operating system and other files.

This process is done by a virtualization layer that runs on top of the physical hardware and is typically referred to as a hypervisor. You install the hypervisor software on to your hardware and then run your virtual infrastructure within that hypervisor. You can manage this virtual infrastructure with a client that you run on your local computer that attaches to the hypervisor over the network. Or in the case of VirtualBox, a client that runs on the same physical computer as the virtual machines.

Chapter 1 – What is Virtualization and VirtualBox?

There is a graphic provided by VMware (figure 1.1) that shows a good example of how this works. As you can see from the graphic, there is a physical server called the host on the bottom and then the hypervisor sits on top of that. Then within the hypervisor, you have the virtual machines (VMs) which are called the guests that run on that hypervisor (6 of them on the graphic). Then on the VMs you can install an operating system (OS) like Microsoft Windows for example and then install your applications within that Windows VM as if you were sitting in front of an actual Windows computer.

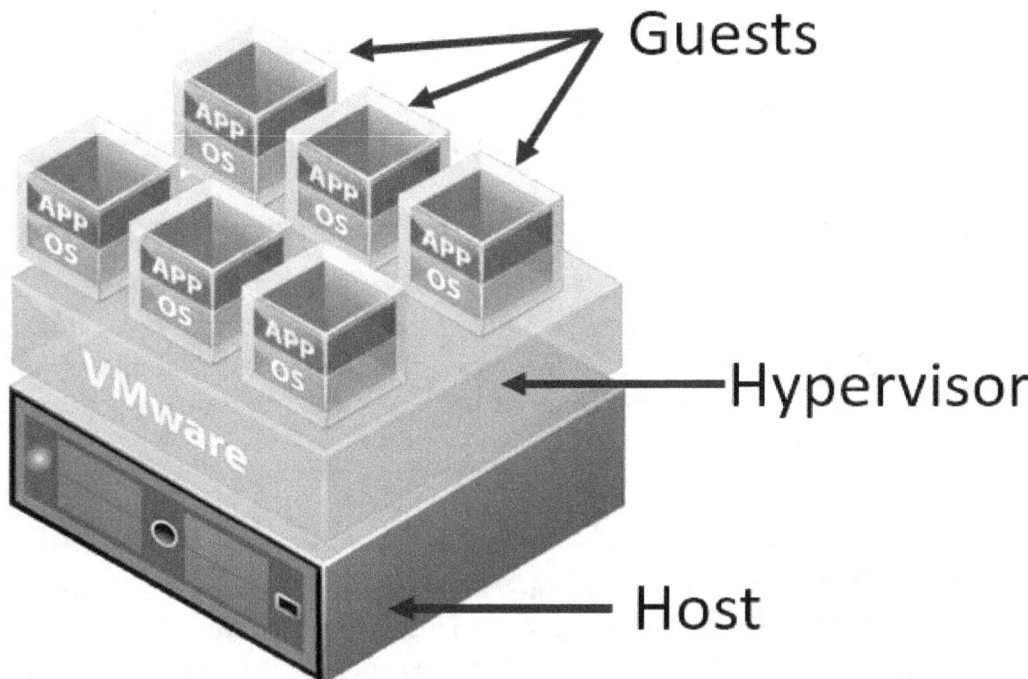

Figure 1.1

The VMs use the server's hardware resources such as CPU, RAM and in some cases, storage as if that hardware was directly attached to the VM itself. This is referred to as shared resources because all the VMs are sharing the same resources. The virtualization resources can even be shared among multiple physical servers allowing you to move your VMs around from host to host without having to shut them down.

Figure 1.2 shows a virtualized environment with three physical servers sharing the same virtualization layer, which will allow you to run your VMs on any physical server without the VMs knowing the difference. This way if you need to perform maintenance on a physical server you can move the VMs that are

Chapter 1 – What is Virtualization and VirtualBox?

running on that server to another server while they are still running and then shut down the physical server to perform your maintenance. The moving of the VMs is done over the network that all three servers are connected to.

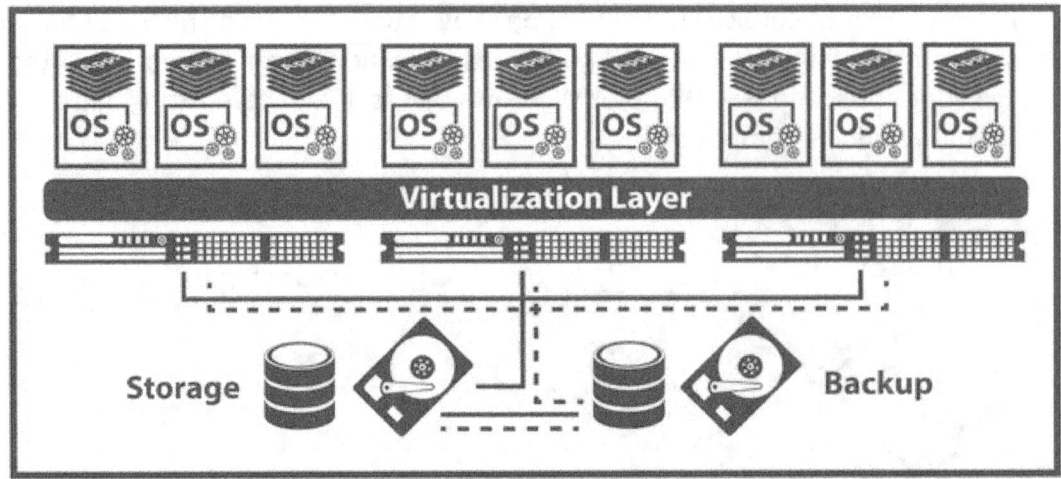

Figure 1.2

This is more of an enterprise level example of virtualization and VirtualBox does not work quite the same way, but I wanted to give you an example of how a more advanced virtualized environment like you would find at on organization works.

 One of the more important things to be aware of when it comes to virtualization is keeping an eye on your shared resources. It's easy to find yourself with slow running VMs because you are low on RAM or CPU power etc. because you are running more VMs than your hardware can

VirtualBox uses your computer's operating system as its hypervisor and the VirtualBox software is also installed on your computer's operating system. Plus you manage your virtual environment from that software installed on your computer. Think of it as an all in one solution on a much smaller scale as shown in figure 1.3. As you can see we have a computer that can be running Windows, Linux or Mac host with VirtualBox installed on that computer. Then the Virtual Machines are created within VirtualBox and use the hardware resources of the

Chapter 1 – What is Virtualization and VirtualBox?

host that has VirtualBox installed on it. Then you can install any supported OS that you like on the VMs running within VirtualBox.

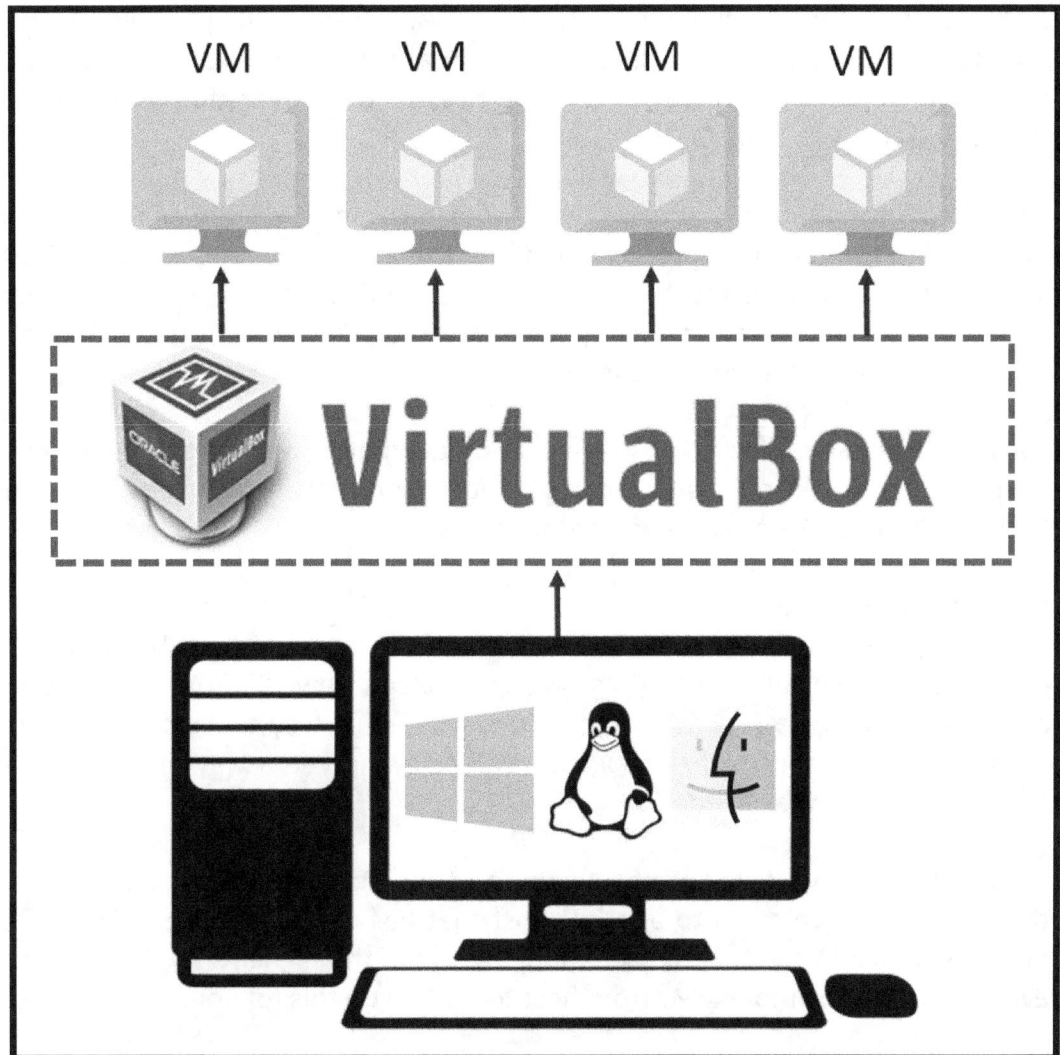

Figure 1.3

Virtualization Benefits
The reason that virtual environments are so popular is that there are so many benefits to having one, especially in a corporate setting. When it comes to advances in datacenter technology, virtualization ranks fairly high on the list of significant innovations.

Chapter 1 – What is Virtualization and VirtualBox?

Cost Savings

One of the reasons for using virtualization for your servers is to save money and we all know how people and businesses like to do that! By being able to run multiple virtual computers\servers on one physical server, it's possible to really save some money on hardware costs. A typical server can easily cost $10,000 depending on its configuration and if you needed ten servers for your business that would cost you $100,000!

Thanks to virtualization you can buy a super high powered server for let's say $20,000 and run ten virtual servers on it and therefore only have to pay $20,000 in hardware costs. In reality, though you would want to have at least two servers to run your VMs for redundancy purposes rather than having to rely on one piece of hardware running all your servers.

Software companies like Microsoft will also have better licensing deals for their operating system (Windows) when you run them on virtual machines rather than having a separate license for each physical server.

Computer Management

Having all of your computer virtualized also gives you the upper hand when it comes to managing all of your VMs because you can view all of their stats from a central location. All virtualization platforms give you a way to check things such as memory, CPU and storage usage as well as giving you a way to log into the console of each VM as needed.

If you have some VMs that are taking up too many resources on a particular host then you can move them to another host that has more available resources to even out your VM resource consumption. Many of the higher end platforms can even automatically move VMs from host to host to do this for you.

Experimentation

If you are the type who likes to try out new operating systems and software then VMs are a perfect platform to do this on. Rather than needing to tie up a physical computer to use for your lab work, you can simply create a VM, install an OS, and then start running your tests.

If you end up messing up the VM, then all you need to do is delete it and start over and it doesn't affect anything in your environment.

Chapter 1 – What is Virtualization and VirtualBox?

Hardware Management
You will see when I get into the process of creating a VM in VirtualBox that you need to assign hardware resources such as processors, RAM and storage to your VMs in order for them to be able to run. When you are creating VMs they will most likely serve different purposes, so the hardware requirements won't always be the same.

One of the best features of using VMs is the ability to add and remove hardware to a VM as needed. So if you notice that your VM that has 8GB of RAM assigned to it is maxing out its memory when running then you can simply add more RAM to it as needed to fix the problem. Of course you will need to have the RAM available in physical host to be able to assign it to your VM.

Backups
Backups are a huge part of keeping your infrastructure running reliably. Sure you can back up your files in case you have some type of data loss but what about the computer itself?

Virtualization allows you to back up your computers and servers by either backing up the entire computer itself as a file or series of files or creating what is called a snapshot which is a point in time backup of the state of a particular computer. If you have an issue then you can revert back to that snapshot and things will be exactly as they were when the snapshot was taken.

Chapter 2 - Installing VirtualBox

If you have experience installing software on your computer such as Microsoft Office or even a video game then you will have no problem installing Oracle VirtualBox on your computer.

All you need to do is go to the VirtualBox website, find the download page and choose the version that is right for your computer. The download link for VirtualBox is listed below.
https://www.virtualbox.org/wiki/Downloads

Once you get there, simply click on the link for the operating system you run on your computer and the setup file will then be downloaded to your computer. The version number listed below will most likely vary depending on when you download the software.

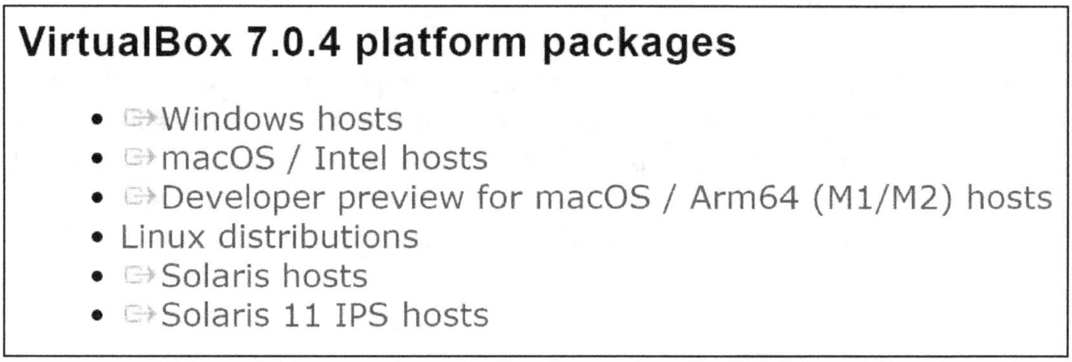

VirtualBox 7.0.4 platform packages

- ⇒Windows hosts
- ⇒macOS / Intel hosts
- ⇒Developer preview for macOS / Arm64 (M1/M2) hosts
- Linux distributions
- ⇒Solaris hosts
- ⇒Solaris 11 IPS hosts

Figure 2.1

System Requirements
Just like with any other software you install on your computer, VirtualBox has its own set of system requirements that your computer must meet in order to use the software effectively. Keep in mind that the requirements to run the software are not the same as what might be needed to run your VMs within the software.

For example, they say you can use any modern x86 Intel or AMD processor and 4 GB of ram but in reality, it's kind of a necessity to have at least 6 GB of RAM just to run Windows effectively. In my opinion, you should have 16 GB or more RAM in order to be able to run multiple VMs at the same time. If you only plan on running one or two at a time then you might be able to get away with 8 GB of RAM.

Chapter 2 - Installing VirtualBox

Going back to the processor requirement, you will need to make sure that your CPU supports *Intel Virtualization Technology (Intel VT)* or *AMD-V* depending on whether you have an Intel or AMD processor. These features allow you to assign CPU resources to VMs running on your computer. Most newer processors should support these virtualization features.

Since your VMs will be sharing the same hard drive space as your host, you need to make sure you have enough room to store the VM files which will consist of the guest operating system files and any software you install on your VMs. With today's huge hard drives, you most likely won't have any issues with storage space unless you are the type that likes to fill up your hard drives with music and movies etc. When creating a VM you have the option to use dynamic storage allocation which only uses storage on your host as needed. I will be getting more into this later in the book.

As for supported host operating systems, as in what you can install VirtualBox on they say they support Windows, many Linux distributions, Mac OS X, Solaris and OpenSolaris.

The Installation Process
Like I mentioned earlier, the VirtualBox installation process is very similar to any other software you might install on your computer. I will be installing version 6.0 on a Windows 10 host and then be using this version for the rest of this book.

Once you download the file and double click it to start the instantiation you will be presented with the Welcome screen that tells you what version you will be installing.

Chapter 2 - Installing VirtualBox

Figure 2.2

Next, you will be prompted to choose what features of the software you want to install. If you click on a specific feature, it will tell you what that feature does. I would just leave them all selected so you make sure you get everything you need installed. If you want to install VirtualBox to a different location than the default, click the *Browse* button and choose your new location.

Chapter 2 - Installing VirtualBox

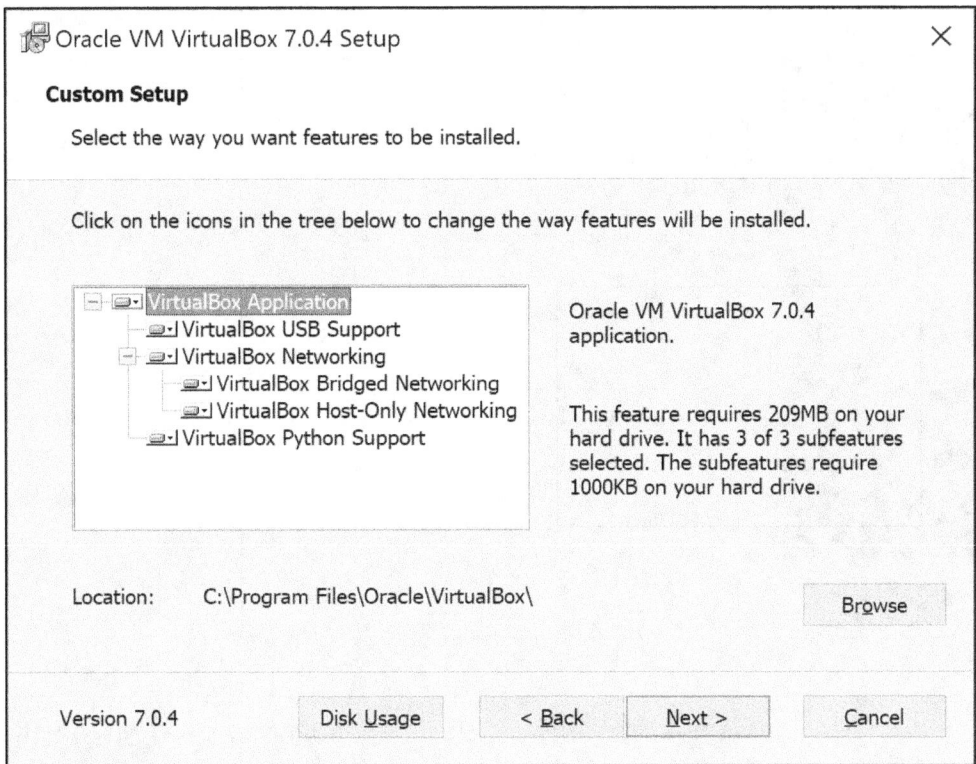

Figure 2.3

During the installation, VirtualBox will reset your network configuration so it can do its own network set up so if you are in the middle of transferring any files over your network or downloading something from the Internet you might want to allow that to finish before clicking on the *Yes* button.

Chapter 2 - Installing VirtualBox

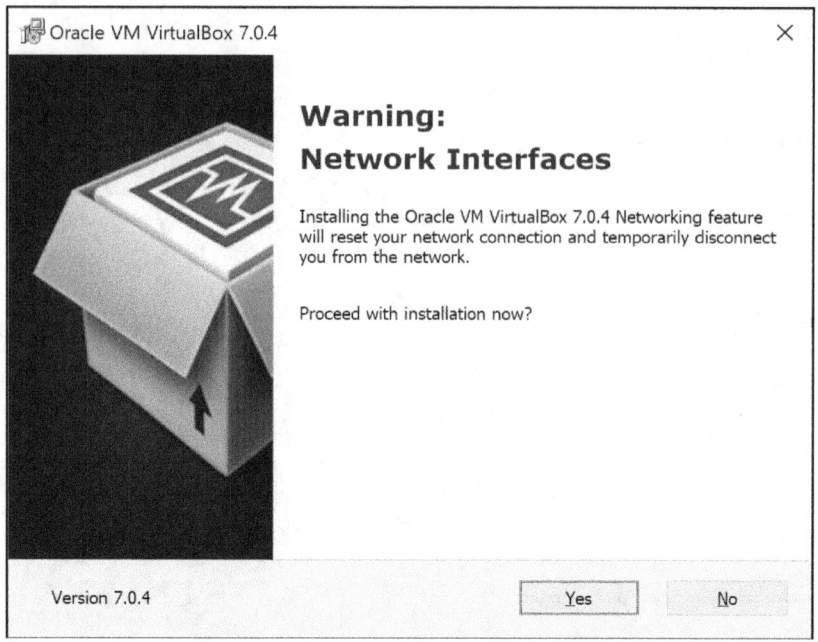
Figure 2.4

Then if you get a message about any missing dependances, click Yes on that screen as well.

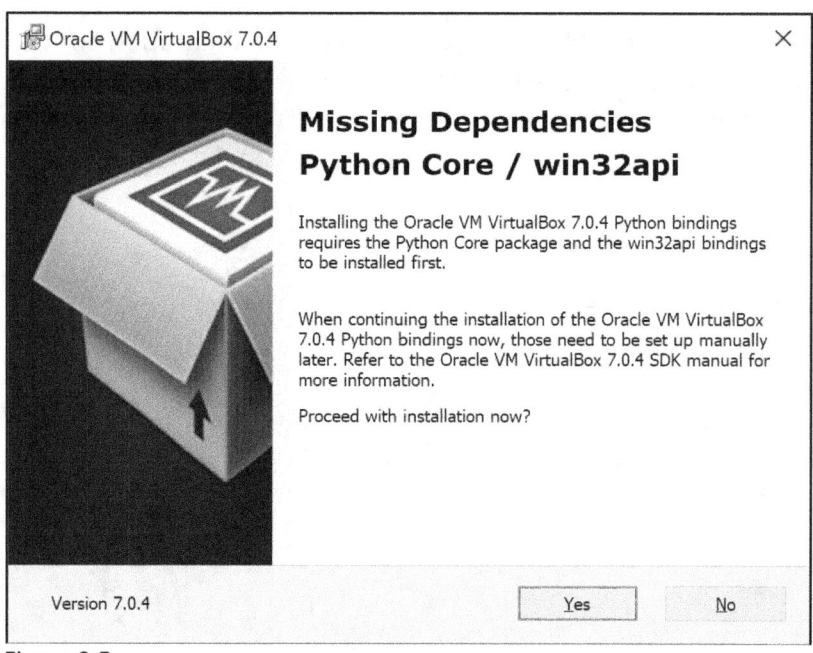
Figure 2.5

Chapter 2 - Installing VirtualBox

Once you have everything in order, all you need to do is click on the *Install* button to begin the installation.

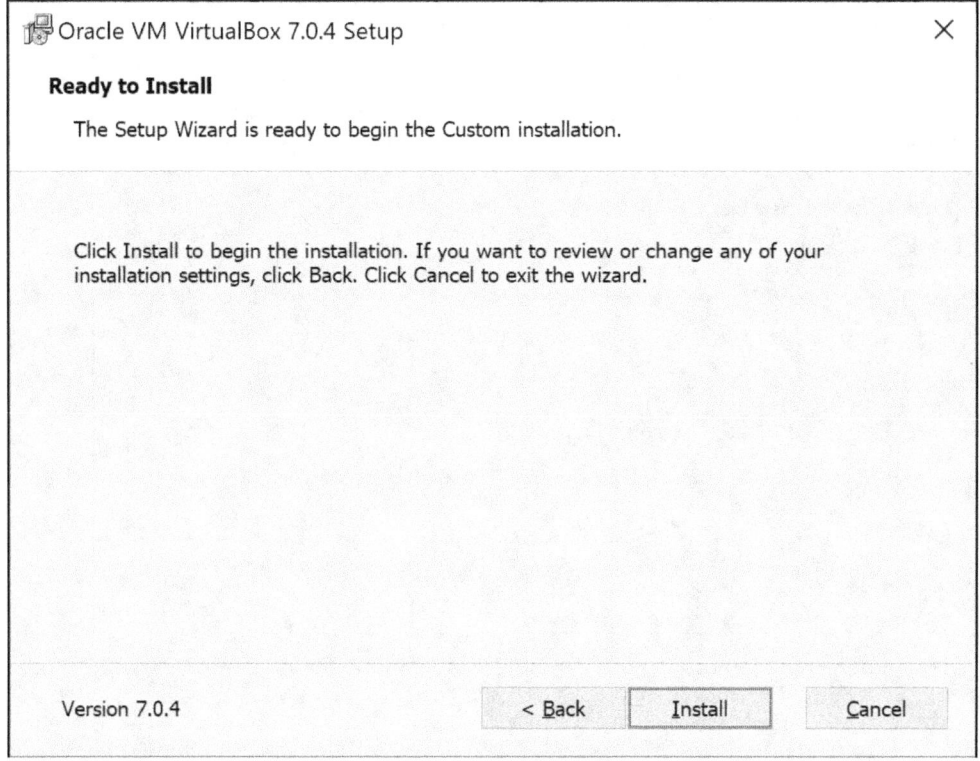

Figure 2.6

You will then see the installation status and it should only take a few minutes to complete.

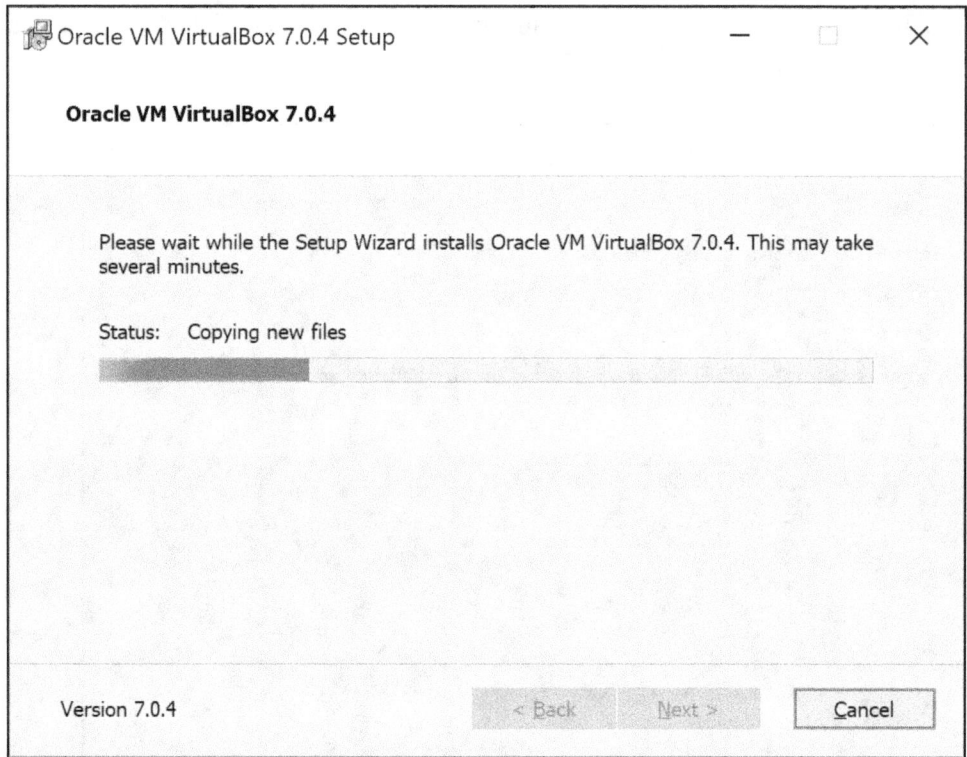
Figure 2.7

Installing the VirtualBox Extension Pack
When the main installation process is complete, you might be prompted to download the *VirtualBox Extension Pack* which is used to extend the functionality of VirtualBox by adding things such as USB 3.0 support and disk encryption. If you already have VirtualBox installed and are doing an upgrade it will ask you to replace your current version.

For a new installation, you can open VirtualBox and go to the *Extension* menu and then click on the *Install* button. But before doing so, you will need to download the extension pack from the VirtualBox website. This can be found on the same page where you downloaded VirtualBox itself. One thing you always need to check before installing an extension pack is that it matches the version of your VirtualBox software. So in my case, I will be installing extension pack version 7.0.4 to match my VirtualBox version.

If you already had an extension pack installed, it will ask you to upgrade, otherwise it will simply ask you to install it.

Chapter 2 - Installing VirtualBox

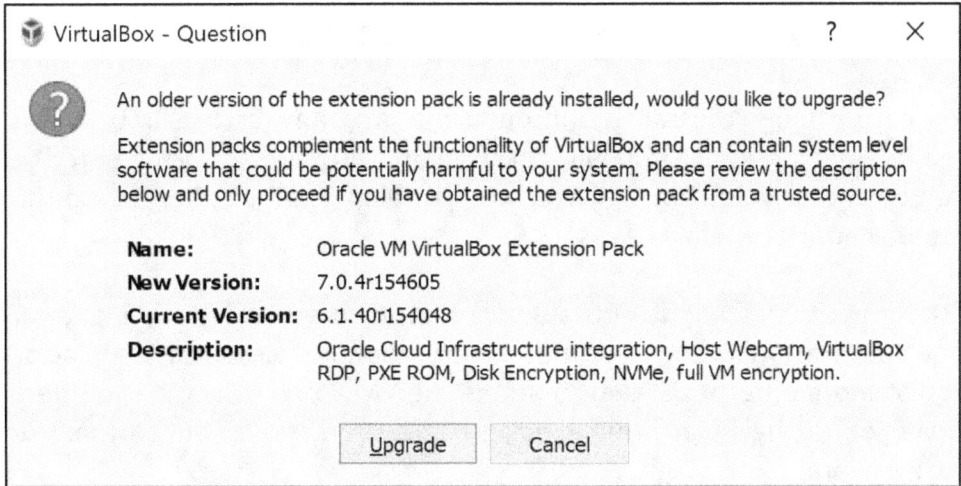

Figure 2.8

After the extension pack is installed, you will see it in the extension pack section in VirtualBox.

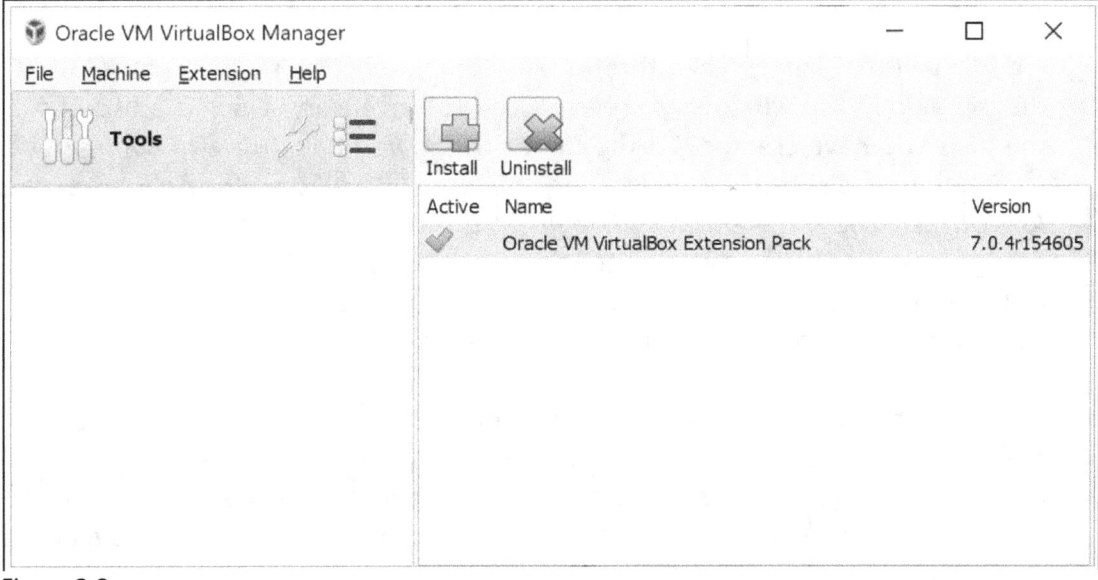

Figure 2.9

Chapter 3 – The VirtualBox Interface

Once you get VirtualBox installed and open the program for the first time you won't see too much because you will not have any virtual machines created yet. But once you create your first VM, you will be able to get a better idea of how the VirtualBox interface is laid out.

One of the great things about VirtualBox is that it is very easy to navigate and find what you are looking for. It's not a very complex virtualization platform compared to more enterprise level solutions like VMware. VMware also offers a desktop version of their platform called VMware Workstation but VirtualBox is easier to use overall.

VirtualBox Manager Interface
Even though you probably don't have any VMs created I want to go over the VirtualBox Manager, so you know what you are looking at once you do have some VMs ready to go.

The VirtualBox Manager has three main components as seen in figure 3.1. On the left side of the window, you have your VM inventory which is a listing of all the VMs you have created. To the right of that, you have the VM configuration summary that is shown for whichever VM you have selected from the inventory. As you can see I have my Windows 2016 VM selected on the left and its configuration summary is shown to the right. Here you will see things such as the installed operating system, hardware configuration, storage capacity and so on. I will bet getting into more detail about VM settings in Chapter 5.

Finally, at the upper right side of the window, you will be shown a small preview of that VMs local console screen. This is used to give you an idea of what is going on with that VM such as whether or not it is logged in or powered on etc. As you can see from my preview screen that the VM is running and has been logged into the desktop.

Chapter 3 – The VirtualBox Interface

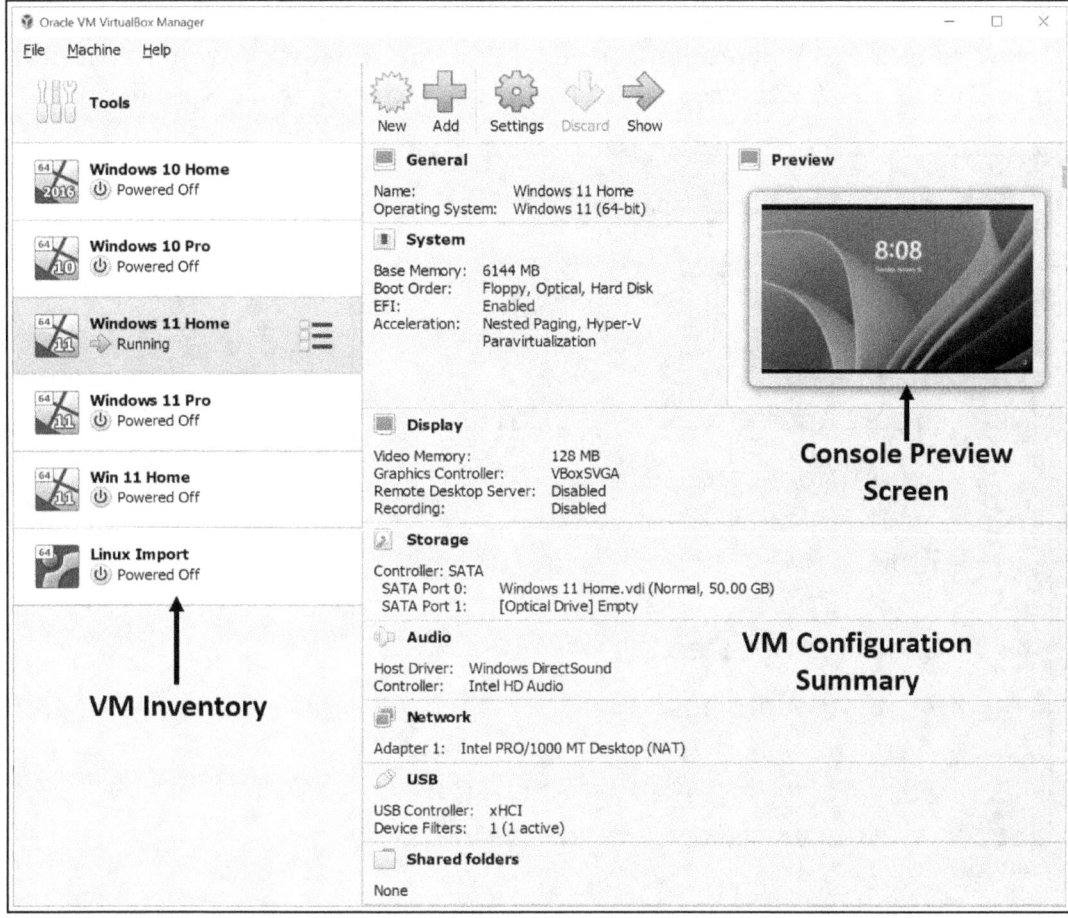

Figure 3.1

Menu Items

The VirtualBox Manager only has three menu items to choose from and I would like to now take a moment to go over these menus. I will be going over most of the items within these menus in more detail in later chapters, so for now I will just give you an overview of what you can expect to see here. Also, keep in mind that many of the actions you can perform from the menu items you can also perform from other locations within the VirtualBox Manager.

The *File* menu (figure 3.2) is where you will find things such as the VirtualBox Preferences, the import and export appliance options and all of the other management tools that are used to change various configurations within the software.

Chapter 3 – The VirtualBox Interface

While using VirtualBox you will occasionally be shown messages warning you about potential configuration issues etc., that you will just close out most of the time. The *Reset All Warnings* choice can be used to bring those warnings back.

Figure 3.2

The *Machine* menu allows you to perform actions on already created virtual machines such as cloning, moving, pausing, resetting them etc. and is also a place you can go to create a new VM or export an existing VM to the Oracle Cloud Infrastructure.

Show in Explorer will open up your Windows Explorer (Windows PCs) to show you the files that make up the VM that you have highlighted (figure 3.4). Remember that your VMs are just files and folders that are kept on the hard drive of your computer. This is the same for enterprise level virtualization like VMware vSphere except the VM files are usually kept on networked storage.

Chapter 3 – The VirtualBox Interface

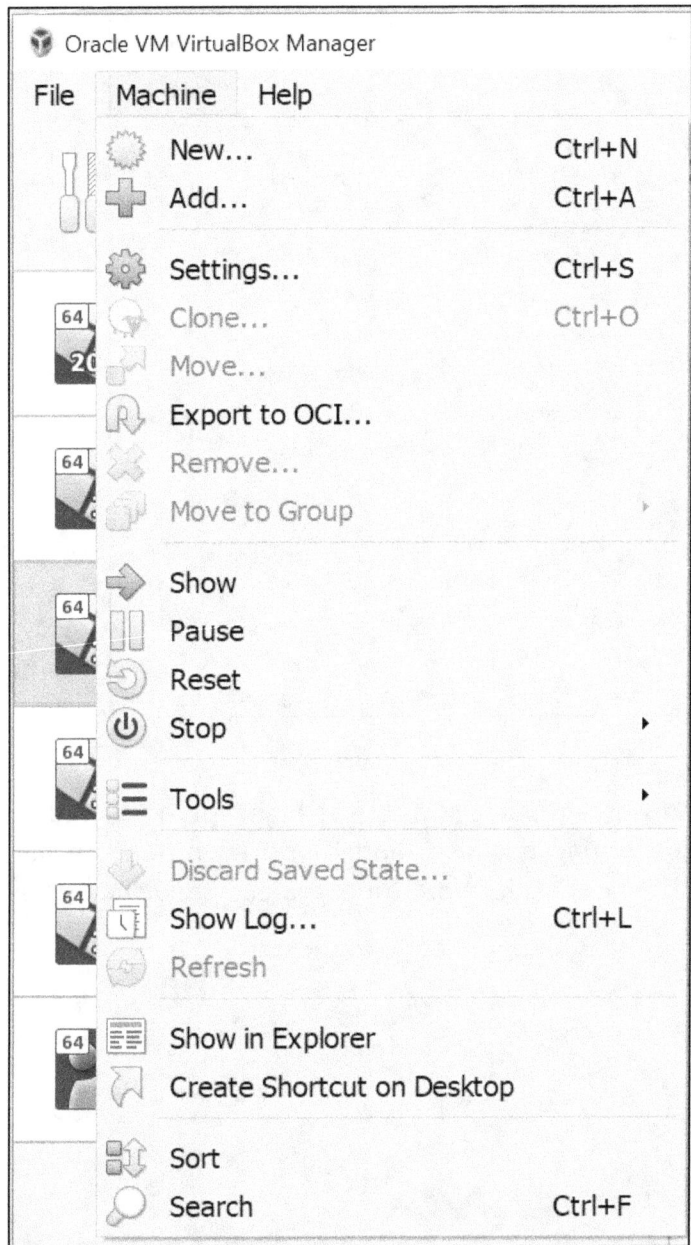

Figure 3.3

Chapter 3 – The VirtualBox Interface

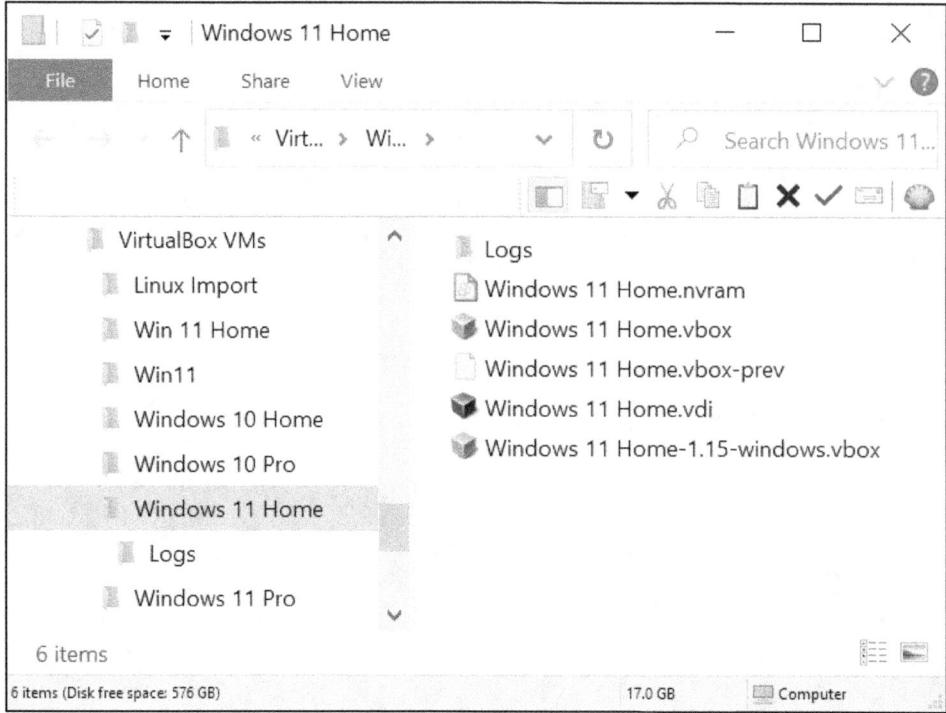

Figure 3.4

Show Log will open up the log viewer (figure 3.5) for the highlighted VM and you can use this tool for troubleshooting purposes and if you even need to have someone else do some troubleshooting for you, then you can send them these logs.

Chapter 3 – The VirtualBox Interface

Figure 3.5

Create Shortcut on Desktop will create a shortcut to the highlighted VM that you can simply double click on to open its console screen. If the VM is not running then it will start after you click on the icon.

Figure 3.6

Chapter 3 – The VirtualBox Interface

Finally, we have the *Help* menu and you have most likely used help menus in the past when using other software so you should have an idea of how they work.

Figure 3.7

Clicking on *Contents* will actually open up a help menu which you don't see too much of these days. Usually, when you click on help in other software it takes to you the software developers' website.

You can then browse the contents of the help menu or click on the *Search* tab to enter in a word or phrase that you are looking for help on.

Chapter 3 – The VirtualBox Interface

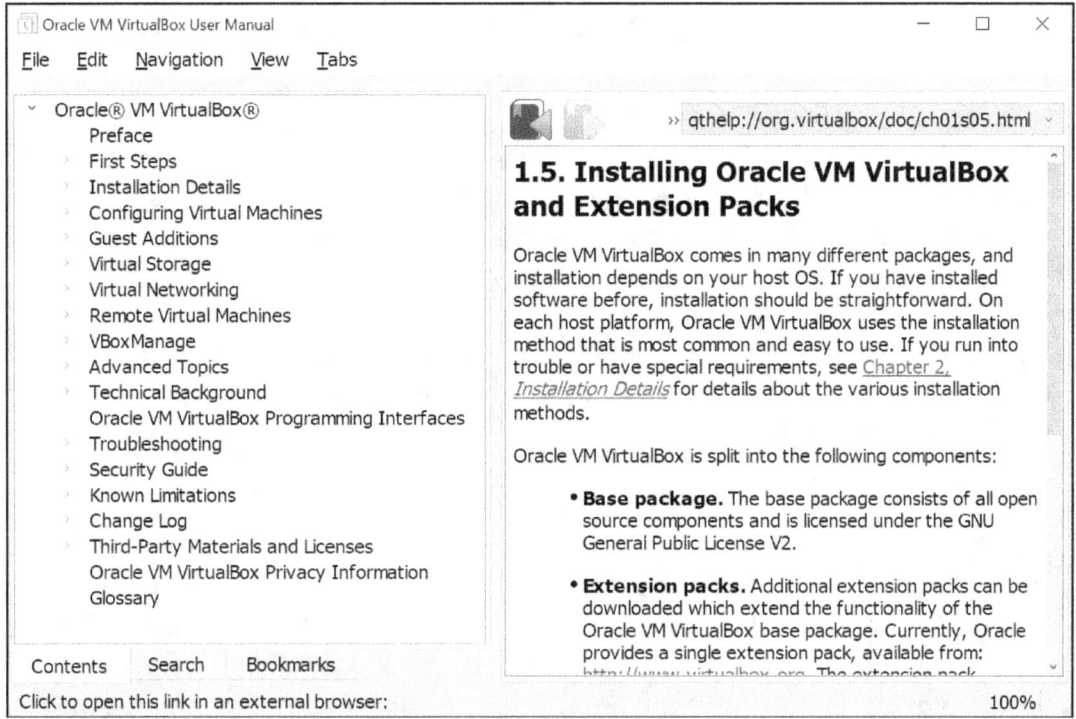

Figure 3.8

There are other help options to choose from such as visiting the VirtualBox forums where you can sign up and discuss issues with other VirtualBox users. Or you can visit the actual VirtualBox and Oracle websites from the help menu if you would like to read up on VirtualBox or other Oracle products. Clicking on *About VirtualBox* will tell you which version of VirtualBox you are running.

Chapter 4 - Creating a Virtual Machine (VM)

Now that you have a basic understanding of virtualization and have seen how simple the VirtualBox interface is, it's time to start creating some virtual machines and growing our inventory. This is where the fun begins, and you will see how easy this process is once you get started.

Before you create a VM you should have the operating system (OS) files handy otherwise you will have no way to install an OS on your VM and it really won't do you much good without one.

ISO Files
When installing an operating system on a VM, the easiest way to do so is by loading an ISO image file into your VM that contains all of the files needed to install the operating system. When you download an OS from a website, it usually comes in the form of an ISO file making it easy to download since everything is in one file. They are usually bootable as well meaning that your computer or VM can boot itself using the ISO image and then start the OS installation process.

It's also possible to take your existing operating system CD\DVD and convert it to an ISO file using third party software if you like. This way, you will have a bootable OS image file stored on your computer that you can use over and over to install the same operating system on multiple VMs. These ISO files can be quite large in size such as 2-4 GB so keep that in mind if you plan on keeping a bunch of different operating system ISO file on your hard drive.

Of course, you can always use your operating system CD\DVD with your DVD drive to install your operating system on your VM if you don't want to use ISO files. To do that, you simply mount the DVD drive to your VM and install your OS using the same method (discussed later).

VM Storage Location
Before you start the process of creating your virtual machines, you might want to take a minute to plan out where you will be storing these VMs since they tend to take up a bit of hard drive space depending on their configuration.

Chapter 4 - Creating a Virtual Machine (VM)

The default location for VM storage is **C:\Users\YourUserName\VirtualBox** VMs for VirtualBox running on Windows. If you don't have enough space on your C drive or maybe want to keep your VM files in a different folder then you should figure this out and maybe even make this folder before starting to create your VMs.

Figure 4.1 shows the properties for my VirtualBox VMs folder that stores my 7 virtual machines. These VMs don't really have much on them besides the operating systems installed and they still take up 158 GB on my hard drive so you can see how things can get out of hand if you create a large amount of VMs and also install a lot of programs on those VMs as well. I keep my VMs on my D drive since I have much more free space there.

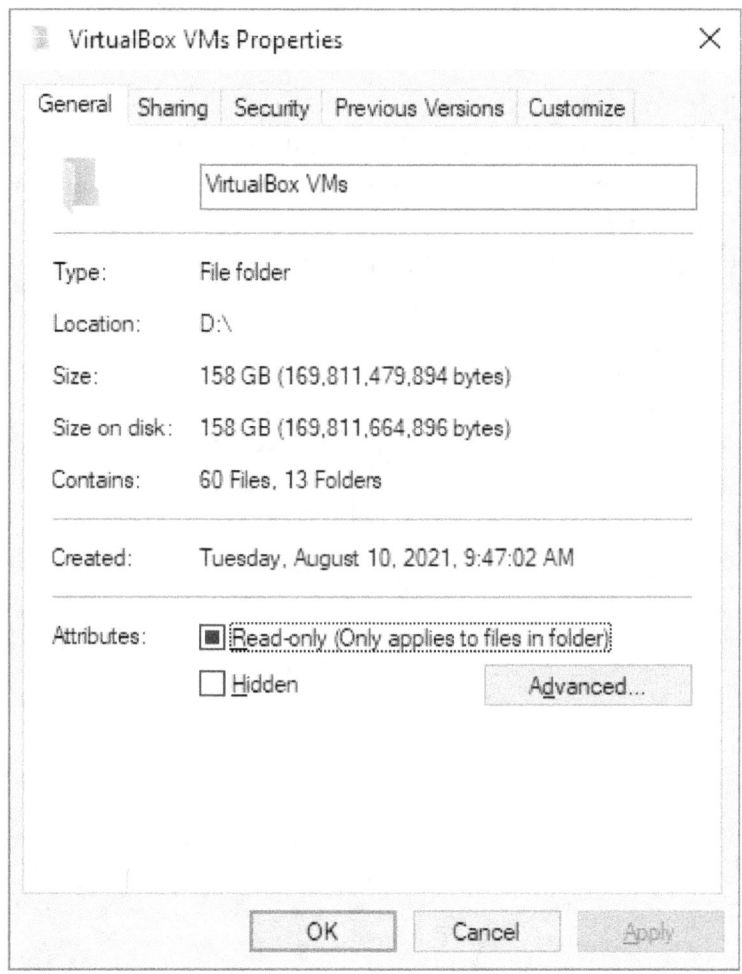

Figure 4.1

Chapter 4 - Creating a Virtual Machine (VM)

Thankfully we have the option of dynamically allocated storage to help keep hard drive usage down. I will be going over this concept when I start the VM creation process.

Creating a Windows VM

Now it's time to have some fun creating a new virtual machine in our VirtualBox environment. For this example, I am going to create a Windows 10 VM and show you the entire process for installing Windows itself. If you have installed Windows before then this might not be too exciting but for those who are new to installing Windows, this should be a good lesson for you. There is a normal VM creation mode and then an *Expert Mode*. For this VM I will be using the normal (Guided) mode and then in the next section I will create a VM using the Expert Mode.

To start the process I will go to the *Machine* menu and choose *New* or just click on the New button in the VirtualBox Manager. I will call my VM **Windows 11 Home 2** since I already have another Windows 11 Home VM and don't want to get things confused. Notice in figure 4.2 in the Machine Folder section how it wants to put the VM files in the default storage location?

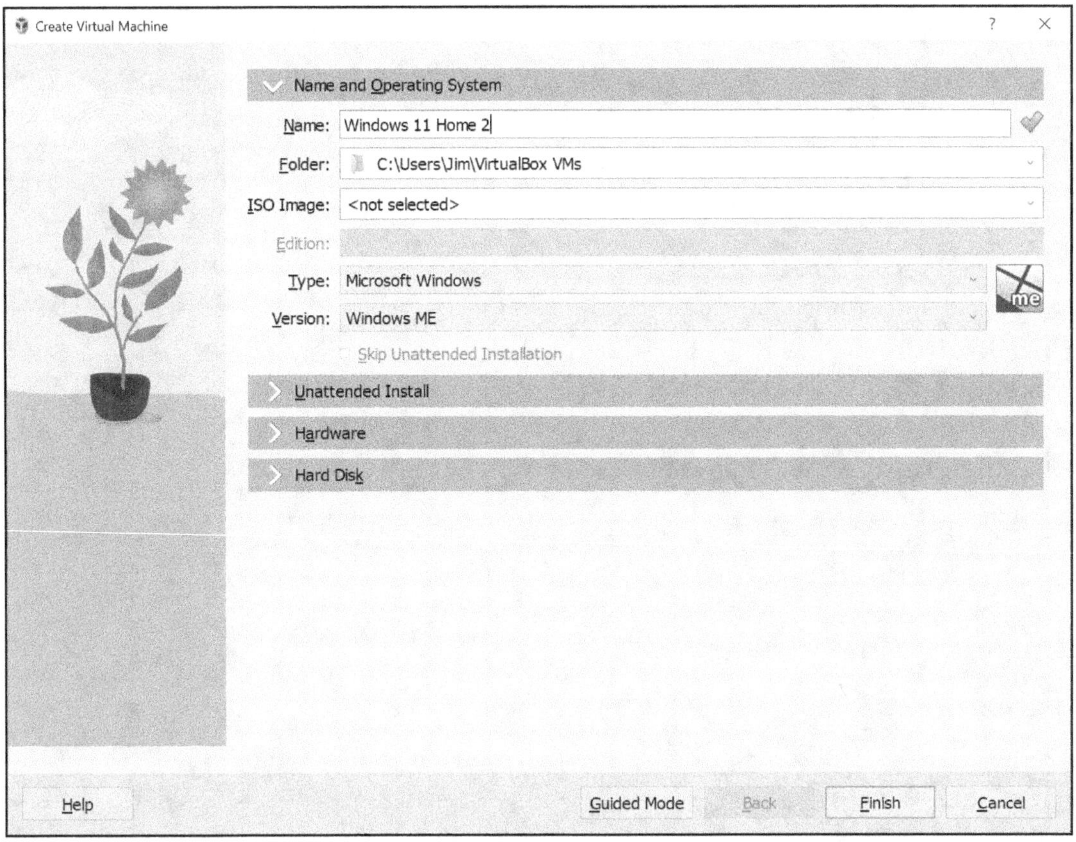

Chapter 4 - Creating a Virtual Machine (VM)

Figure 4.2

Since I don't want this, I will click on the down arrow at the end of the folder path and click on *Other* to browse to a new location. Then I will browse to my VirtualBox VMs folder on my D drive and then click on the *Select Folder* button.

I will then select my Windows 11 ISO file that I will use for the installation (figure 4.3).

When choosing the OS type for your new VM, you might run across a situation where there is not an exact match shown for what you are trying to install. When this happens you can just choose the closest match and you should be just fine.

31

Chapter 4 - Creating a Virtual Machine (VM)

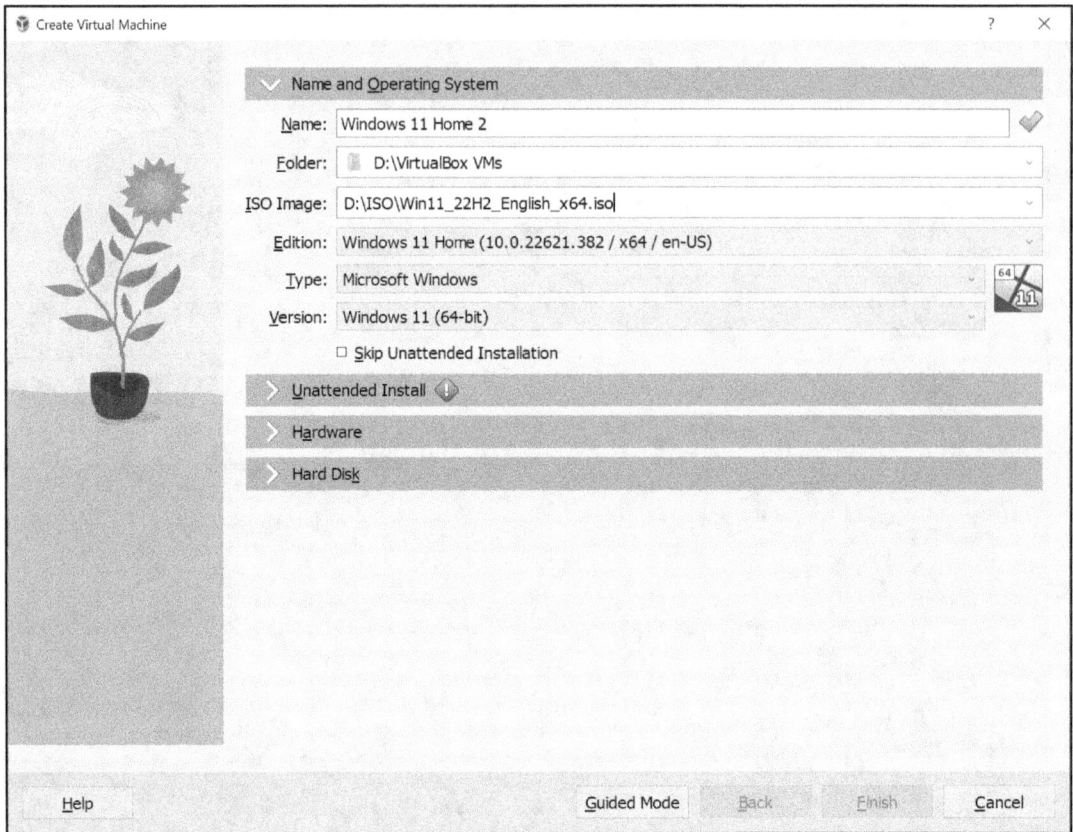

Figure 4.3

VirtualBox 7 does a much better job at reading the information from the ISO file to figure out what operating system it contains compared to previous versions. As you can see in figure 4.3, it detected that it was a Windows 11 ISO image and automatically filled in the *Edition* section.

The Unattended Install section is optional and can be used to preconfigure the new virtual machine with information such as a username and password, product key, hostname and domain name. You can also check the box to have the VirtualBox Guest Additions installed automatically. I haven't had too much luck with this working smoothly but by the time you are reading this, maybe they will have improved the process. If you don't want to use this step, you can check the box that says Skip Unattended Installation as seen in figure 4.3.

Chapter 4 - Creating a Virtual Machine (VM)

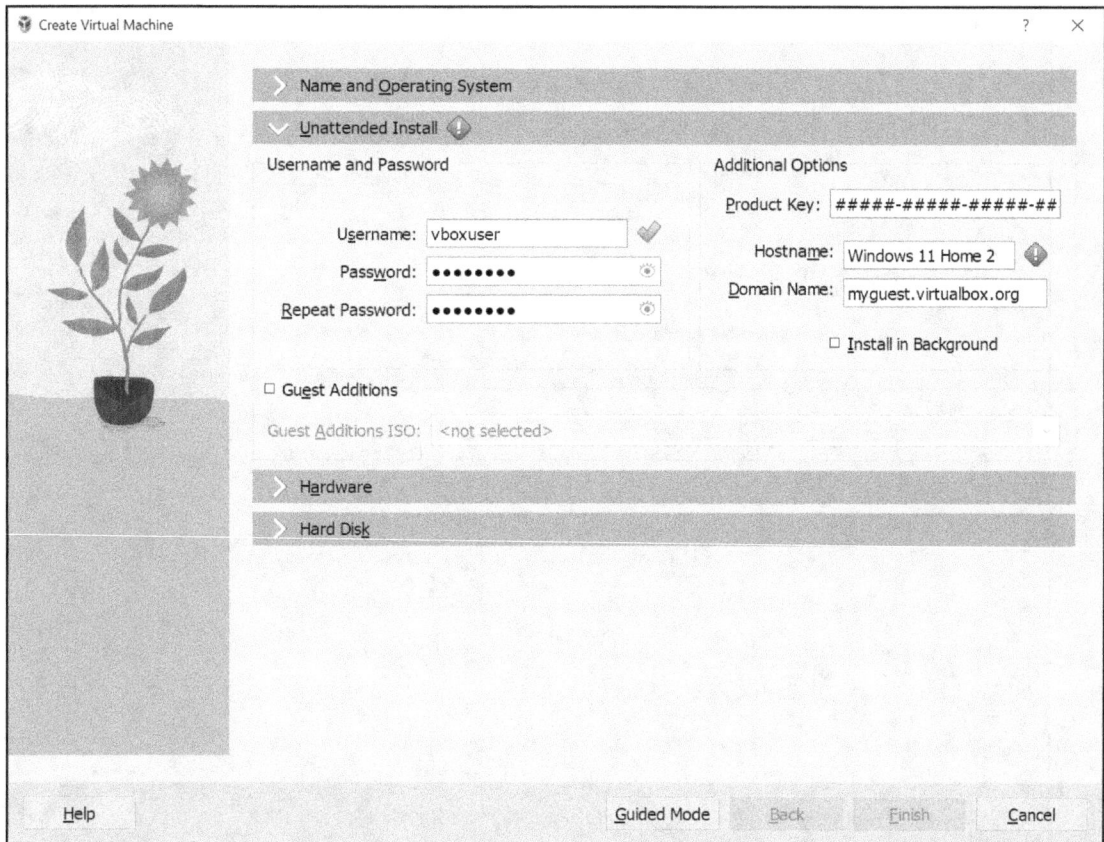

Figure 4.4

Next, I will be prompted to select how much memory and how many processors I will be allocating to my new VM. In this section, VirtualBox is referring to Random Access Memory (RAM) and not hard drive storage space. VirtualBox will give you a recommended memory allocation setting but I find that most of the time it's too low and should be increased. Just remember that this can be changed later so if you discover you need more or less RAM in the future it's easy to adjust.

For my new VM, VirtualBox is suggesting 4096 MB of RAM which translates into 4 GB since 1 GB = 1024 MB. When moving the slider to adjust the amount of RAM you don't have to keep it in increments of 1024 MB, but I like to anyway to keep things uniform. I am going to bump it up to 6 GB (6144 MB). I will leave the default selection of 2 CPUs since that is plenty for my needs. The values at the very right of the slider (32768 MB and 16 CPS) will vary based on the configuration of your host computer. Mine has 32 GB of RAM so that is way it shows 32768 MB for the maximum value.

33

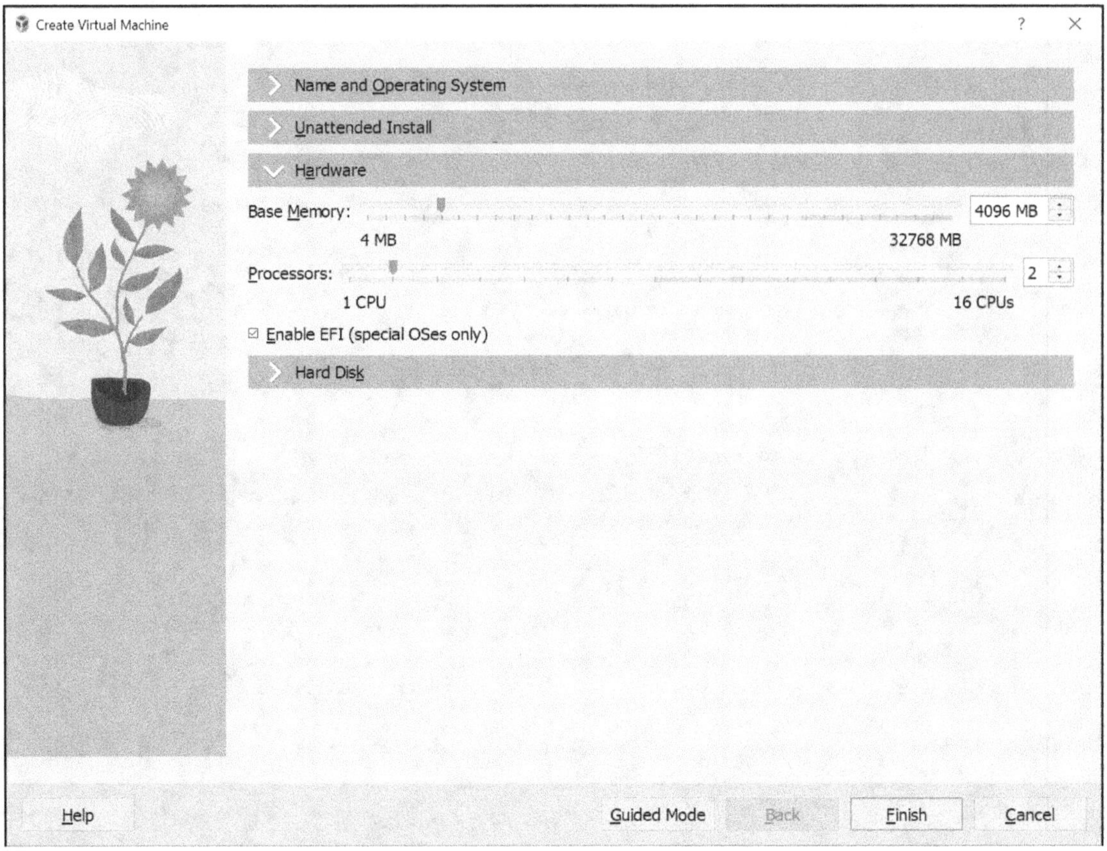

Chapter 4 - Creating a Virtual Machine (VM)

Figure 4.5

Now I need to choose a hard disk (hard drive) size for my new VM. Here I have three options as shown in figure 4.6.

- **Create a virtual hard disk now** – Here you can choose to add a new hard disk and attach it to your VM. VirtualBox gives you a recommended size based on the type of VM you chose to install (Windows 11 in my case).

- **Use an existing virtual hard disk file** – If you have a virtual disk leftover from another VM or one that you detached from an existing VM then you can use it for your new VM and run your OS assuming it has one already installed.

- **Do not add a virtual hard disk now** – You don't need to add a hard drive to your VM when creating it but you will need to add one later to install an operating system on unless you just plan on booting it with CDs to do things like run utilities or run a temporary OS that goes away when you shut down the VM.

Chapter 4 - Creating a Virtual Machine (VM)

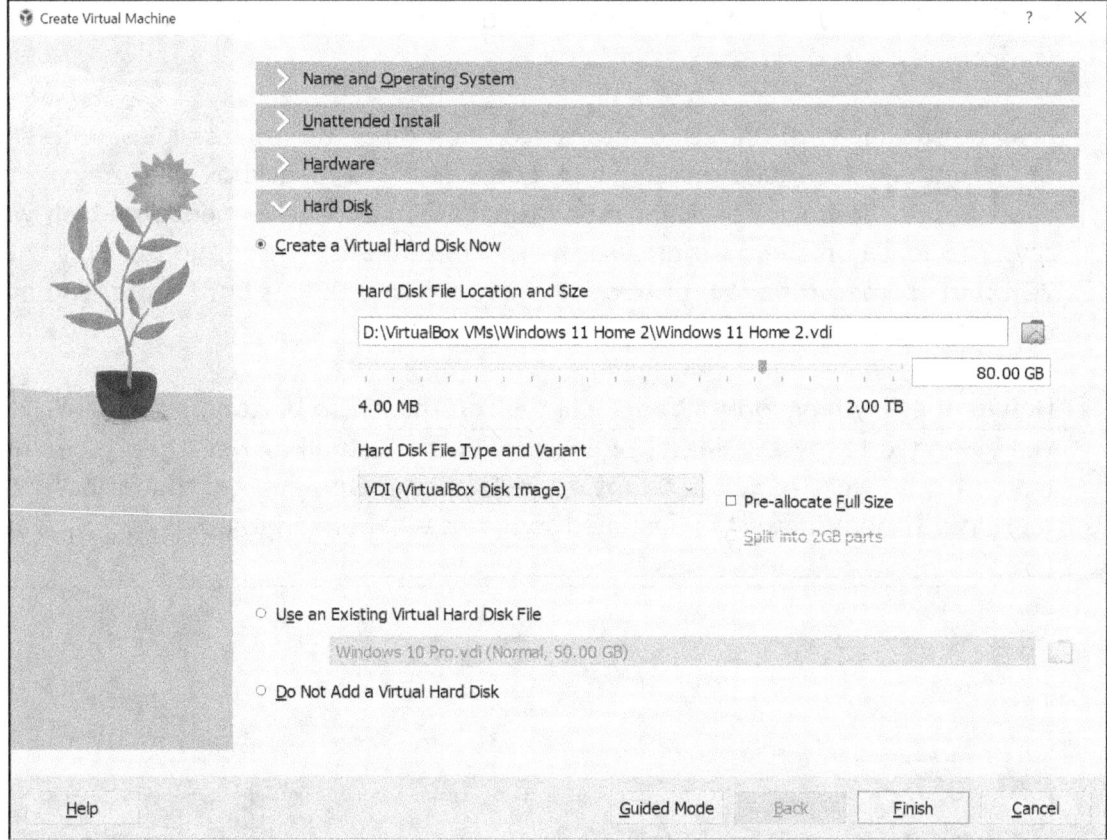

Figure 4.6

For my new VM, I am going to create a new virtual hard disk so I will choose the first option

For the hard disk file type and variant dropdown, we get six choices to choose from.

- **VDI** – The default VirtualBox disk image type.

- **VHD** – A VM disk format that can also be used with Microsoft Hyper-V.

- **VMDK** - A VM disk format that can also be used with VMware products.

- **HDD** – Used for the Mac Parallels virtualization software.

- **QCOW** – This is a file format for disk image files used by QEMU, a hosted virtual machine monitor.

Chapter 4 - Creating a Virtual Machine (VM)

- **QED** – This is a disk image file saved in the QEMU Enhanced Disk Image (QED) format.

I will be sticking with the VDI option since I don't plan on using this VM with any other virtualization platforms. I will not select the checkbox that says *Pre-allocate full size* because I want my virtual disk to expand as needed which will save me space on the hard drive of my host computer. The option to split into 2GB parts comes in handy for backing up your VM disk files but I prefer to have one virtual disk file.

Now that everything looks good, I will click on the *Finish* button and my new VM will be added to my existing VM inventory in the VirtualBox Manager as seen in figure 4.7. If I were to power on my new VM then it wouldn't get too far because there is no operating system installed so that is what I need to do next.

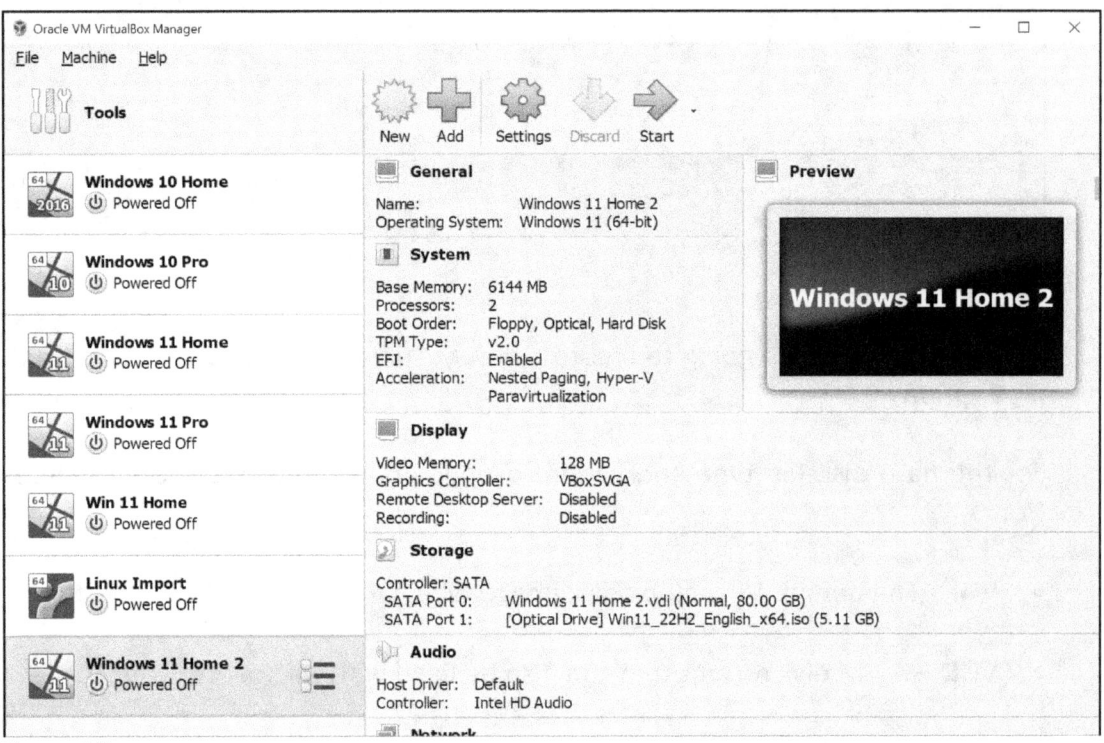

Figure 4.7

Chapter 4 - Creating a Virtual Machine (VM)

If I need to adjust any hardware settings or add additional hardware, I can highlight my new VM and click on the *Settings* button in the VirtualBox Manager or go to the *Machine* menu and then Settings.

For example, if I didn't select my ISO file during the virtual machine's creation, I can go to the Storage area and then click on the virtual optical drive and choose an ISO file I have on my computer or use one of the other attached drives\CD drives installed on my computer (figure 4.9).

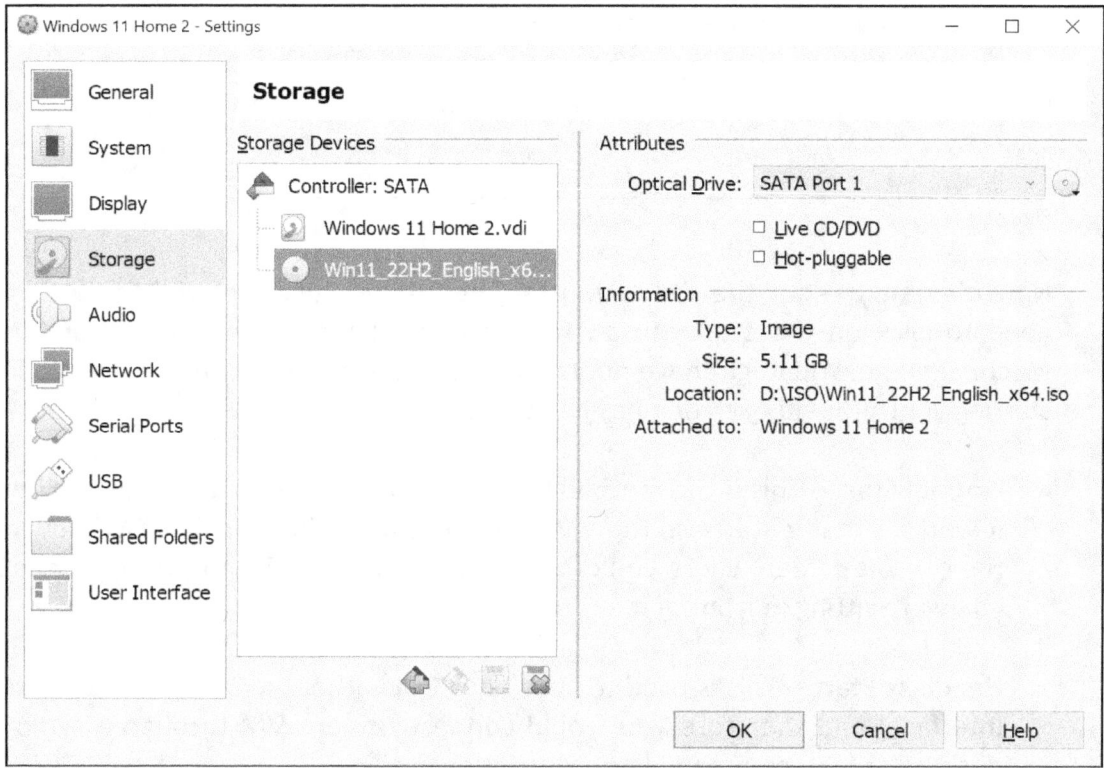

Figure 4.8

Chapter 4 - Creating a Virtual Machine (VM)

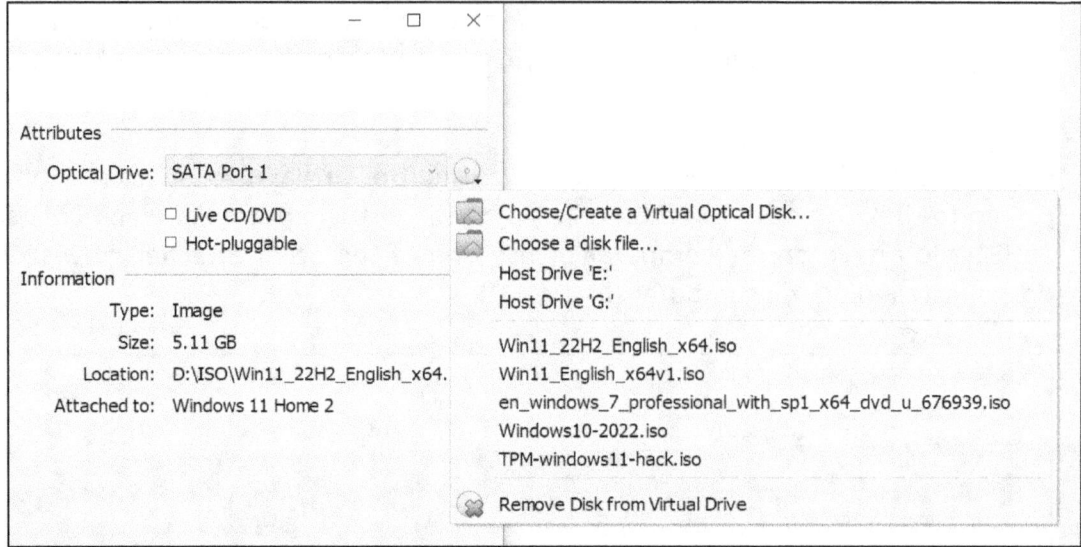

Figure 4.9

Now it's time to start the VM and install the operating system and to do that I need to click on the *Start* button from the VirtualBox Manager or from the Machine menu. You might have noticed that there are three different options for starting your VM and each one has its purpose.

- **Normal Start** – This is the method that you will use most of the time and how it works is that it starts up the VM and opens a window for that VM showing the console screen where you can log in and interact with the computer as if you were sitting in front of it.

- **Headless Start** – This is used to start your VM without a GUI (Graphical User Interface) and therefore you would connect to your VM through a remote desktop or SSH (command line) connection.

- **Detachable Start** – When you start a VM in normal mode, it will open a separate window for that VM and when you close that window it will shut down that VM. When you start a VM in Detachable mode, you can close out the window but leave the VM running.

After clicking on Start and then Normal Start, my VM reads the attached Windows 11 ISO file and loads the setup program to install Windows. Now I will walk you through the process of installing Windows 11.

Chapter 4 - Creating a Virtual Machine (VM)

 Since Microsoft is always changing or "upgrading" Windows as they call it, the steps listed here might vary a little depending on what build (version) of Windows 11 you are installing but the process should be very similar.

The first screen will ask you to confirm your language, time and currency format as well as your keyboard type. Then you will click on *Next* and then click on the button that says *Install Now* on the next screen.

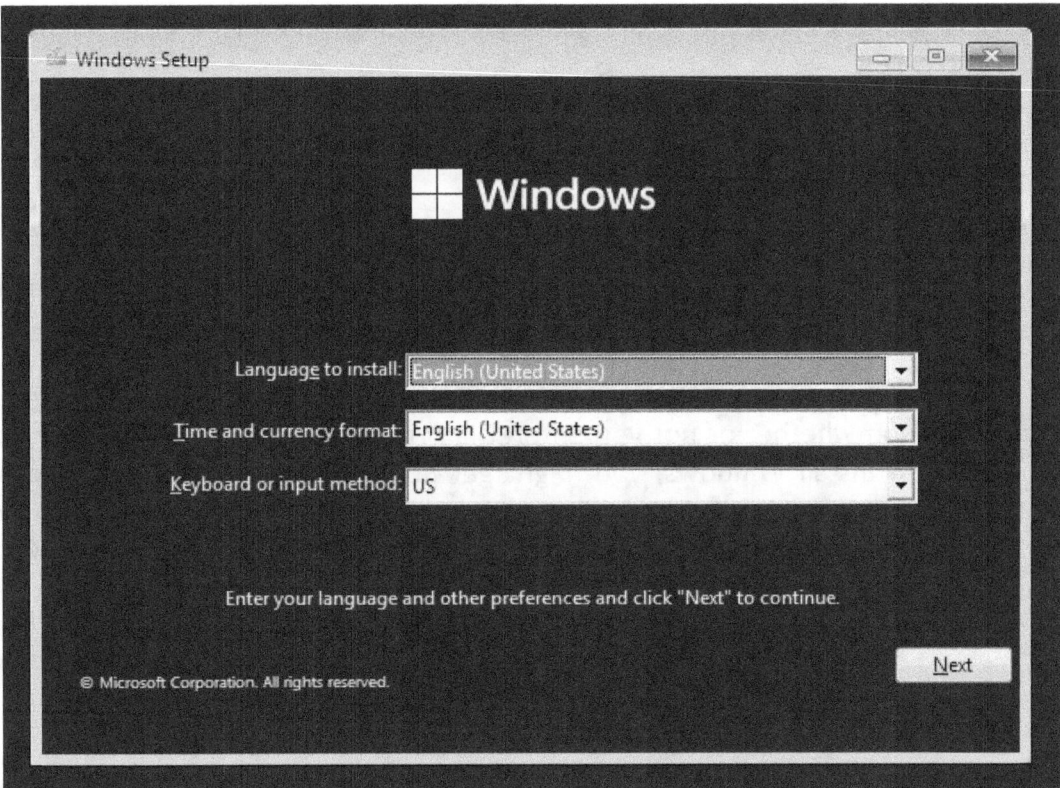

Figure 4.10

To use Windows you will need a valid product key that will come with your copy of Windows. If you are just installing Windows as a test and don't plan on using it for an extended period of time you can just click on the *I don't have a product key* link. Windows 11 will let you use it without a valid product key but certain features will be disabled until you successfully activate it.

Chapter 4 - Creating a Virtual Machine (VM)

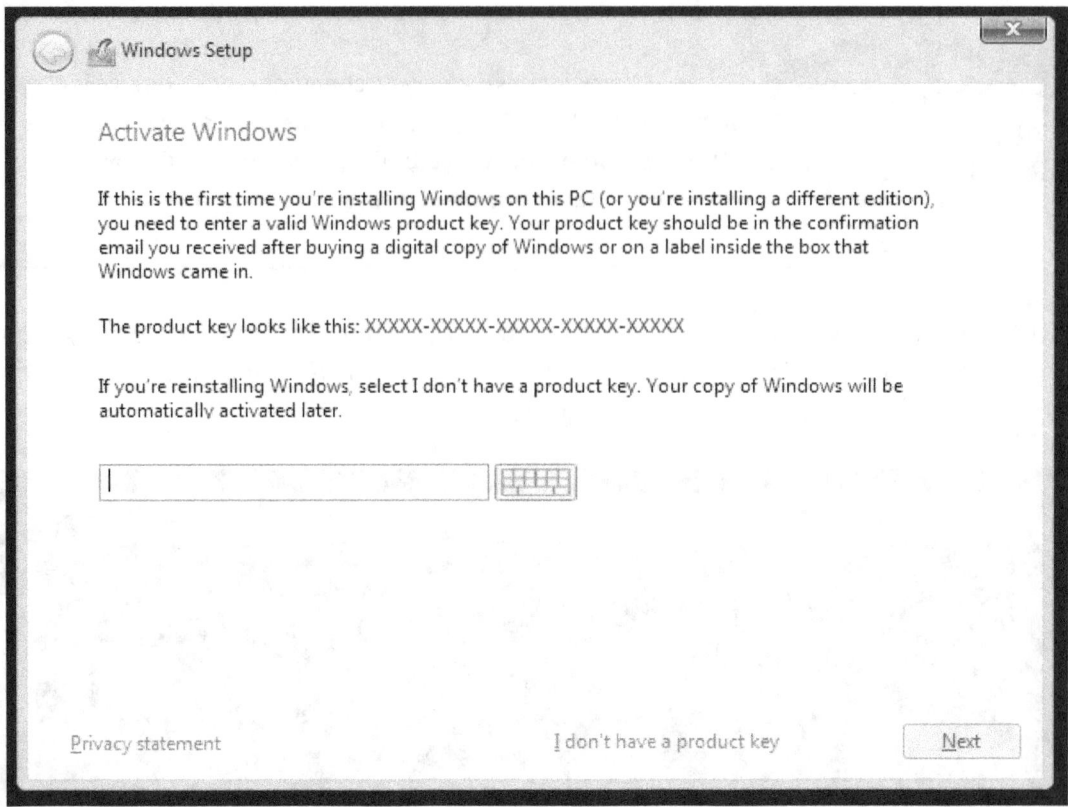

Figure 4.11

Depending on whether or not you entered a product key and what ISO file you are using to install Windows, you might get prompted to choose a version of Windows that you wish to install. If you plan on using a product key later on to activate Windows, then you should choose the version that matches your key. For my example, I will be using Windows 11 Home Edition. After you click on Next you will be asked to accept the terms of the license agreement.

Chapter 4 - Creating a Virtual Machine (VM)

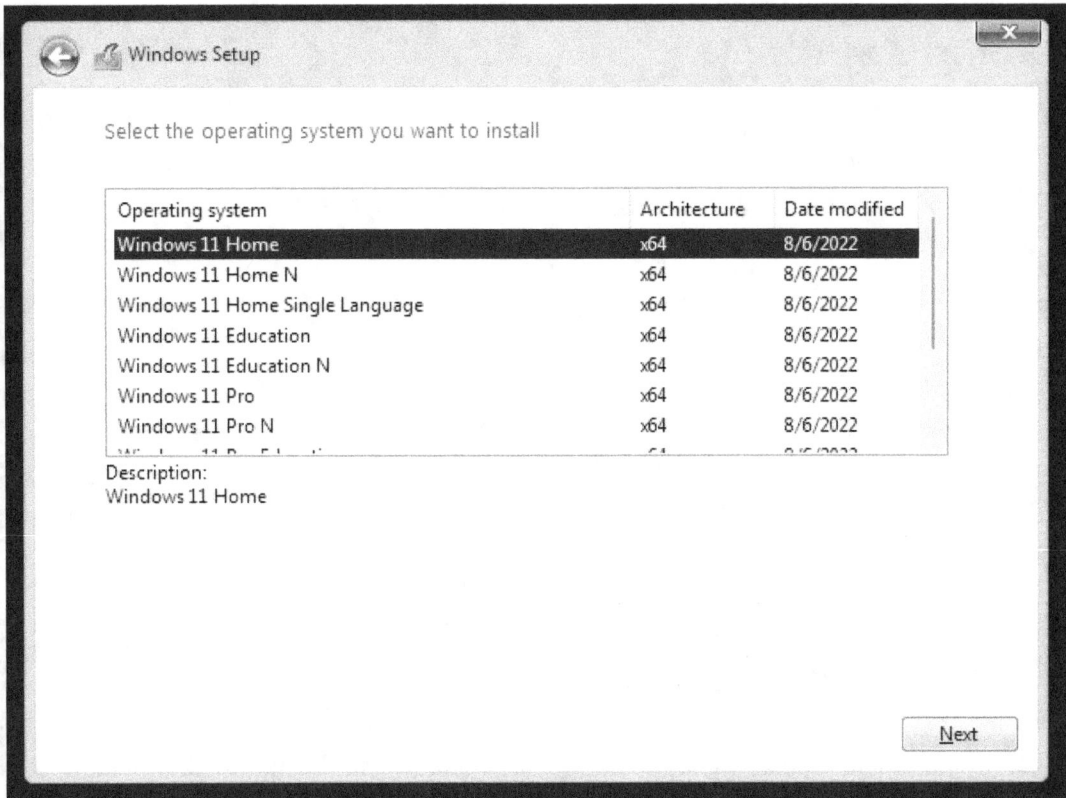

Figure 4.12

If this is a new installation of Windows which it most likely is rather than an upgrade you will need to choose the *Custom* option for the installation type.

Chapter 4 - Creating a Virtual Machine (VM)

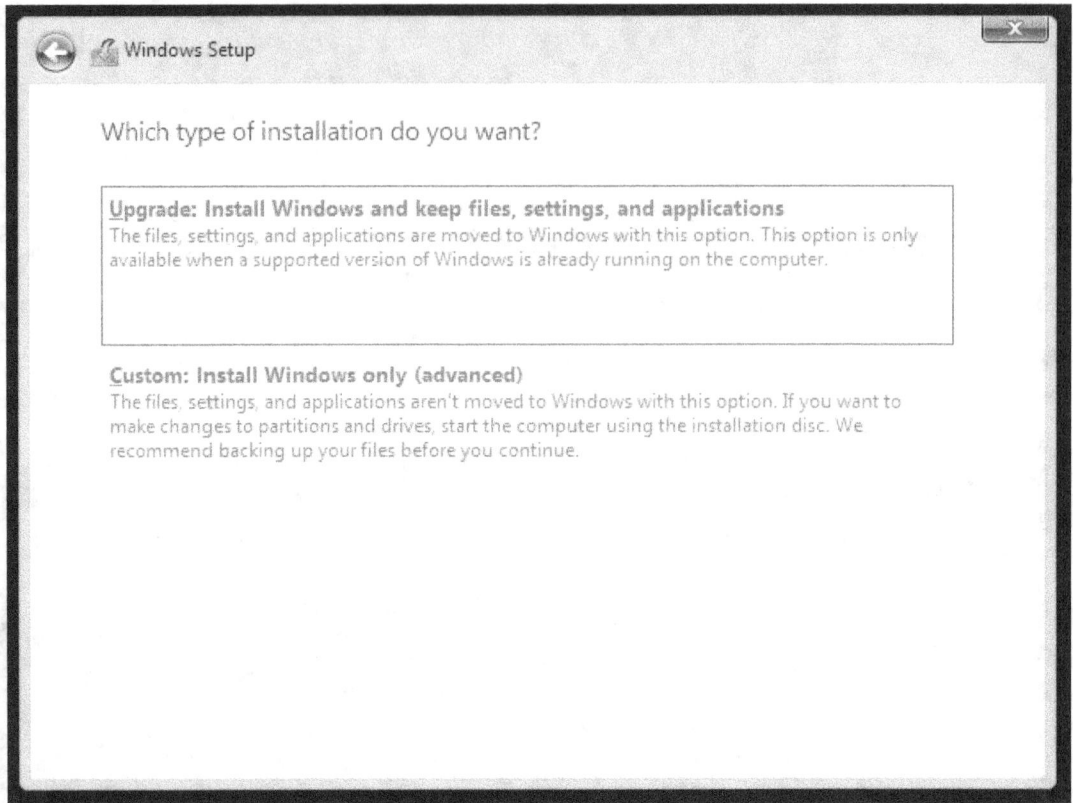

Figure 4.13

Now you can choose how much of the new virtual hard disk you want to allocate to Windows by clicking on *New* or if you just want to use the entire disk then you can click on Next.

Chapter 4 - Creating a Virtual Machine (VM)

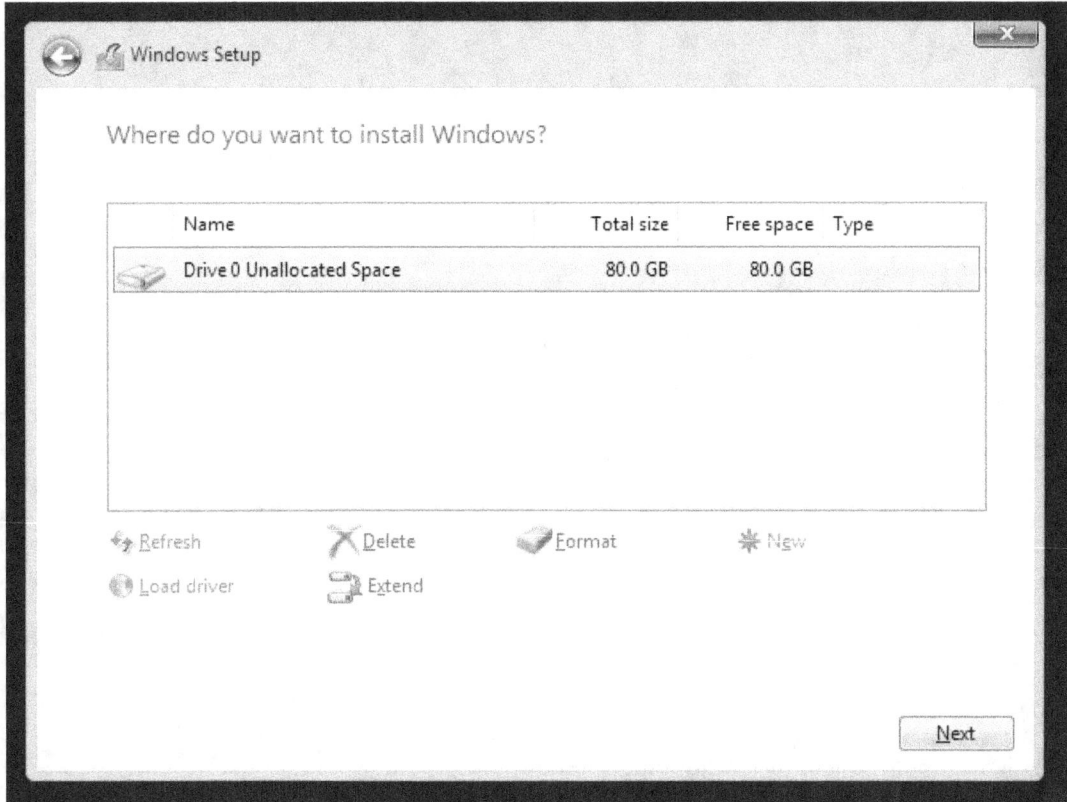

Figure 4.14

Then the installation process will begin, and this will take a bit of time depending on how fast your computer is.

Chapter 4 - Creating a Virtual Machine (VM)

Figure 4.15

Once Windows starts for the first time you will be required to answer a bunch more questions and this is where things will start to vary depending on what build of Windows you are installing.

 Once the initial Windows installation is complete you might want to unmount the ISO file from your VM, so it doesn't start the installation again from scratch when you go to reboot the computer. You can do this by choosing *Remove Disk* from Virtual Drive from the same menu you used to attach the ISO file.

The first thing you will notice is the Windows 11 virtual assistant named Cortana telling you how she will be guiding you through the setup process. You can mute her by clicking on the microphone icon if you choose to do so.

Chapter 4 - Creating a Virtual Machine (VM)

Then you will need to choose what region you are located in from the available options. Most of the time, the correct region will be chosen for you.

Next, you will need to choose your keyboard layout from the available options. Once again, the correct choice should already be highlighted for you. It will also ask you if you would like to add a second keyboard layout to your new computer. If not, simply click on the *Skip* button. Then Windows will check for some updates online.

Then you will need to wait a bit while Windows does its thing and sets itself up on your new computer. This part might take a few minutes so now is the time to go get some coffee!

After the updates, you will be asked to name your computer and if you don't, Windows will give it a generic name that won't make much sense. You can rename it later if you are unsure of what you want to call it during the installation.

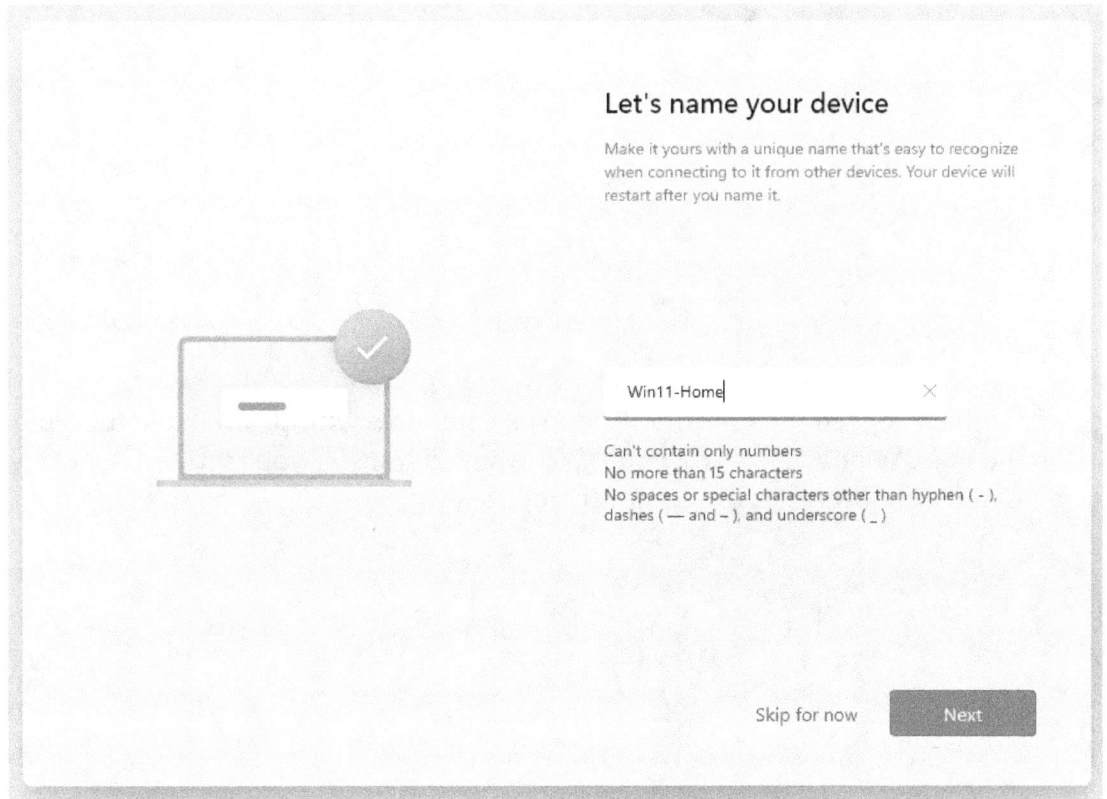

Figure 4.16

Chapter 4 - Creating a Virtual Machine (VM)

Windows prefers that you sign in with a Microsoft account to your computer so that all of your settings and other information will transfer over to your new Windows installation so you will be asked to sign in on for the next step. If you don't have a Microsoft account you can create one from this screen by clicking on the *Create one* link.

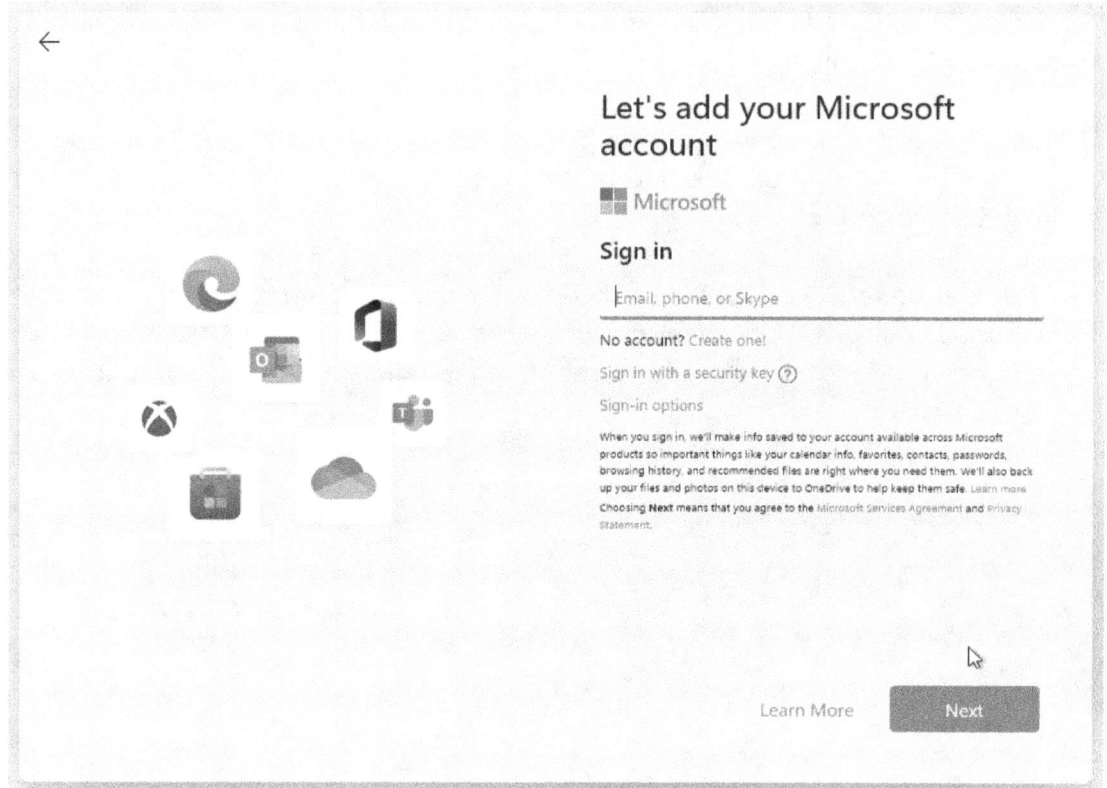

Figure 4.17

If you have logged into another Windows computer with this Microsoft account in the past, Windows will ask you if you want to transfer your settings, OneDrive files and Windows apps to this new computer.

Chapter 4 - Creating a Virtual Machine (VM)

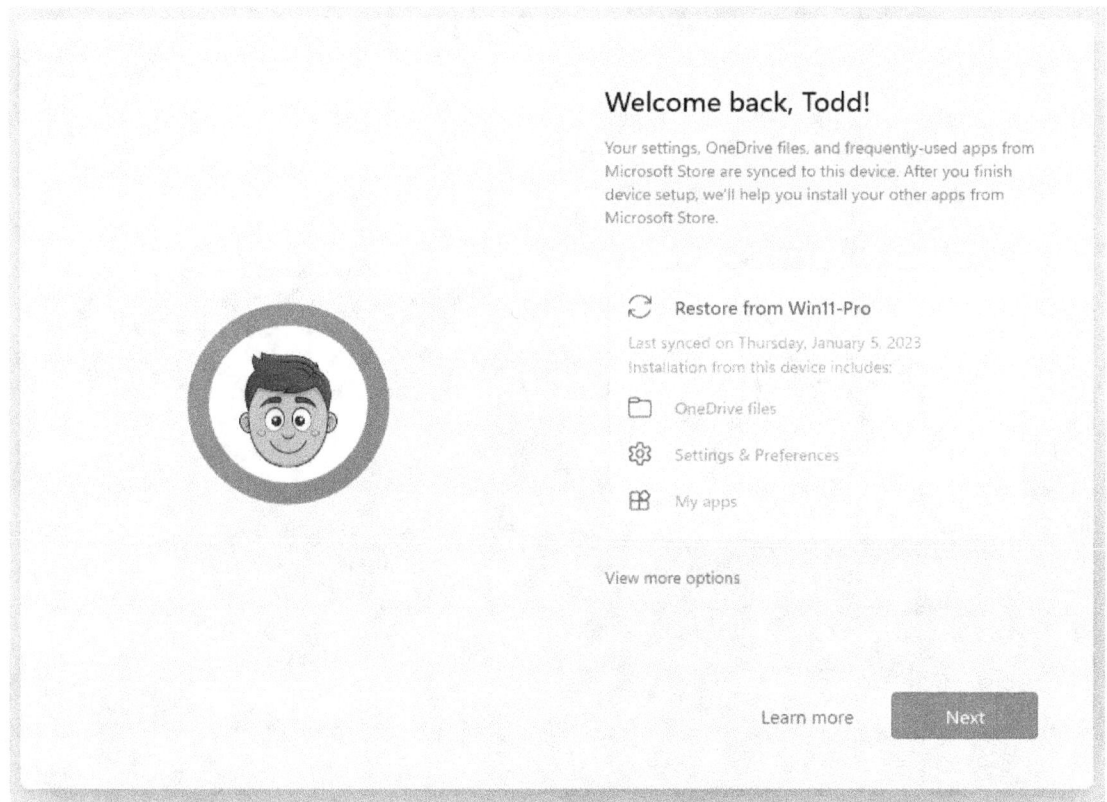

Figure 4.18

If you don't want to do this, simply click on the link that says *View more options*. Then you will be shown other computers that you have logged into and also have an option to setup this computer as a new device without transferring any of the settings which is what I will be doing.

Chapter 4 - Creating a Virtual Machine (VM)

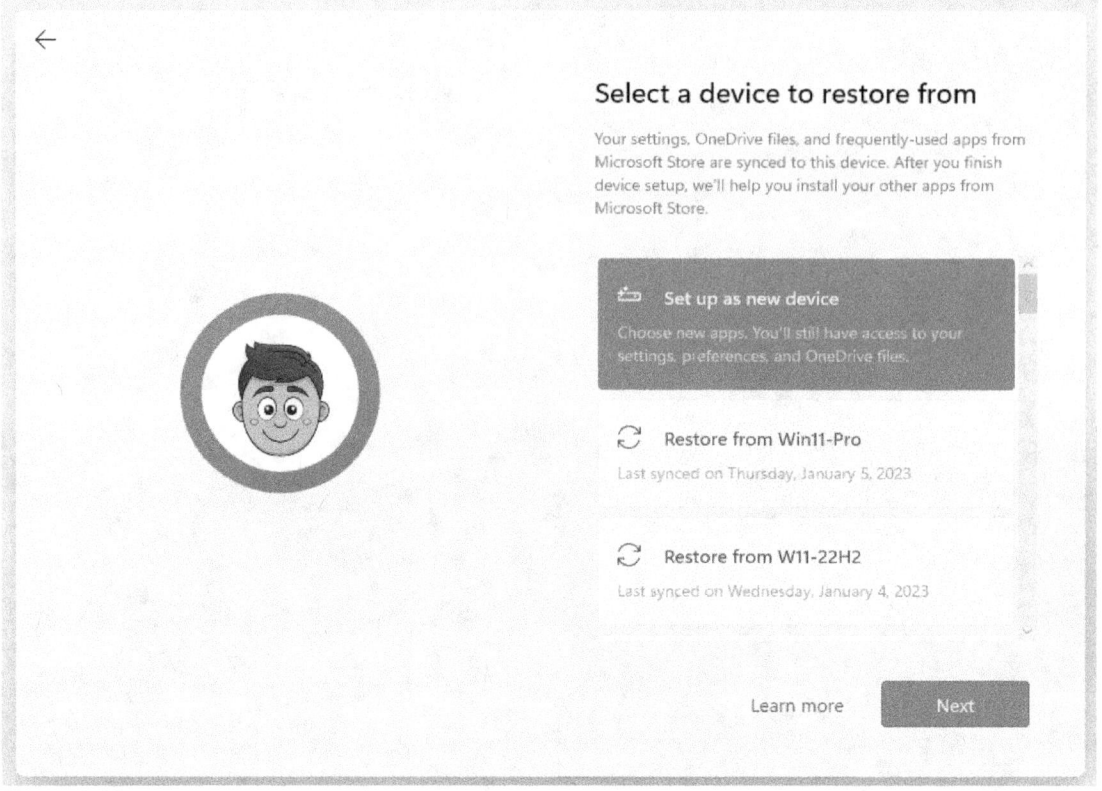

Figure 4.19

Windows will then give you the option to create a PIN number that you can use to sign into your new computer, so you don't need to enter your password. This PIN number will be unique to this computer only and won't work for any other devices that you use the same Microsoft account to sign in to.

Chapter 4 - Creating a Virtual Machine (VM)

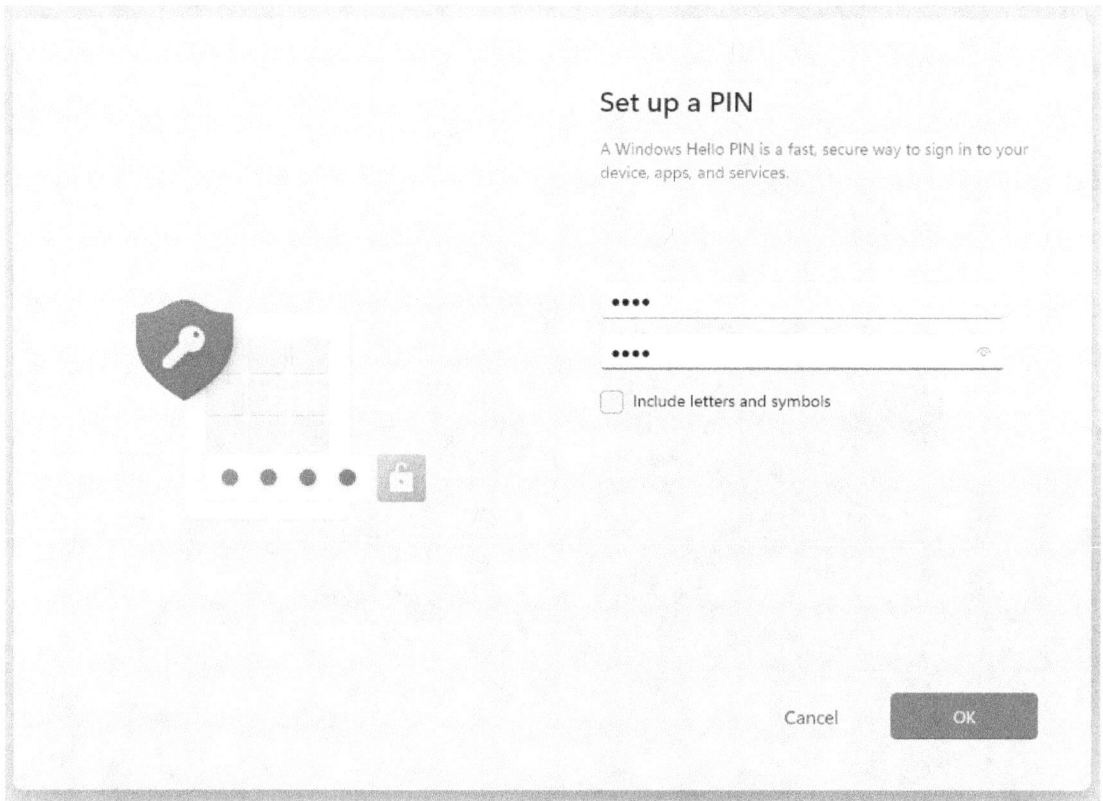

Figure 4.20

Next, you will be asked to choose your privacy settings for things such as tracking your location and sending diagnostic data to Microsoft. You should read through these and decide which ones you want to leave on and which you want to turn off. I always turn all of them off.

Chapter 4 - Creating a Virtual Machine (VM)

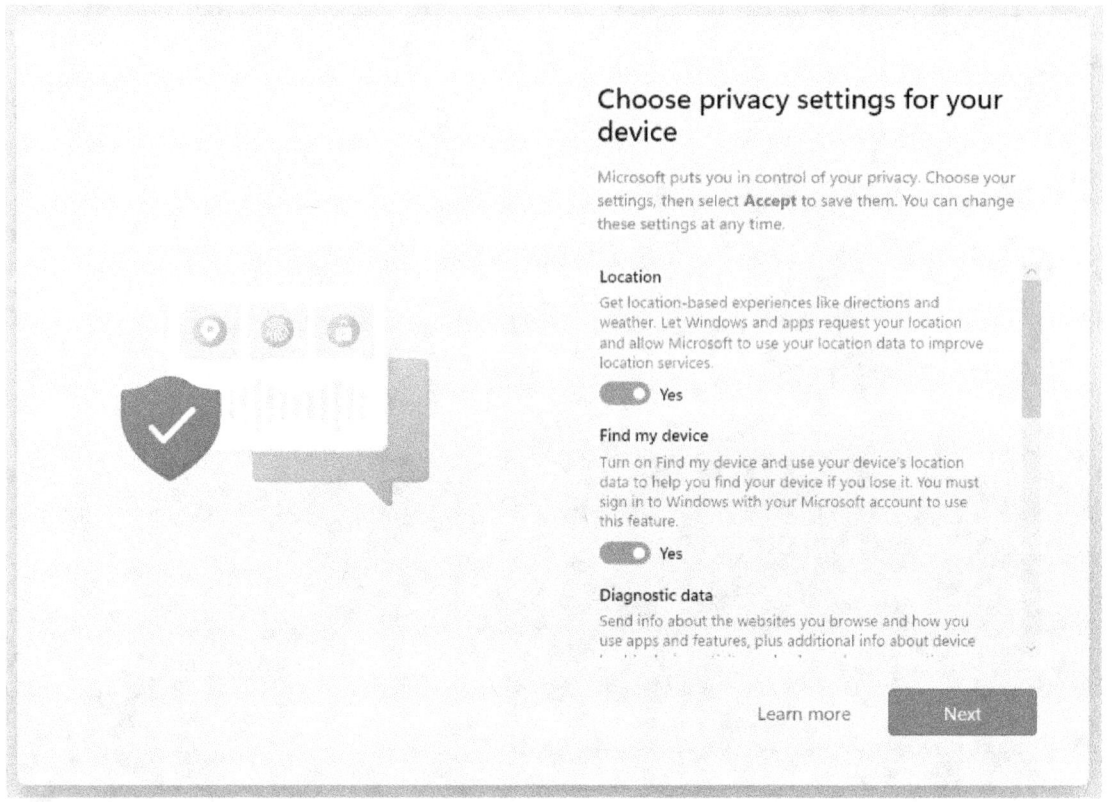

Figure 4.21

Windows will then want to customize your new computer with personalized tips and ads. I always skip this part any time I install Windows.

Chapter 4 - Creating a Virtual Machine (VM)

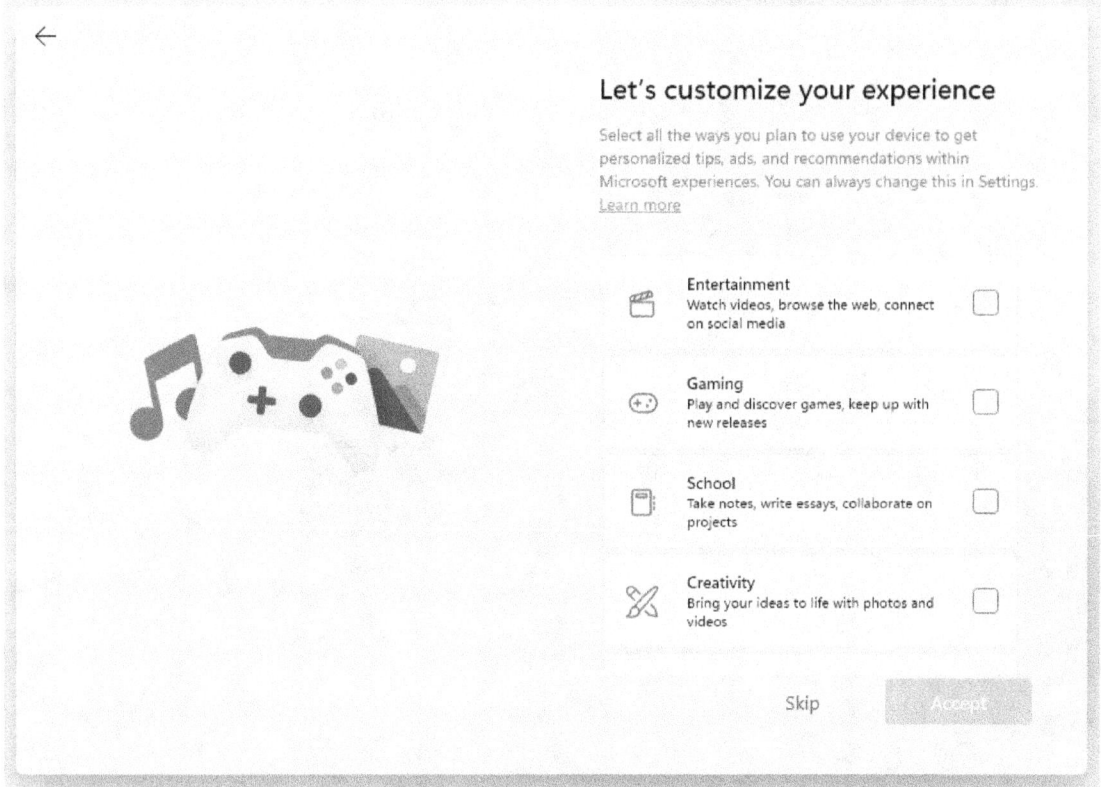

Figure 4.22

If you have an Android based smartphone, you can get photos, text messages and the notifications that are on your phone sent to your computer as well but have to give Microsoft your phone number so once again I'm going to pass!

Chapter 4 - Creating a Virtual Machine (VM)

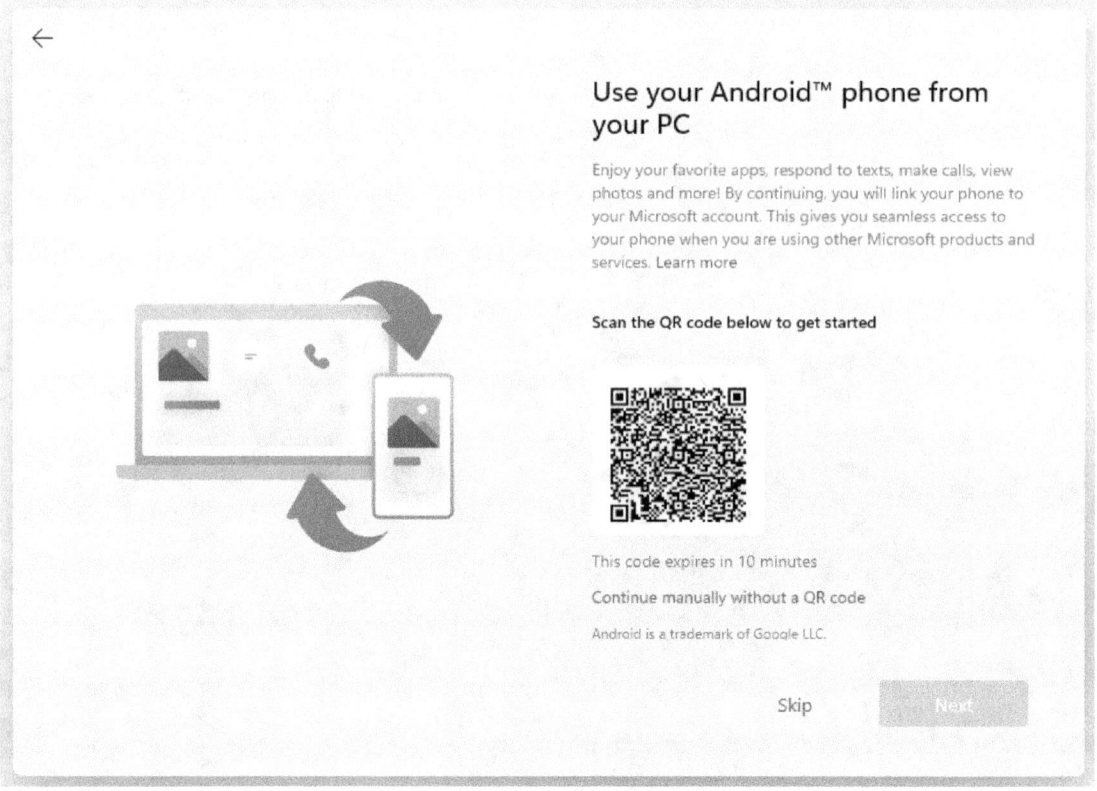

Figure 4.23

I am also going to pass on joining the Microsoft Game Pass which you should see on the next screen. After this, Windows will check for updates once again and then you will get to a user account configuration screen which can take several minutes to complete.

Chapter 4 - Creating a Virtual Machine (VM)

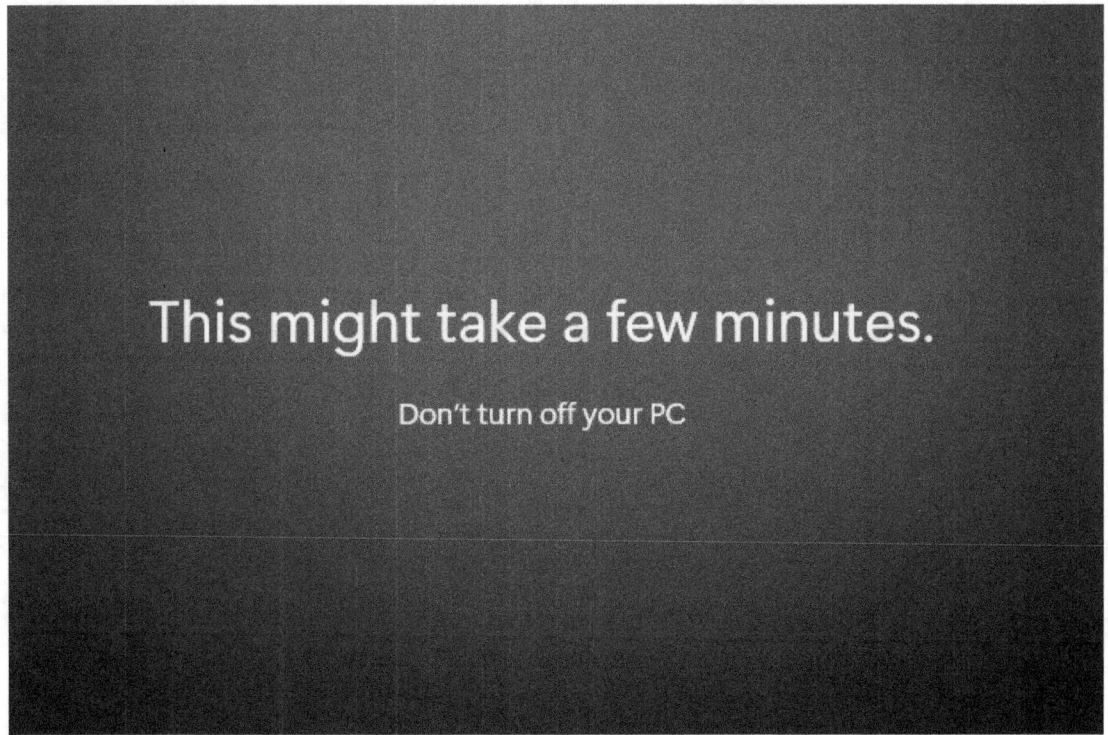

Figure 4.24

During the Windows installation you might also be asked to configure your OneDrive account. Just be sure to pay attention to this and choose the *Only save files to this PC* option if you don't want everything synced with the OneDrive cloud storage app.

 If you are interested in learning about online cloud storage services and how they work then you might want to check out my book called **Cloud Storage Made Easy - Securely Backup and Share Your Files**.
https://www.amazon.com/dp/1730838359

You might also be asked if you want to set up your Office 365 trail which is Microsoft's latest version of their Office productivity suite which includes programs such as Word, Excel, Outlook and so on.

After all of these steps, you will then be logged into your new Windows VM!

Chapter 4 - Creating a Virtual Machine (VM)

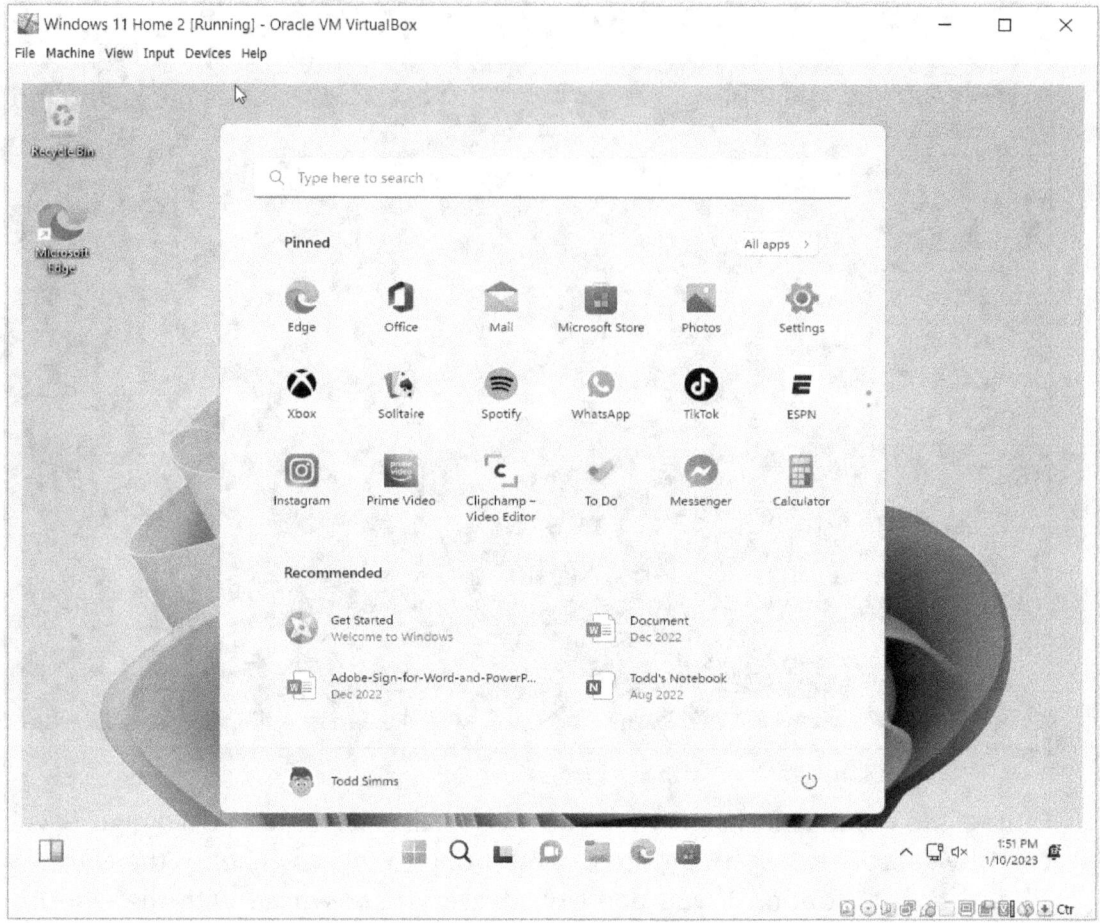

Figure 4.25

Installing a Linux VM
You might not be aware of this, but Windows is not the only game in town when it comes to operating systems. Sure you have Apple with their Mac OS but another big player in the OS game is Linux, which is an offshoot of the popular UNIX operating system that has been used in enterprise environments for years.

Linux is a free OS and there are many upon many versions, or flavors as they are commonly called to choose from. For the most part, Linux is free to use by anyone who wants to install it on their computer and most versions offer a bunch of different preinstalled apps allowing you to do pretty much anything you can do on a Windows computer. Just keep in mind that you can't install your Windows software on a Linux computer unless you have a Linux version of that software.

Chapter 4 - Creating a Virtual Machine (VM)

For this example, I am going to be using the Ubuntu Linux OS since it's one of the more user friendly versions. Of course, I will need my Linux OS installation files so I will go to their website and download the appropriate ISO image file to my local computer. For this download, it's going to be a 3.7 GB ISO file.

To begin I will click the *New* button again and type in the name of my VM, make sure my folder location is correct and select my ISO image. As you can see, VirtualBox can't read the edition of the ISO file but did recognize that it was Ubuntu Linux. I will also check the *Skip Unattended Installation* box since I won't be using it for this installation.

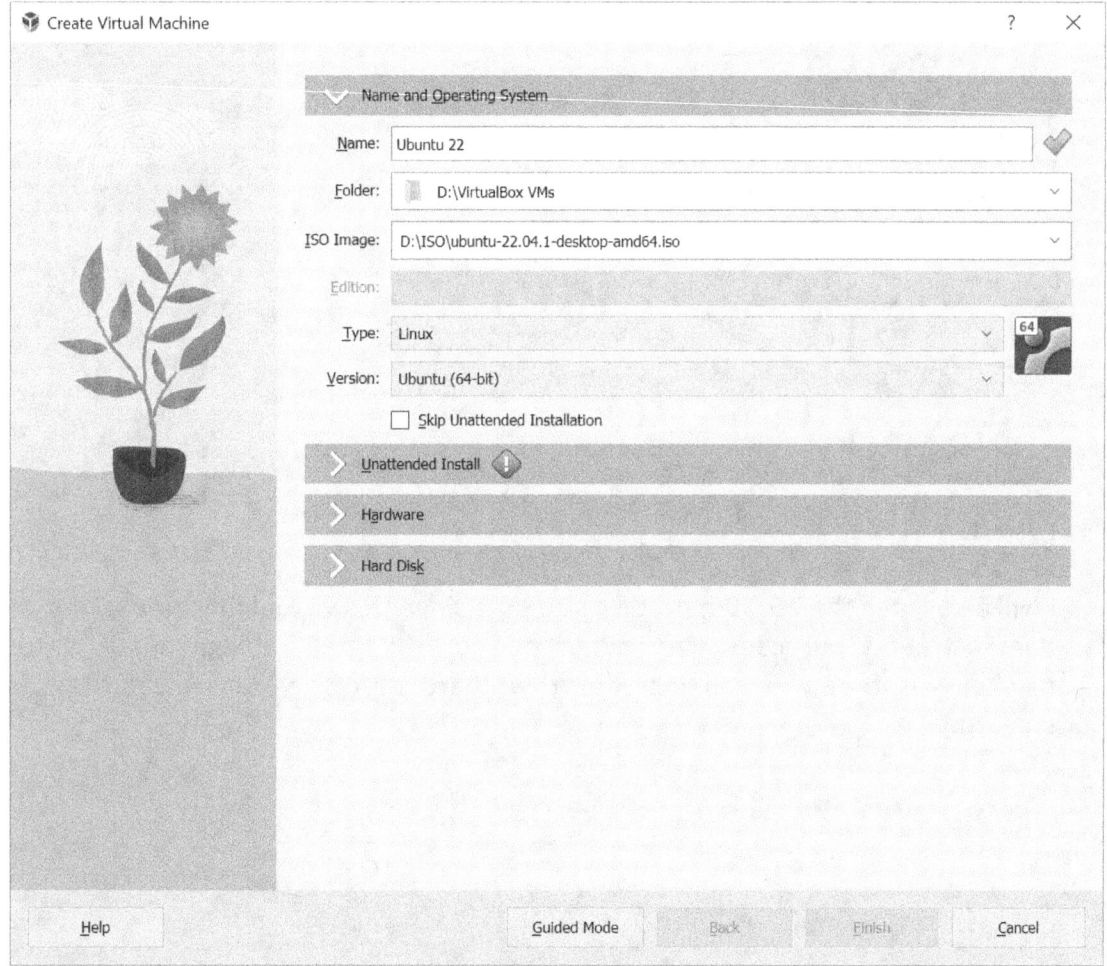

Figure 4.26

I will then bump up the RAM to 4GB and leave the single CPU selection as is.

55

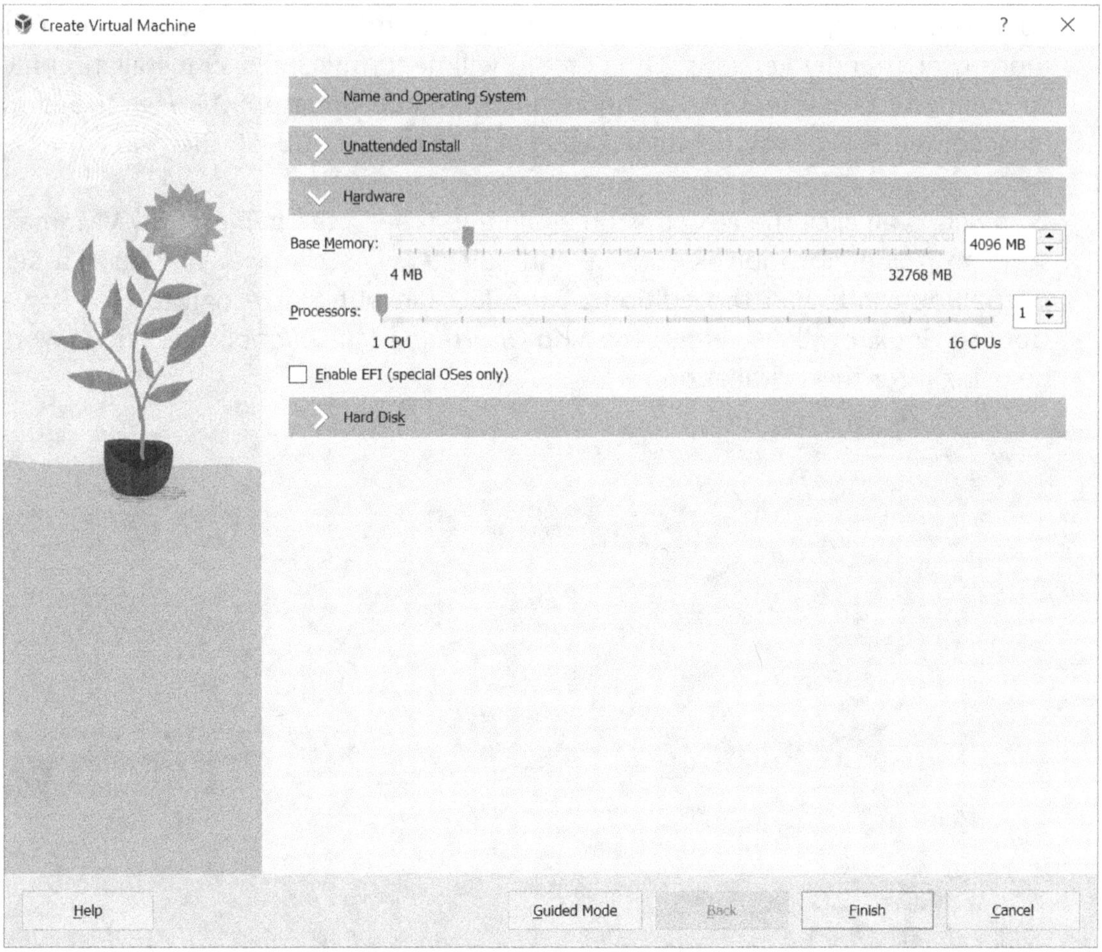

Chapter 4 - Creating a Virtual Machine (VM)

Figure 4.27

I will also leave the 25 GB hard disk size as is since this virtual machine is only for demonstration purposes. Of course one of the great things about virtual machines is that you can increase their hard disk size even after they are created.

Chapter 4 - Creating a Virtual Machine (VM)

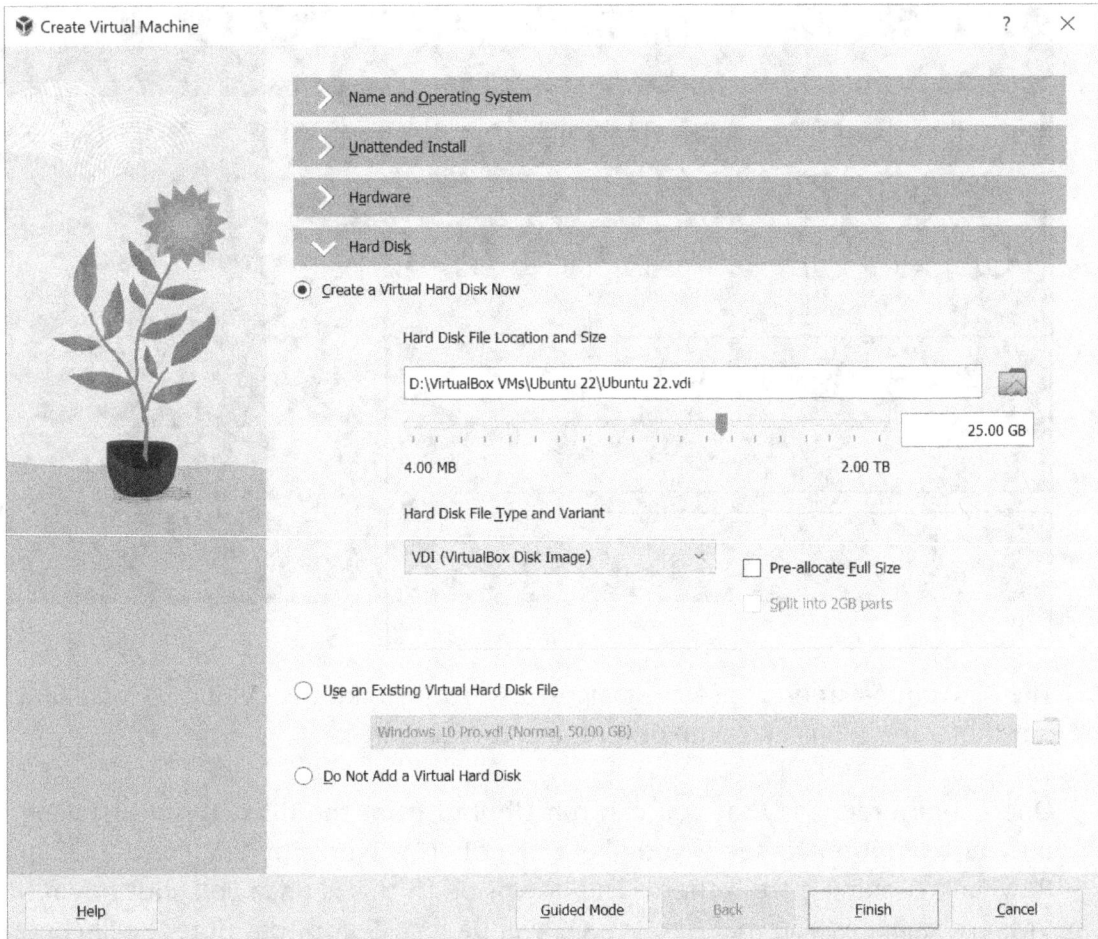

Figure 4.28

When the Ubuntu OS first loads, I will need to select the *Try or install Ubuntu* option.

Chapter 4 - Creating a Virtual Machine (VM)

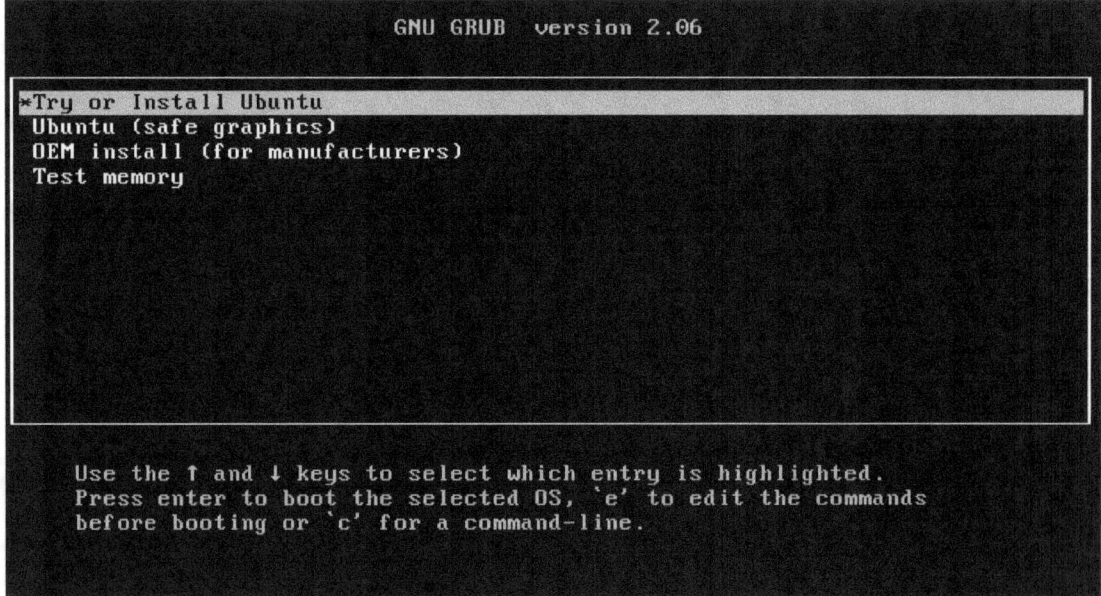

Figure 4.29

The Linux installation is pretty straightforward just like the Windows installation but there are definitely some differences to be aware of.

One big difference is that you can run Ubuntu from the CD without installing it on your computer to see if you like it or not. This works by loading the OS into RAM and running it from there. The downside to this is once you shut down the VM, any changes you made to the OS will be lost. So on that note, I will choose the *Install Ubuntu* option on my virtual hard disk.

Chapter 4 - Creating a Virtual Machine (VM)

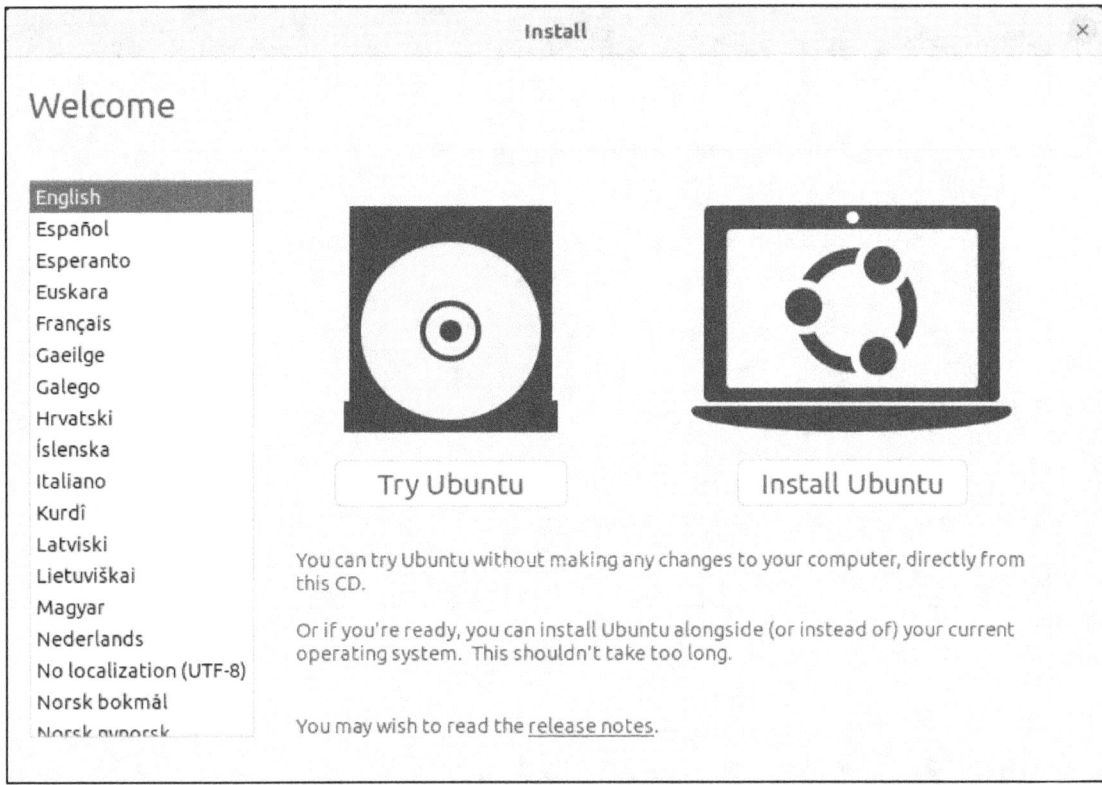

Figure 4.30

I will also need to select the appropriate language setting just like I did for Windows.

Next, I can choose what type of installation I want to perform. If I want the normal installation with all the apps and utilities I can choose *Normal installation*. If I just want the basics like a web browser then I can choose *Minimal installation*. If you really want to check out Linux and see what kind of apps come with the OS then you should go for the Normal installation.

Just like with Windows, Linux has regular updates such as fixes and security patches so if you want to have these updates downloaded during the installation you can check the box to do so.

Chapter 4 - Creating a Virtual Machine (VM)

Updates and other software

What apps would you like to install to start with?
- ● Normal installation
  - Web browser, utilities, office software, games, and media players.
- ○ Minimal installation
  - Web browser and basic utilities.

Other options
- ☑ Download updates while installing Ubuntu
  - This saves time after installation.
- ☐ Install third-party software for graphics and Wi-Fi hardware and additional media formats
  - This software is subject to license terms included with its documentation. Some is proprietary.

Figure 4.31

 If you find your mouse getting "stuck" inside of your VM screen and you can't get it back out to be used on your main computer then press the Ctrl key on the right side of your keyboard (Command for Mac) to get your mouse control back.

The way Linux creates partitions on your hard drive for installing the OS differs from Windows so if this is a new VM with a blank hard disk then I would just go with the first option that says *Erase disk and install Ubuntu* under *Installation Type*. Then you will click the *Install Now* button.

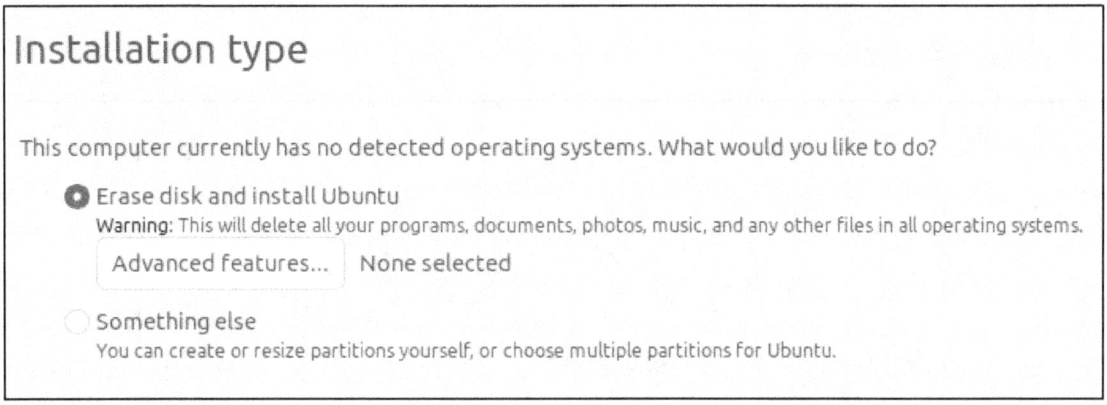

Chapter 4 - Creating a Virtual Machine (VM)

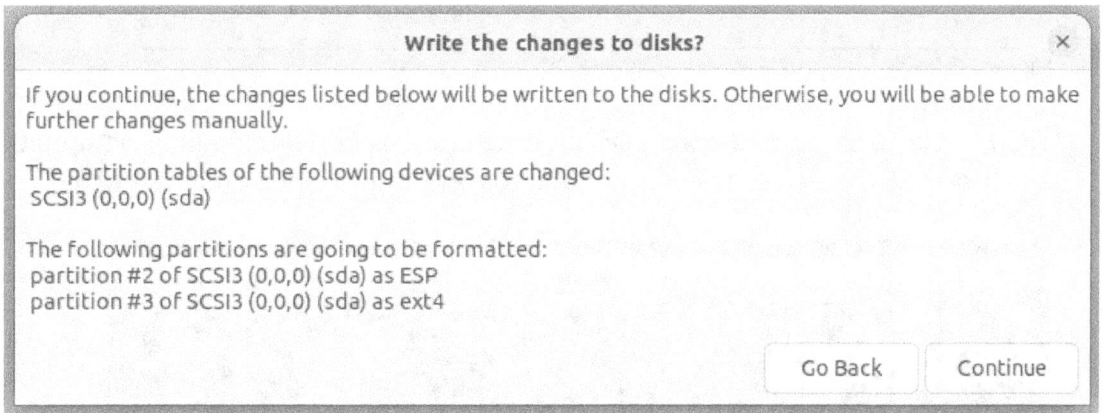

Figure 4.32

You will then get a warning saying the changes you have selected will be written to the disk and you can click on the *Continue* button to have them applied.

Figure 4.33

You will then be asked to choose your time zone before continuing.

Before using Linux for the first time you will need to create a username and password that will be used as your login account for the OS. Here you can also choose a name for the computer\VM itself that will be seen on the network if you plan on doing any networking with this VM.

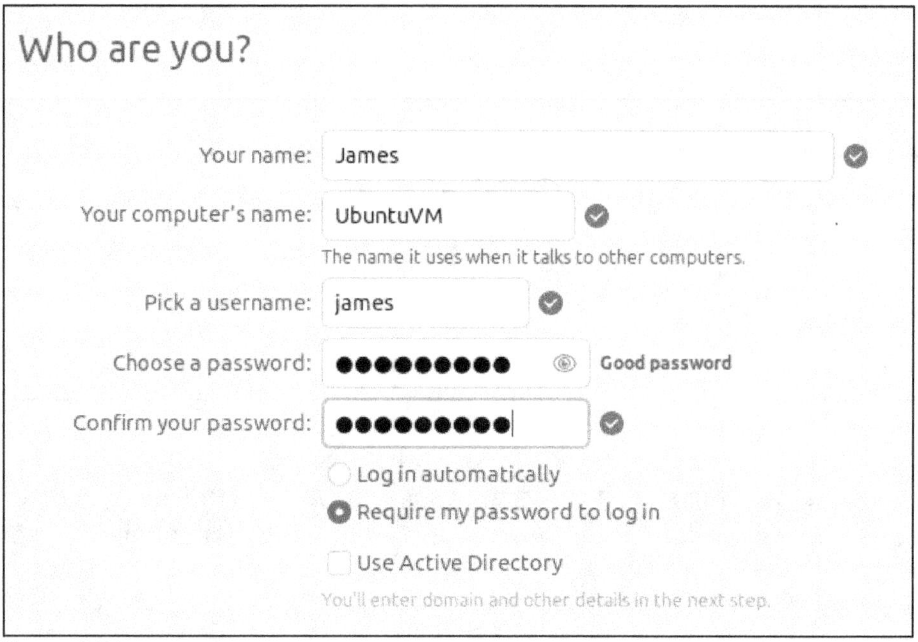

Chapter 4 - Creating a Virtual Machine (VM)

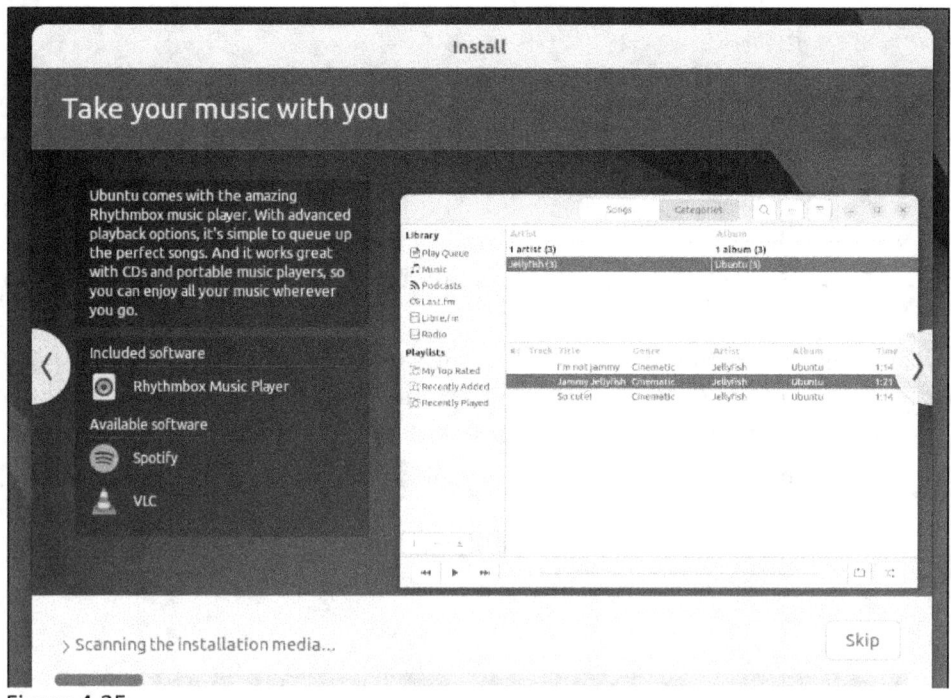

Figure 4.34

Then it will go through the installation procedure after downloading the updates and install all the necessary files needed to run Ubuntu Linux on your VM.

Figure 4.35

Chapter 4 - Creating a Virtual Machine (VM)

After a quick reboot, you will have your brand new Ubuntu Linux VM ready to go and you can then login and see how you like Linux.

Figure 4.36

Installing the Guest Additions Software
One thing you might have noticed when using your new virtual machines is that the mouse movement is kind of choppy and depending on the OS on your VM, you might be pressing your Ctrl key to get the mouse control back to your main computer which can get old quick.

Fortunately, VirtualBox has what they call their *Guest Additions* software which consists of device drivers and other applications which gives your VM better performance and usability. It will also allow you to use higher resolution display settings for your VMs. This software is contained in an ISO file that can be loaded

Chapter 4 - Creating a Virtual Machine (VM)

into your VM so it can then be installed on the guest computer's operating system. Installing this software will greatly improve the experience when working inside of your VMs.

To install the Guest Additions simply click on the *Devices* menu while on the VMs console screen and choose *Insert Guest Additions CD image*. The virtual machine will need to be running to install the Guest Additions.

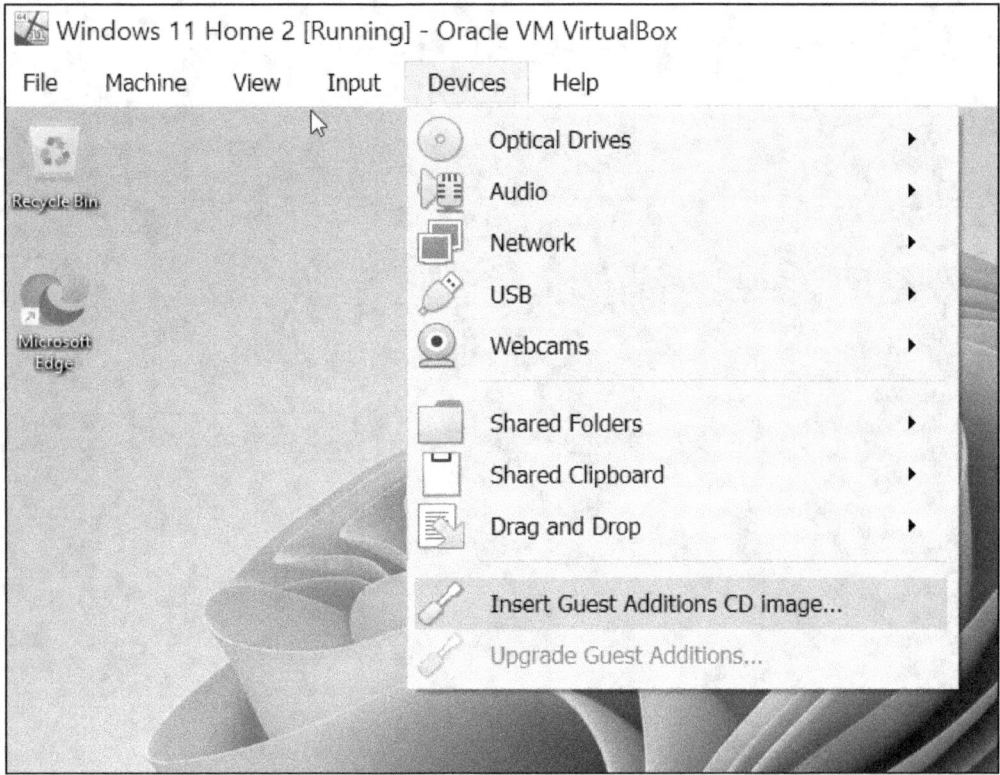

Figure 4.37

Your computer should then ask you if you would like to run the Guest Additions software and install it on your computer. Choose *yes* and then simply follow the prompts to install the software just like you would any other software for your computer. I have included some screenshots of the installation process just so you can see what's involved and also see how easy it is to perform.

If the installation process doesn't start automatically then go to Windows Explorer on the VM and see if you can run it from the mounted CD on the computer (figure 4.38).

Chapter 4 - Creating a Virtual Machine (VM)

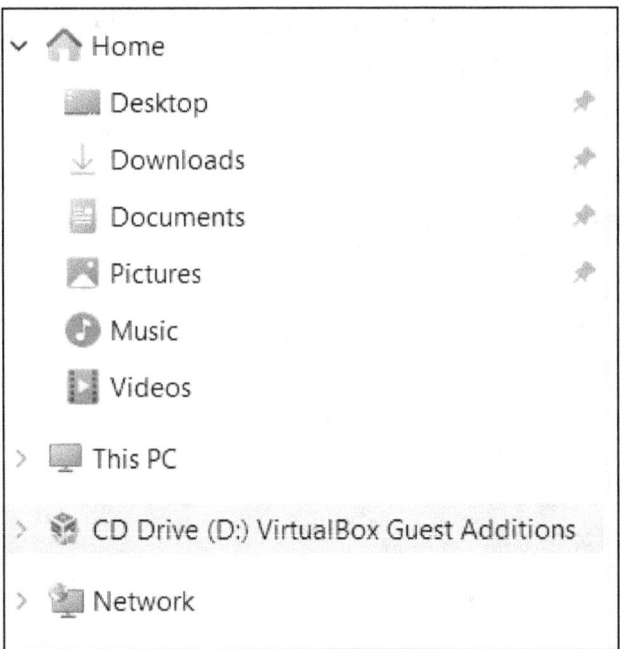

Figure 4.38

If you click on this drive, you should get some folders that have executable files that you can manually double click to start the installation.

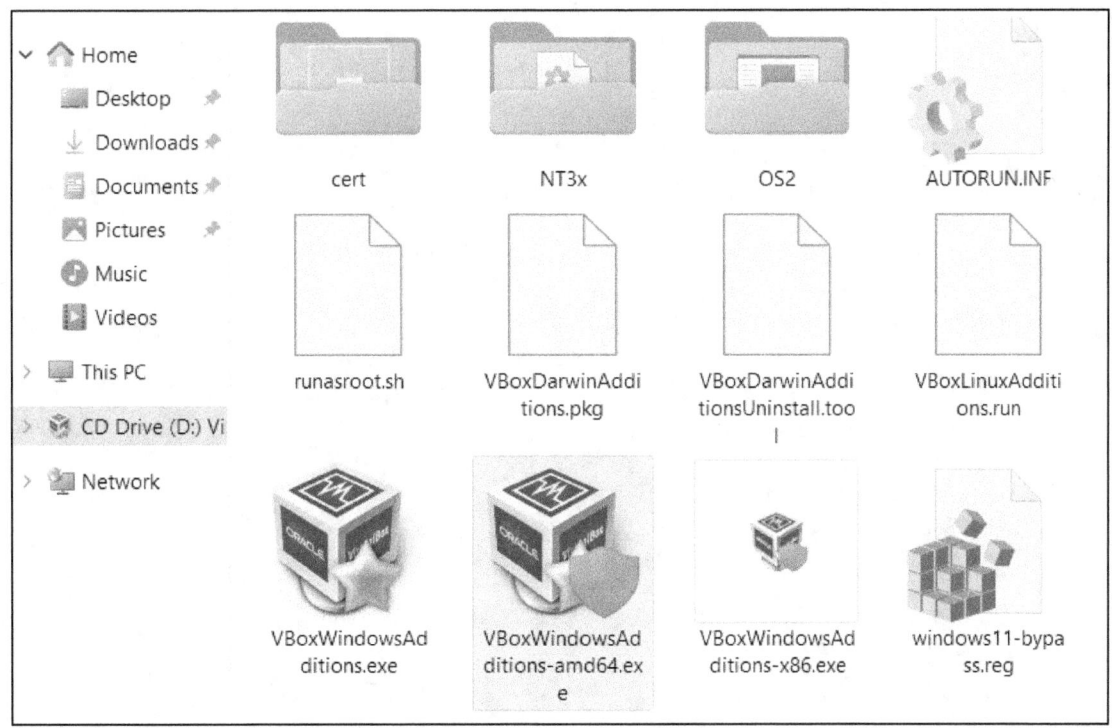

Figure 4.39

Chapter 4 - Creating a Virtual Machine (VM)

Installing the Guest Additions is simply a process of clicking Next through all the installation screens and rebooting when the installation is complete.

Figure 4.40

Chapter 4 - Creating a Virtual Machine (VM)

Figure 4.41

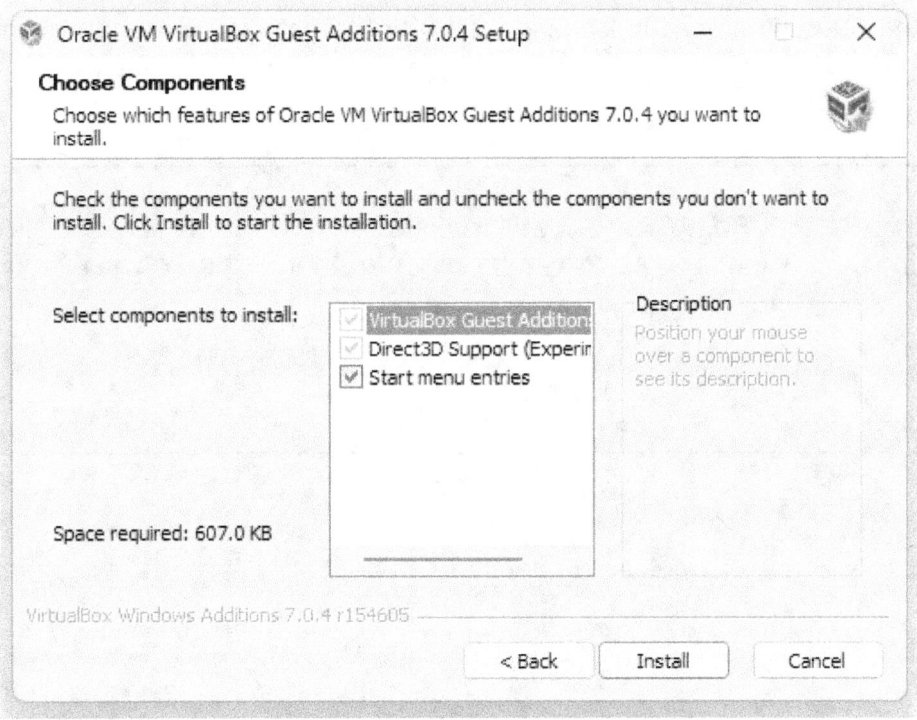

Figure 4.42

Chapter 4 - Creating a Virtual Machine (VM)

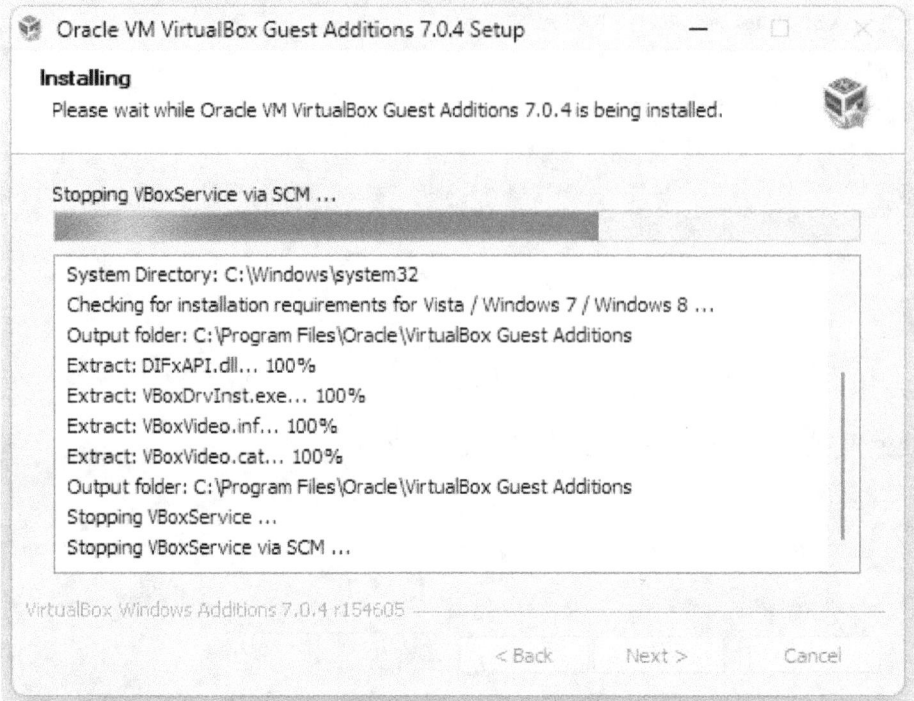

Figure 4.43

Installing the Guest Additions in Linux looks a bit different than in Windows and how this looks will vary even more depending on what version of Linux you are running on your VM.

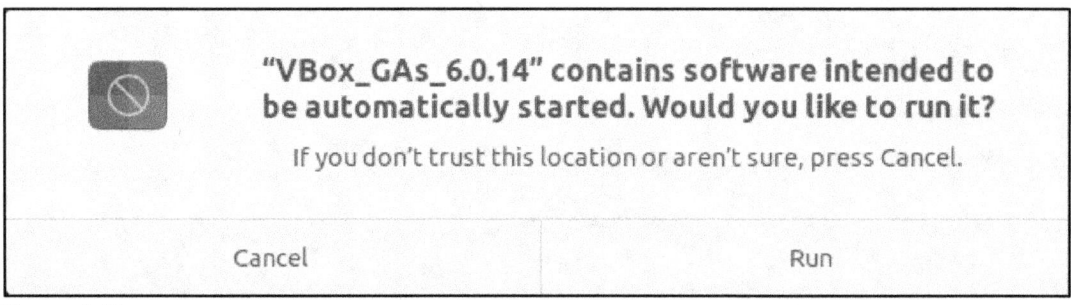

Figure 4.44

Chapter 4 - Creating a Virtual Machine (VM)

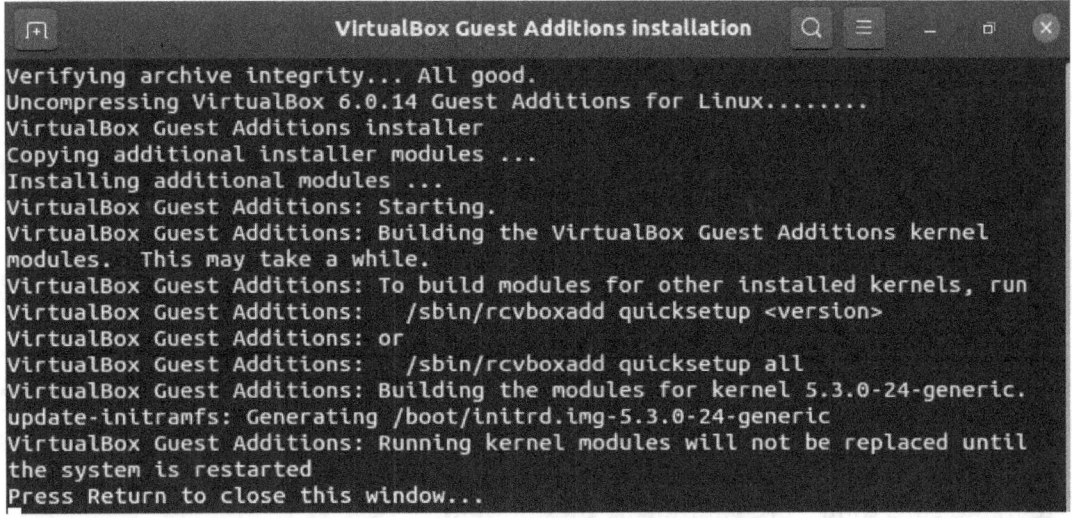
Figure 4.45

Chapter 5 – Virtual Machine Settings

Knowing how to create a virtual machine is crucial when it comes to using VirtualBox (obviously) but there is more to the process than just the initial VM creation. Once you have your VMs in use, you will most likely find that they need to be modified to perform at their best.

There are many settings that can be changed on a VM allowing you to fine tune it for optimum performance. And for the most part, there is more than one way to get to these settings. In this chapter I will be discussing the various VM settings as well as some of the other ways you can check the status of your VMs to make sure things are running as they should.

Virtual Machine Status Icons
When you start up a VM and it opens its console window, you will see a bunch of icons at the lower right hand corner of the windows itself. These icons are there to show you the status of the various aspects of your VM and give you a way to get a lot of useful information all from one place.

Figure 5.1 shows the status bar of the Windows 11 VM that I created in the last chapter and its associated icons.

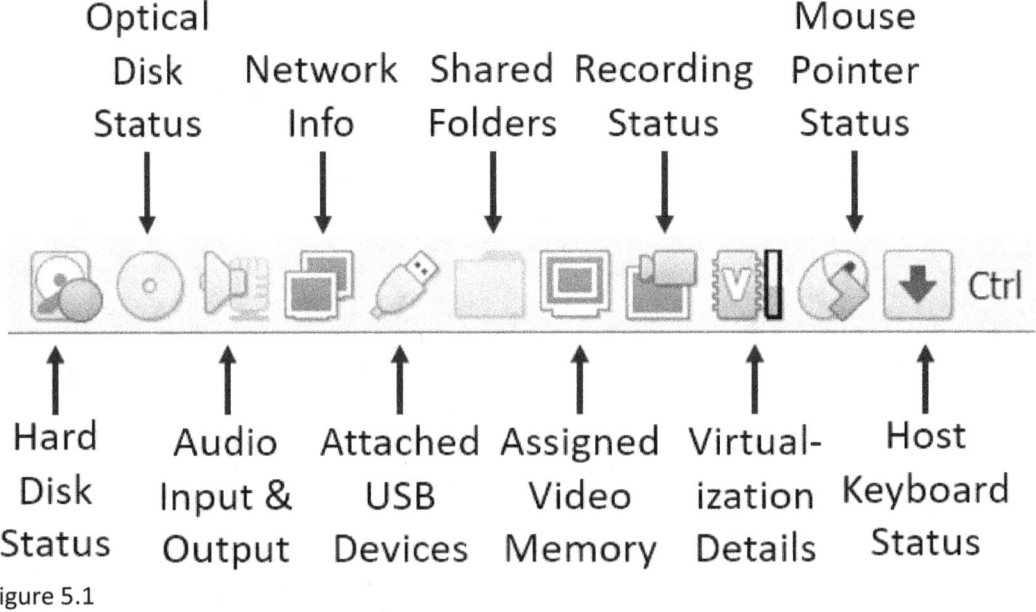

Figure 5.1

Chapter 5 – Virtual Machine Settings

Now I would like to take a moment and explain what each of these status icons will tell you when you hover your mouse over each one of them.

- **Hard disk status** – Shows hard disk activity and also the path on your computer to where the hard disk file is located.

- **Optical disk status** – Shows optical disk activity (CD\DVD drive) and also the path on your computer to where any mounted ISO files reside.

- **Audio input & output** – If you have VM audio input or output enabled it will tell you the status here.

- **Network information** – This will show the network adapter name as well as its assigned IP address and connection status.

- **Attached USB devices** – If you have attached any USB devices from your host computer to be used on your guest computer (VM), they will be shown here.

- **Shared folders** – Shared folders allow you to transfer files between the host computer and your VM. Any shared folders will be shown here.

- **Assigned video memory** – Just like with RAM memory, you can adjust the video memory assigned to a VM to increase its performance. The amount of video memory assigned to the VM is shown here.

- **Recording status** – VirtualBox allows you to create a video recording of the OS as it runs if you would like to do something such as create a training video etc. Here you will see whether recording is on or off at the moment.

- **Virtualization details** – This shows various virtualization parameter details and you most likely won't find this too useful.

- **Host mouse pointer status** – This tells the status of the mouse integration with the VM such as if it's on or off and whether or not mouse input is being captured by the VM.

- **Host keyboard status** – This shows whether or not keyboard input is being captured by the VM.

Chapter 5 – Virtual Machine Settings

As you can see, you get a lot of useful information here even though you can't make any actual changes from these status icons.

Virtual Machine Console Menu Items
At the top of the VM console you will see various menu items just like you have within the VirtualBox Manager, and when you click on each one of these you should notice that you many of the same choices as you do within the VirtualBox Manager itself.

Even though many of these menu items are repetitive, there are still some that are unique to the VM and I will now take some time to go over each of the specific menu items and what they contain.

File Menu
From here you can access the preferences of the VM as well as use the Reset All Warnings option and close down the VM which is the same as clicking the X on the console window.

When you close a VM, you will be prompted to make a choice as to what you want to do with the state of the VM.

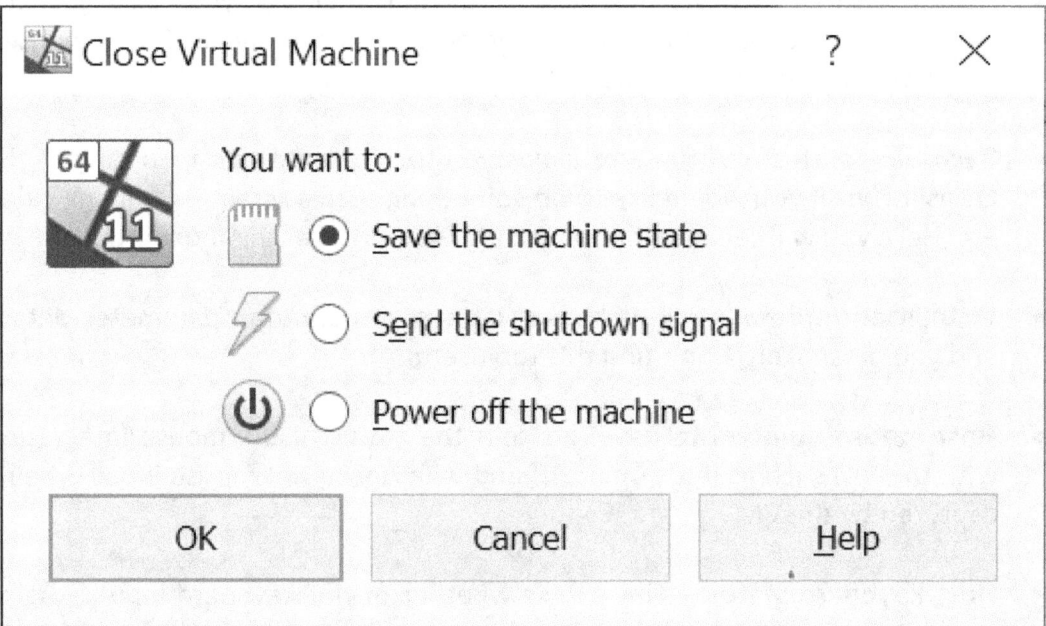

Figure 5.2

Chapter 5 – Virtual Machine Settings

Here is what each of the three choices will do.

- **Save the machine state** – Using this option will "freeze" the virtual machine's state and save it to disk so the next time you turn it on, it will continue exactly where you left off.

- **Send the shutdown signal** – This will send a signal to the guest operating system to have it perform its normal shutdown process as if you were to manually do a shutdown yourself.

- **Power off the machine** – This will simply kill the power as if you were to pull the power cord on the computer.

Machine Menu
The choices here are specific to the VM itself and some of them should be pretty obvious as to what they do. For example, from here you can get to the settings that apply to the particular VM which I will be discussing in the next section.

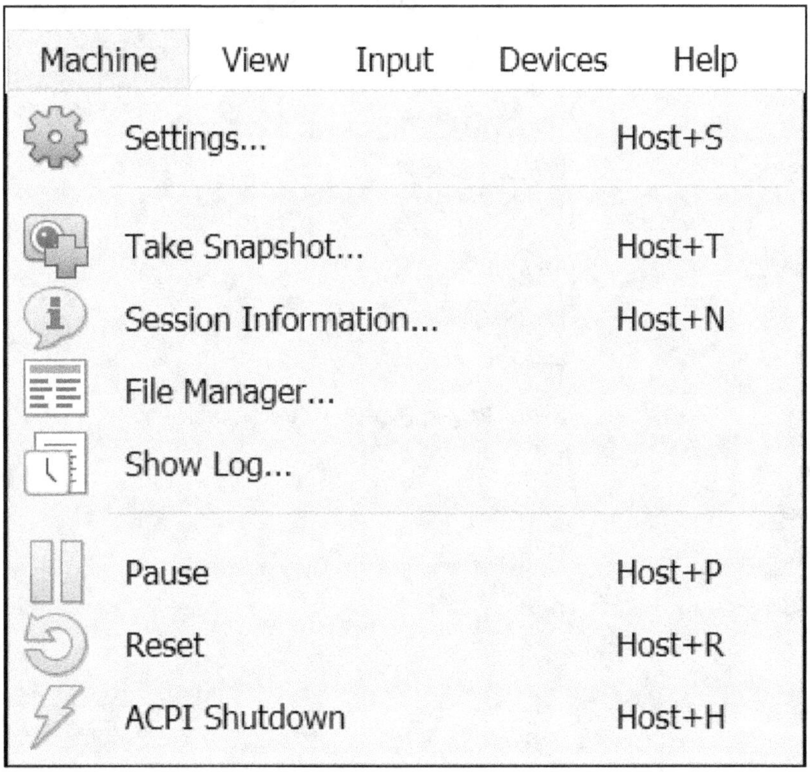

Machine	View	Input	Devices	Help
Settings...				Host+S
Take Snapshot...				Host+T
Session Information...				Host+N
File Manager...				
Show Log...				
Pause				Host+P
Reset				Host+R
ACPI Shutdown				Host+H

Figure 5.3

Chapter 5 – Virtual Machine Settings

You will also have shutdown options similar to those you saw in figure 5.2 including a *Pause* option that puts the VM on hold but keeps it running rather than shutting it down like the Save the machine state option does. *ACPI Shutdown* is similar to the Send the shutdown signal option. *Reset* will perform a hard reset of the VM without shutting it down and can be used when the guest OS is not responding, and you don't have any other choice to reset the VM.

Session Information shows you a lot of useful information about the particular VM and is broken down into *Configuration Details* (figure 5.4) and *Runtime Information* (figure 5.5).

Configuration Details will show you some general information such as the guest OS type, how much RAM is assigned to the VM, how large the virtual disk is and so on.

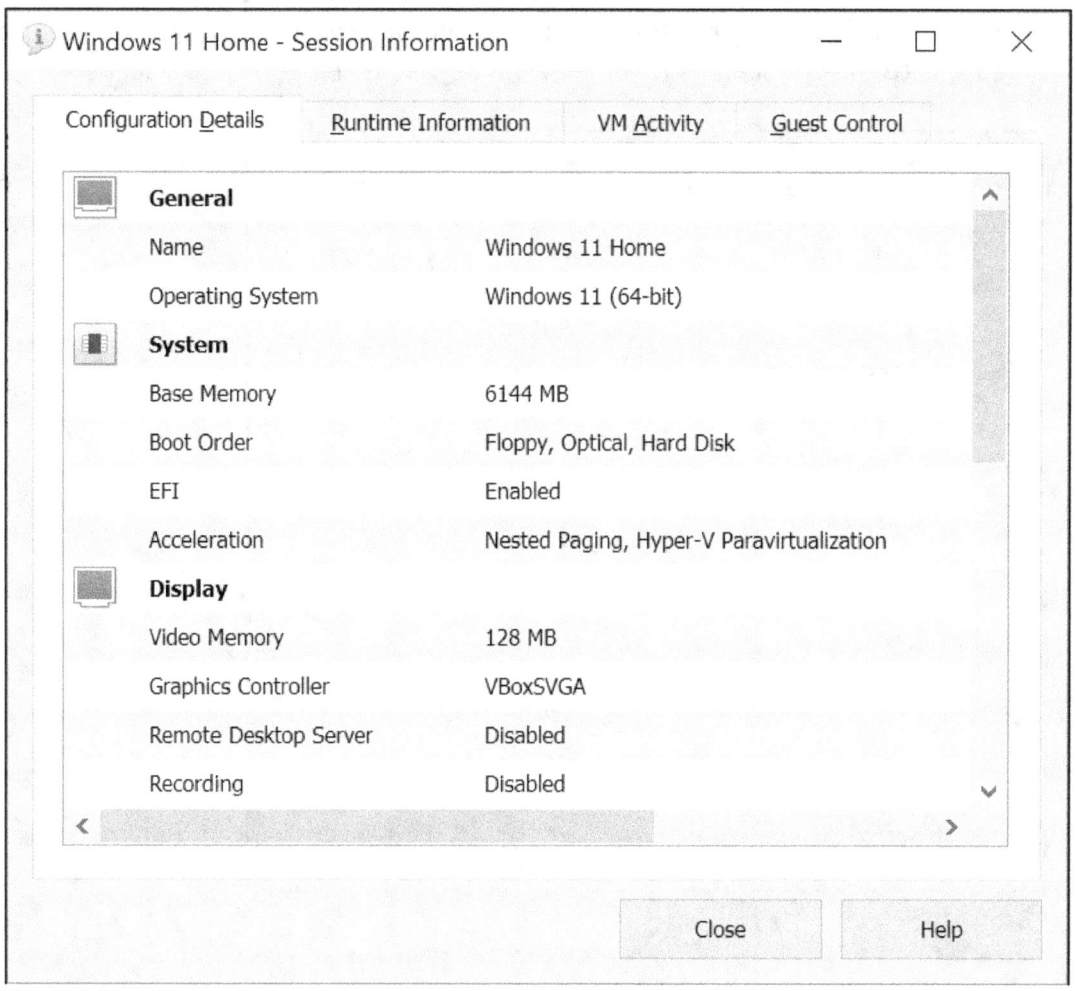

Figure 5.4

Chapter 5 – Virtual Machine Settings

Runtime Information shows things such as how long the VM has been running, how much data has been sent and received over the network and how much data has been read and written to the virtual hard disk.

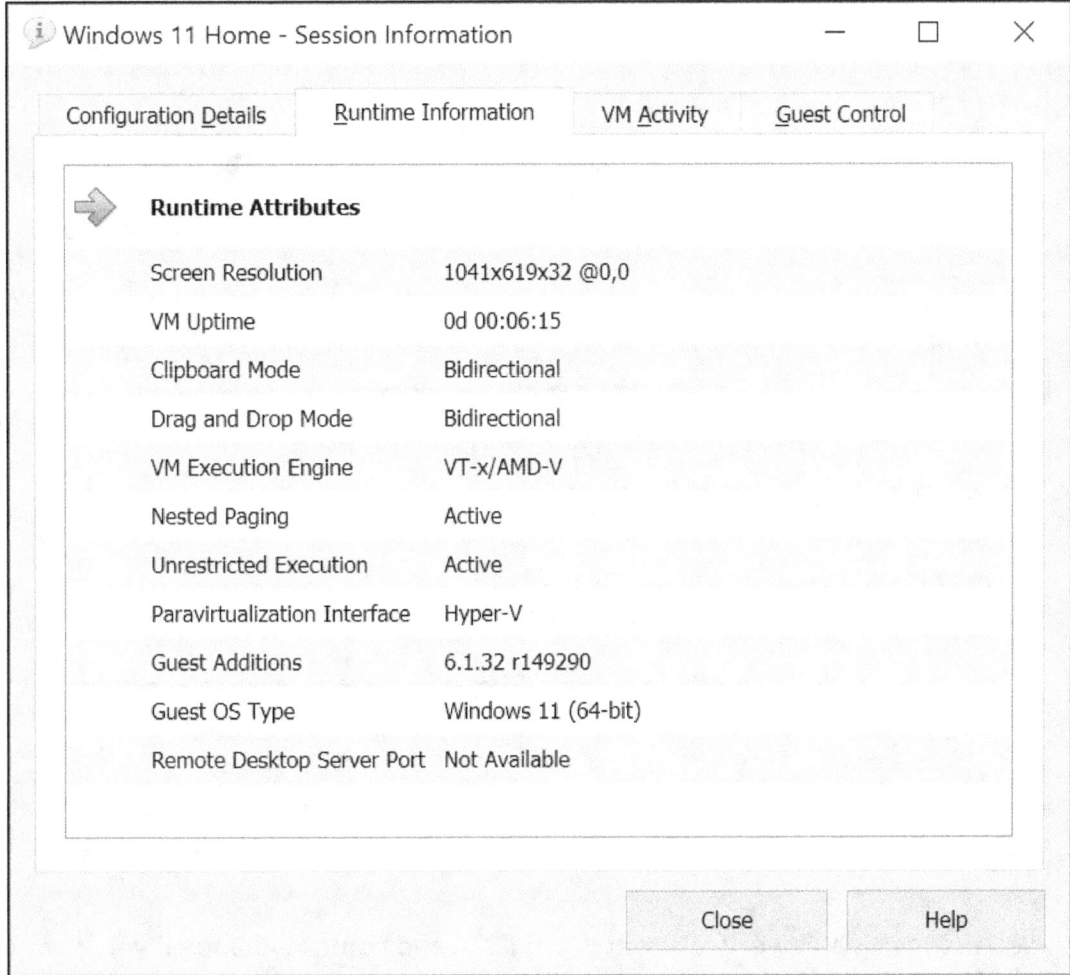

Figure 5.5

Chapter 5 – Virtual Machine Settings

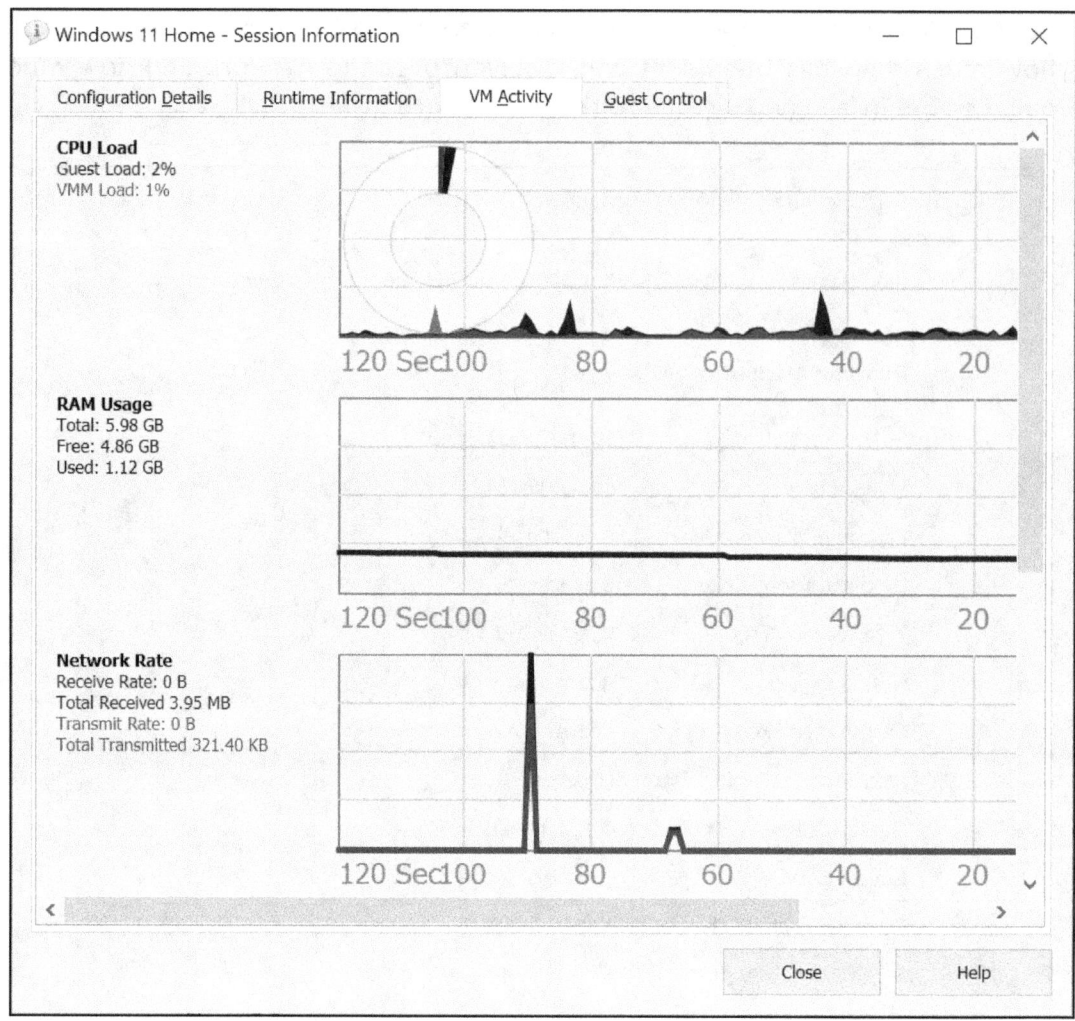

Figure 5.6

File Manager is a newer feature to VirtualBox and comes in handy if you want to transfer files to and from the host and guest computers. If you have ever used an FTP program to transfer files then this should look pretty familiar. Figure 5.7 shows a File Manager session between my host computer and my Windows 11 guest VM. The host drive folders are on the left and the guest on the right.

Chapter 5 – Virtual Machine Settings

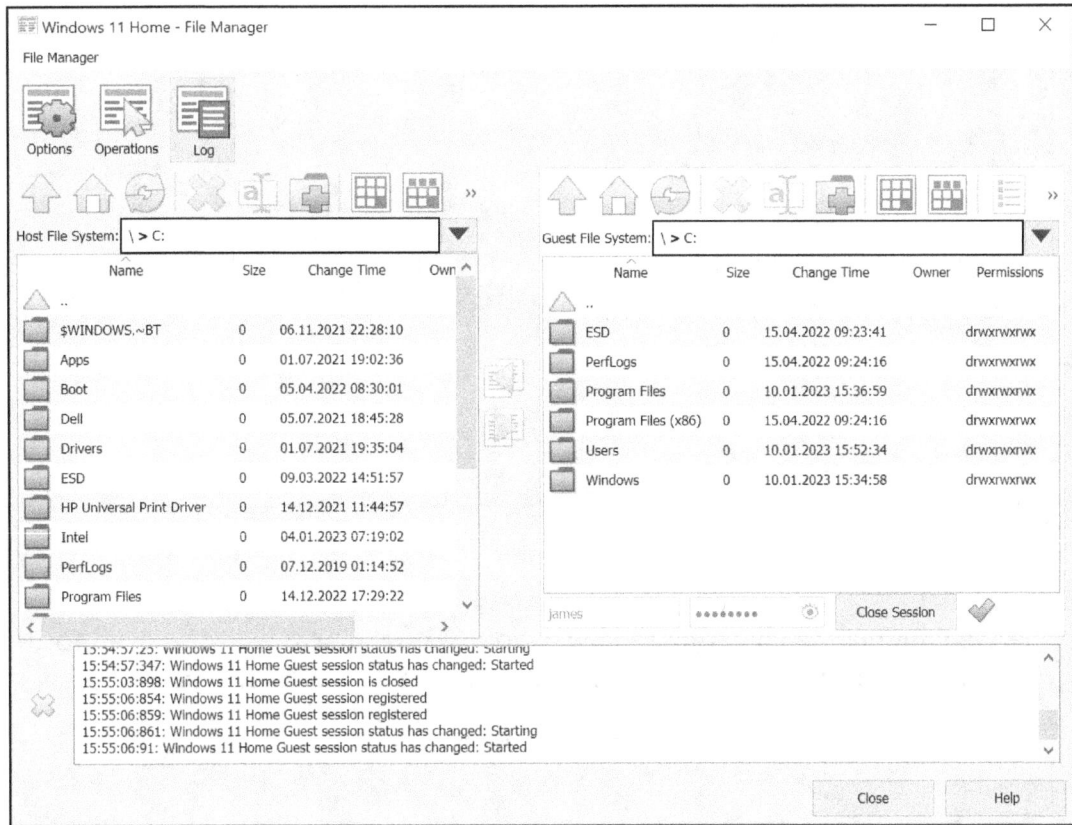

Figure 5.7

In order to use the File Manager feature, you will need to establish a connection between your host computer and the OS of the guest by clicking on the *Session* button. Then at the bottom of the window you will need to type in the name of a user account on the guest system and its password. Then click on *Create Session* and if you have the credentials correct, it will log on and show you the file from that guest computer.

To transfer files between the host and guest simply navigate to the appropriate folders on each one and then use either the host to guest transfer button or the guest to host transfer button in the middle of the panes to transfer any highlighted files between the two systems.

The *Session*, *Options*, *Operations* and *Log* buttons on the top will display their associated information at the bottom of the screen as shown in figure 5.8. You can click the X next to each one to close the particular view. To close out the session itself, you can click on the *Close Session* button or just close out the File Manager window itself.

Chapter 5 – Virtual Machine Settings

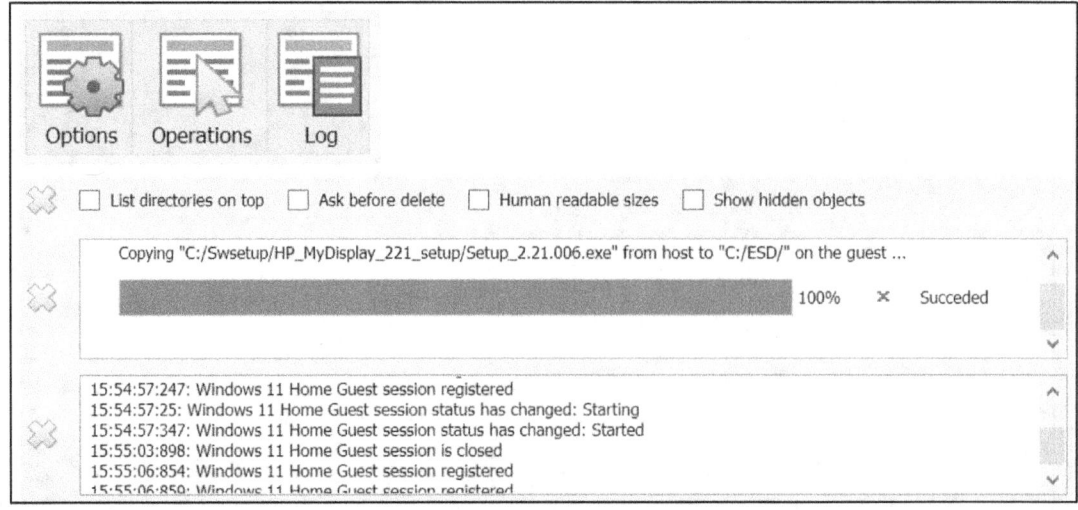

Figure 5.8

View Menu

The View menu lets you adjust the way your virtual machine is displayed for the most part but also has some other functionality that you should know about.

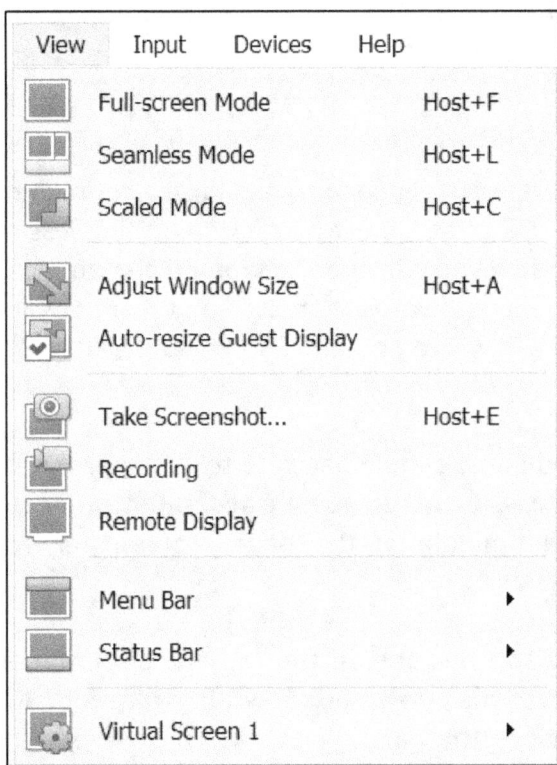

Figure 5.9

Chapter 5 – Virtual Machine Settings

The first five options are used to determine how the VM's console screen is displayed on your host computer.

- **Full-screen Mode** – This mode makes the VM console take up the entire screen on your computer and makes it look as if you were using that VM locally.

- **Seamless Mode** – This mode tries to make it look like the VM environment is integrated with the host environment as if you were running everything on one computer. You really need to try this for yourself to get the idea of how it works and decide if it's something you would like to use.

- **Scaled Mode** – This is used to make the virtual machine's screen be scaled to the size of the window. Normally if you were to stretch out the size of a virtual machine's console window you would end up with a border around the actual OS screen as seen in figure 5.10. Using Scaled Mode will force the VM screen to "scale" as you stretch it out, so the size of the OS screen adjusts automatically to the window size as shown in figure 5.11.

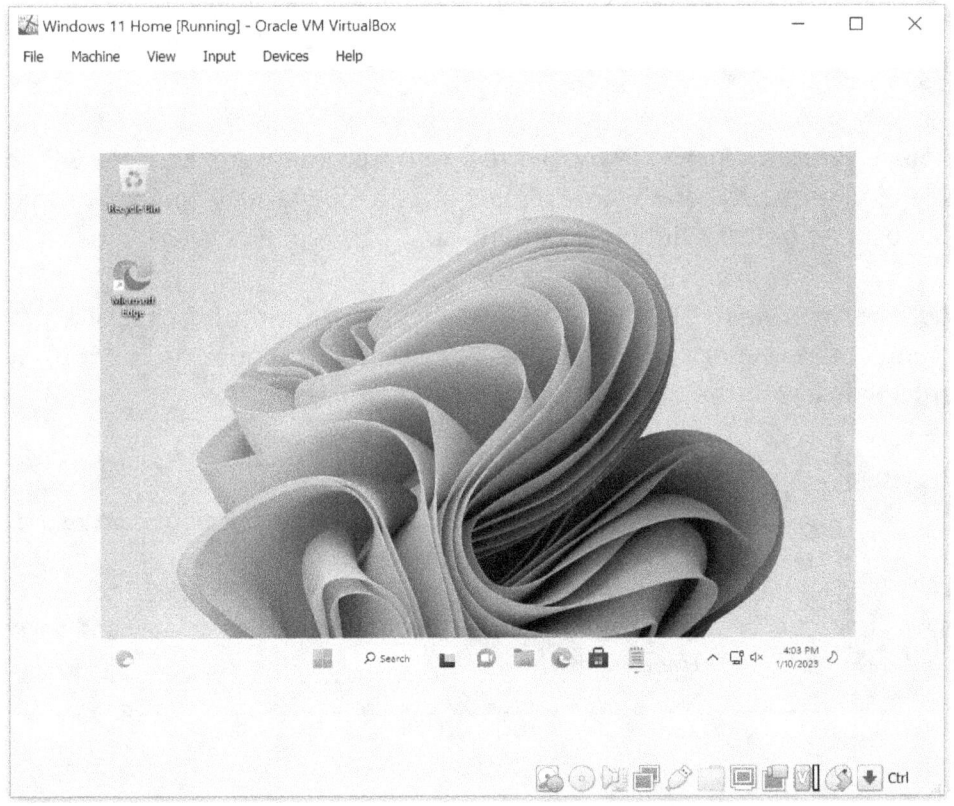

Figure 5.10

Chapter 5 – Virtual Machine Settings

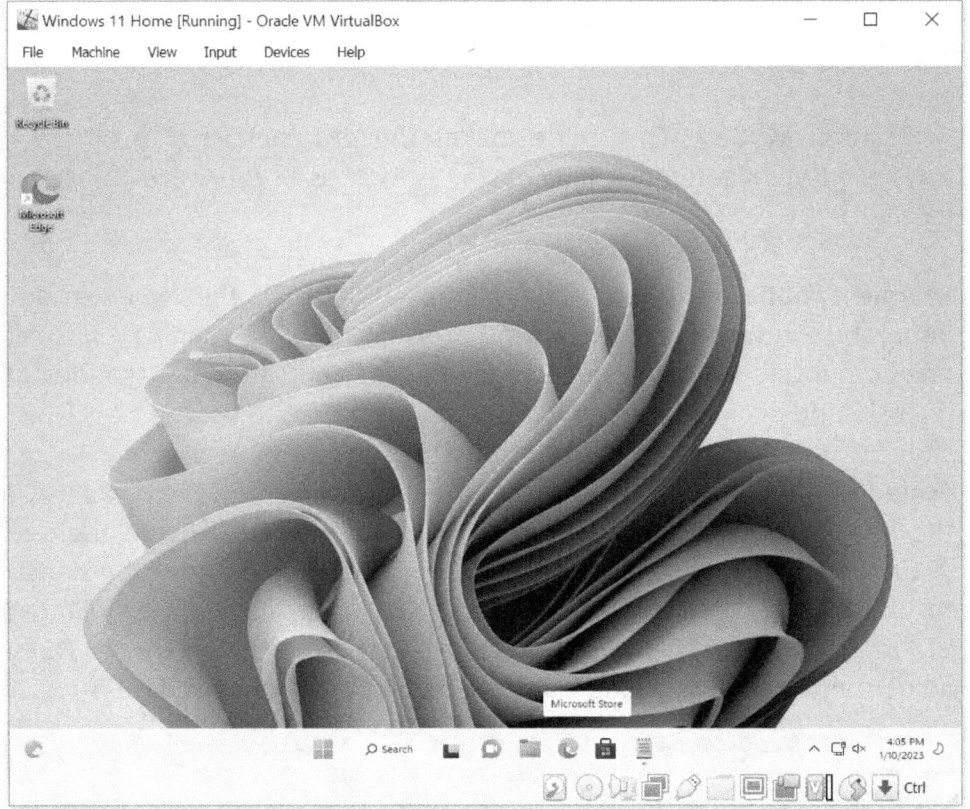

Figure 5.11

- **Adjust Window Size** – If you were to stretch out your console window as seen in figure 5.10 and want to get things back the way they were then you can use the Adjust Window Size to do so.

- **Auto-resize Guest Display** – If you select this option by checking it in the menu then every time you resize the VM's consoles screen, it will automatically fit the new size of the window.

 When you use these various display options make sure to pay attention to the message you get when enabling them. It will tell you what key combination you need to press on your keyboard to get out of that particular view and back to the default view.

Chapter 5 – Virtual Machine Settings

Some of the other functions from the View menu include the *Take Screenshot* feature which will take a picture of the VM's console screen and allow you to save it as an image file on your computer. There is also the *Recording* option which I mentioned earlier in the chapter that will record everything that is going on within the VM's console.

To enable recording, simply click on the *Recording* choice in the *View* menu and you will notice that the recording status icon for the VM will turn into an animated old school tape reel as seen in figure 5.12.

Figure 5.12

When you are done recording, you can go back to the Recording option in the View menu and uncheck it or you can right click the recoding status icon to stop the recording.

To view your recordings you will need to navigate to the folder that contains the virtual machines files on the hard drive of your computer (the host). The recording files will end with the *.webm* file extension and can be viewed in some video players and should also be viewable in your web browser. They will also have the date of the recording in the file name.

Chapter 5 – Virtual Machine Settings

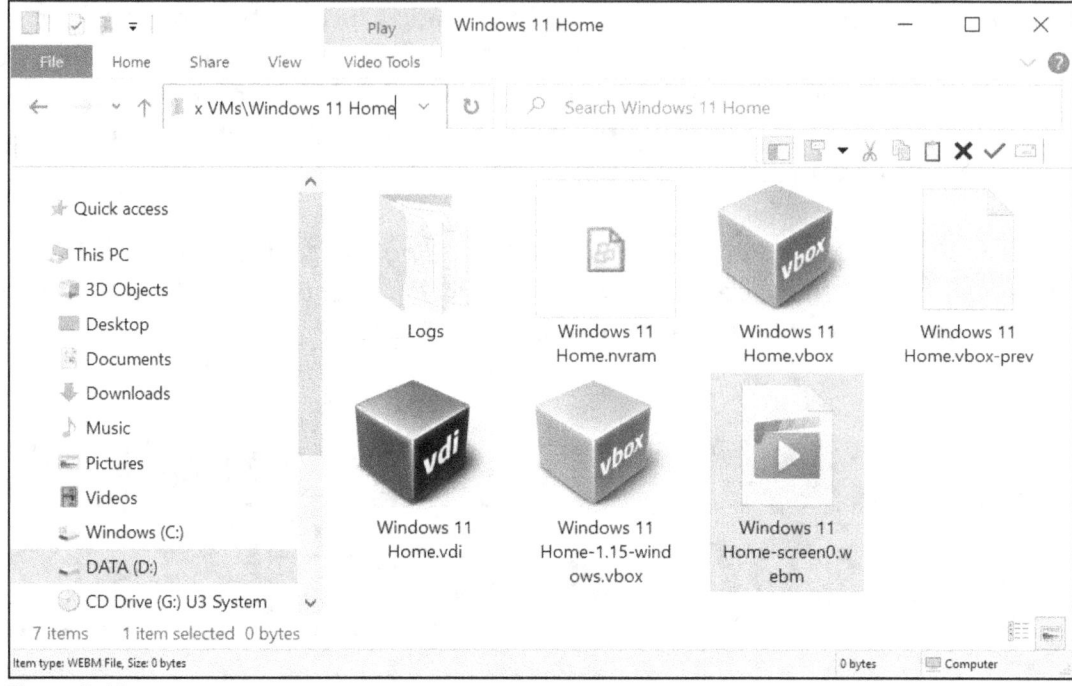

Figure 5.13

If you have ever used the Windows Remote Desktop client to connect and control Windows based computers over the network or Internet then you might be interested to know that you can initiate an RDP session to your VM right from the View menu by clicking on *Remote Display*.

There are a couple of caveats to using this feature. This first one is that you need to have Remote Desktop enabled within Windows on your VM and your VM also needs to be running a version of Windows that supports Remote Desktop which my Windows 10 Home VM does not. The Remote Display setting should be enabled on your VMs by default but if not then you can enable it from the *Display* setting and then the Remote Display tab within that VM's settings.

The *Menu Bar* and *Status Bar* choices are there in case you would like to hide either the Menu items on top or the Status icons on the bottom right. The problem with hiding the Menu items is that if you want them back you can't get to the menu items to re-enable it! To get around this press the right *Ctrl* key on your keyboard and the *Home* key at the same time and it should pop up a menu in the middle of your screen. Then you can go to the View menu and turn the Menu Bar back on.

Chapter 5 – Virtual Machine Settings

Finally, the *Virtual Screen* option lets you change the video resolution of the VM itself or the scale size of the console window in case you want things larger or smaller.

Input Menu
The Input menu only has a couple of settings, but the *Keyboard Setting* is one you will want to know about.

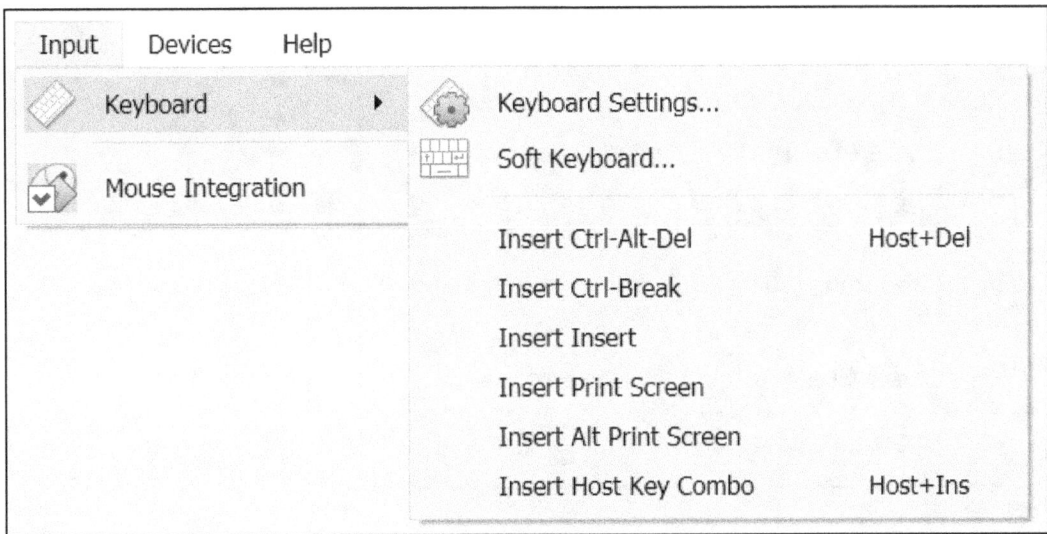
Figure 5.14

The Keyboard Settings are used to send keyboard commands to your VM that normally won't work since the command will be applied to your host computer rather than your VM when pressed. For example, you might know that you need to press Ctrl-Alt-Del when logging into Windows computers in a domain/corporate environment or when using Windows Server operating systems.

If you had a Windows VM running and pressed Ctrl-Alt-Del then that would send that command to your local (host) computer and not the VM. But if you need to send that Ctrl-Alt-Del command to the VM then you can do so from the Keyboard Settings menu item.

Devices Menu
The Devices menu lets you configure or change settings for various devices that you may have attached to your VM.

Chapter 5 – Virtual Machine Settings

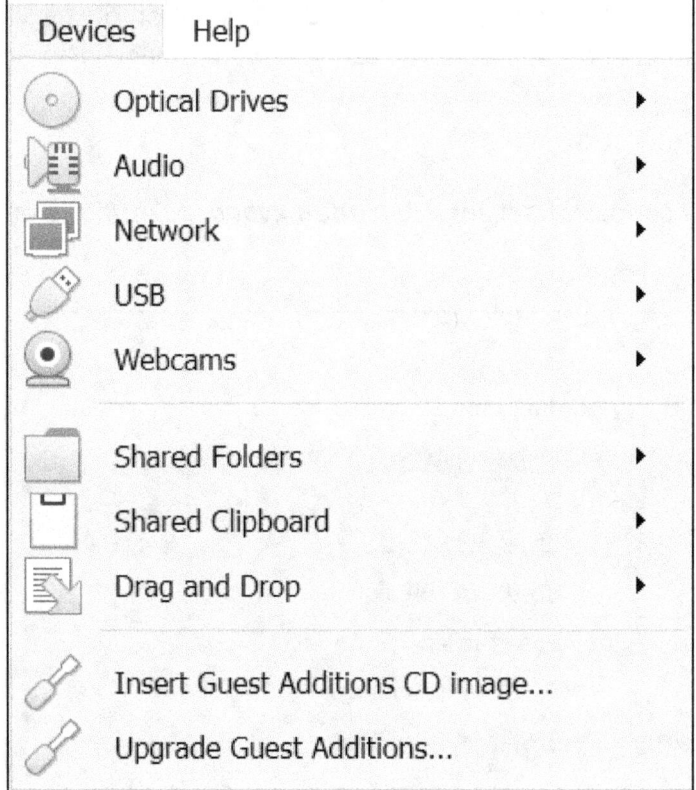

Figure 5.15

For example, you can click on *Optical Drives* and attach a CD or ISO image file to your virtual DVD drive so you can use it within your VM. Or if you want a quick way to check your network settings you can do so from the *Network* menu item.

I will be discussing *Shared Folders* later in this chapter so I will skip that for now, but the *Shared Clipboard* option can be used to share things you copy such as text so you can paste it from host to guest or guest to host. It is disabled by default so if your copy and paste operations are not working then that is most likely why.

The *Drag and Drop* feature is really handy because it lets you drag and drop files from host to guest or guest to host by simply dragging a file from one computer to the other as if you were working in two different folders on the same computer. It is also disabled by default.

Chapter 5 – Virtual Machine Settings

General Settings

Now it's time to get into some of the more important virtual machine settings that you might find yourself needing to adjust to get your VMs running smoothly. In the following sections I will be accessing the VM settings from the Machine menu but you can also access them from the VirtualBox Manager by selecting the VM you want to adjust and then clicking on the Settings button. You might notice that the Network settings will be missing from this chapter and that's because I will be covering Networking in Chapter 6.

The *General* settings section consists of four tabs and there isn't too much that can be changed from any of them.

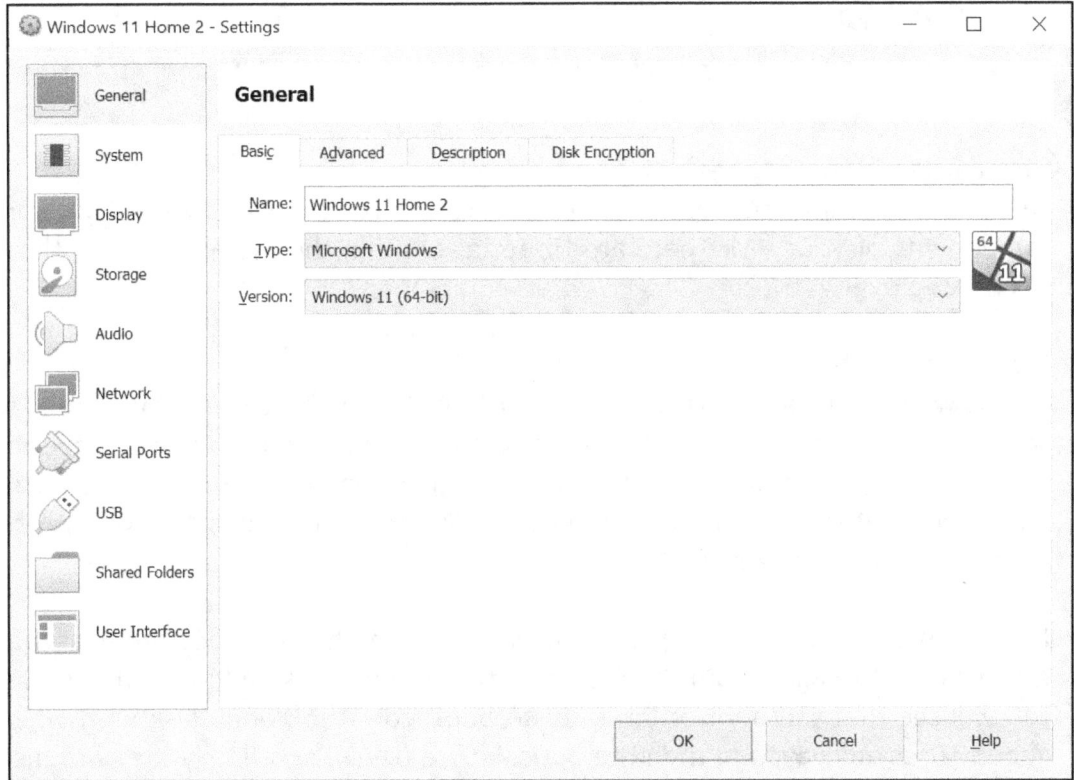

Figure 5.16

Here is a brief overview of what each tab does.

- **Basic** – Shows the VM name, its OS type and the OS version.

- **Advanced** – Tells you the location of any snapshots (discussed in Chapter 7) and also gives you a place to enable the Shared Clipboard and Drag and Drop features.

- **Description** – Here you can type in any information or notes you want to make for the VM.

- **Disk Encryption** – If you have the need to protect your virtual machine's files then you can apply disk encryption to that VM from here.

 If you see that a particular setting or settings are greyed out that is most likely because the VM is running and you can't make any changes to those settings unless you shut down the VM first.

System\Hardware Settings
The System settings section is where you can make changes to the hardware components of your VM. There are three tabs within the System settings that I will now go over.

Motherboard Tab
Here is where you can adjust the amount of RAM your VM is using if you need to add more or take some away to allocate to another VM. You can either move the slider to make your adjustment or type in an exact number in the box. Just remember that the number is in megabytes (MB) and not gigabytes (GB) so you will need to do your conversion (1024 MB = 1 GB).

Just like with your host computer, virtual machines have a boot order as well which can be changed from the System settings. If you take a look at figure 5.17 you will see that the boot order is set to boot from the floppy disk first, which nobody uses anyway, and then the optical drive (DVD), and finally the hard disk. To change the boot order simply click on the device you want to move and use the up or down arrow to move it wherever you like in the boot order list.

Chapter 5 – Virtual Machine Settings

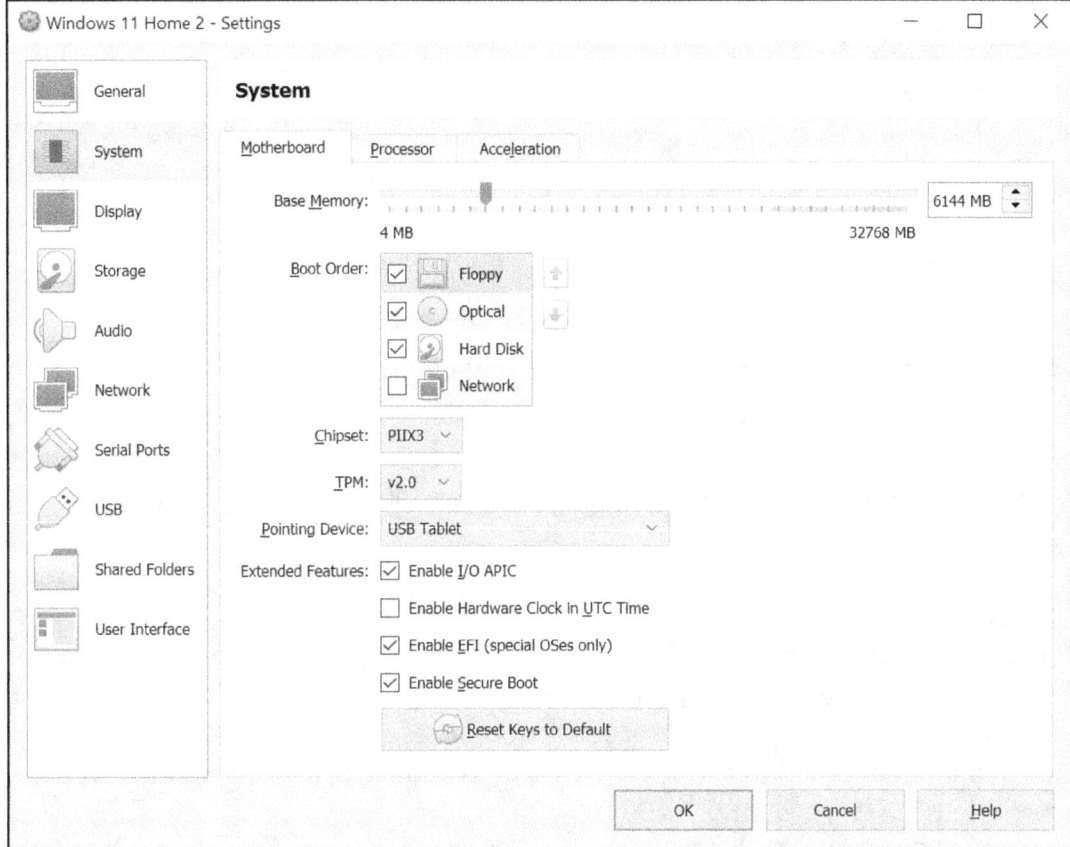

Figure 5.17

The *Pointing Device* setting is chosen by VirtualBox based on the VM type and for newer operating systems it will most likely use the *USB Tablet* option and for older OS types it will use *PS/2 Mouse*. If you want to change the setting and see if it affects the way your mouse performs you can give it a shot.

The *Extended Features* settings should be configured for you by VirtualBox, but you can change them if needed. For example, the I/O APIC setting will usually be checked when you are running a 64-bit version of Windows on your VM. On the Linux VM I created in Chapter 4 the *Hardware Clock in UTC Time* box was checked automatically by VirtualBox since Linux usually uses Coordinated Universal Time.

Processor Tab
The settings here have to do with the VMs processor or CPU as it is also called. Here you can add additional processors to your VM if you plan on running processor intensive applications on your VM. I usually find a lack of RAM to be more of a performance issue that processor power in my VMs.

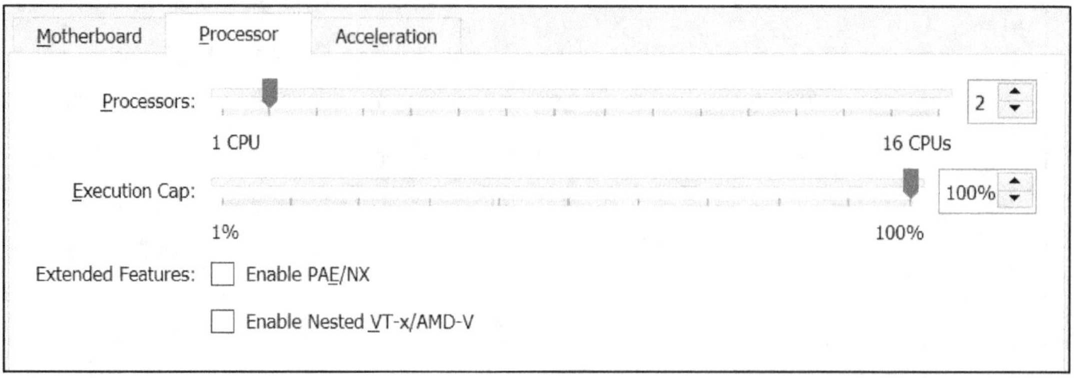

Chapter 5 – Virtual Machine Settings

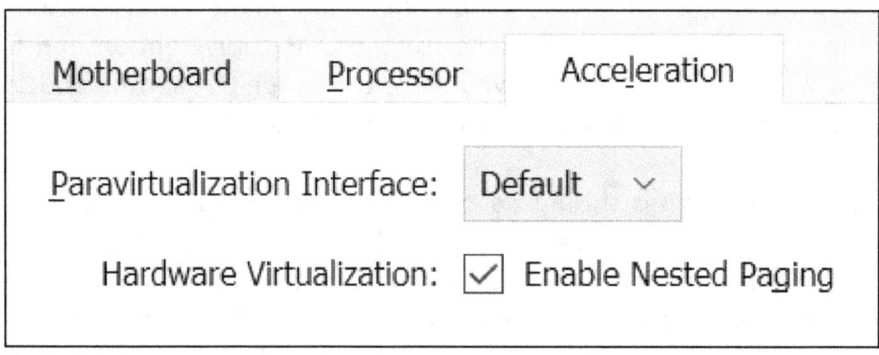

Figure 5.18

The *Execution Cap* setting limits the amount of time a host CPU spends to emulate a virtual CPU. The default setting is 100%, meaning that there is no limitation.

Acceleration Tab
The settings here will be configured based on the OS type you are using for your VM and you shouldn't change any of the settings unless you run into a specific problem relates to hardware acceleration. These settings are CPU specific so changing them can affect how your VM runs or make it so it doesn't run at all.

If you think you might benefit from making changes here, you will need to know your CPU model and do a little research to see what features it supports.

Figure 5.19

Display Settings
Just like your host computer, virtual machines need video memory to be able to use higher resolutions and color depths and the options you have here will be based on the video card you have installed in your host computer. There are other display related settings you can adjust from here which I will now go over.

Chapter 5 – Virtual Machine Settings

Screen Tab
Video Memory is how much memory you have allocated from your host to be used on the VM. The maximum setting will be based on the video hardware you have in your host computer. Since I am just using a standard video card that comes built into the motherboard, I only get a maximum setting of 128 MB. If I were to check the box that says *Enable 3D Acceleration* then my Video Memory maximum would increase.

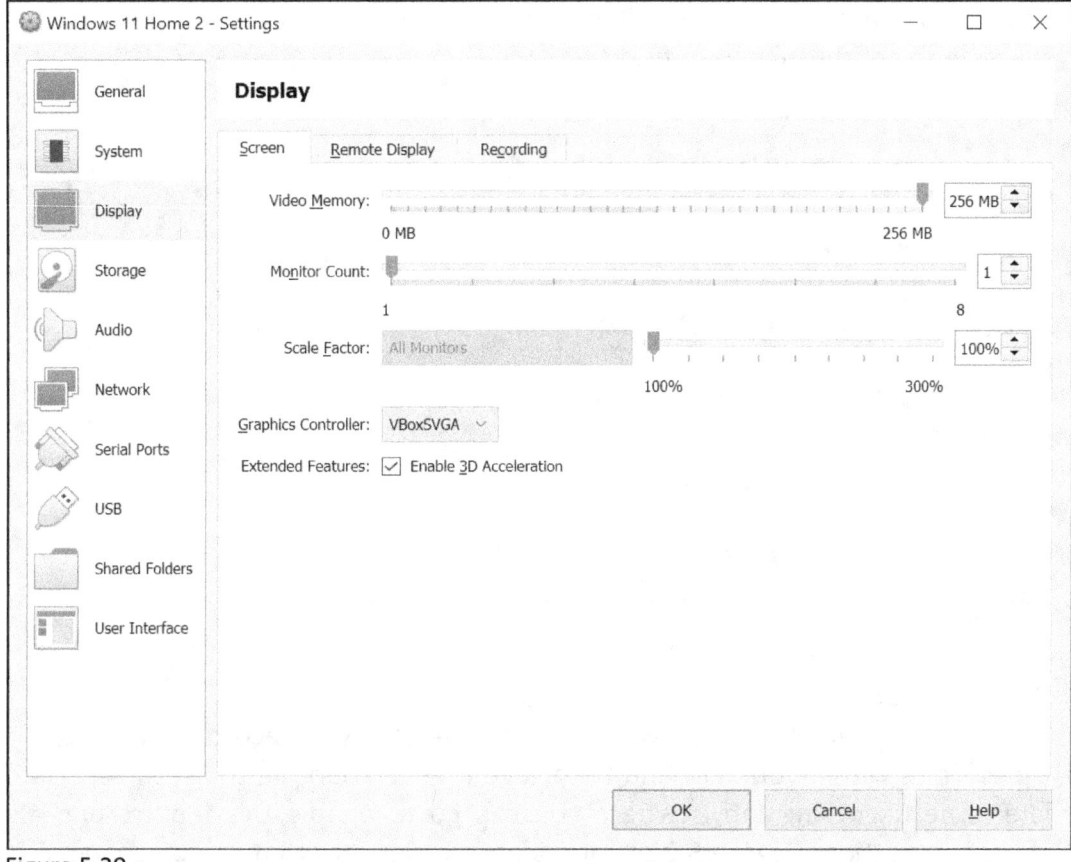
Figure 5.20

Monitor Count is used to allocation additional virtual monitors to your VM just like you might have on your physical host computer. The guest OS needs to support multiple monitors to use this feature.

Scale Factor can be used to increase the display size of the VM making things like text easier to read. This can be applied to all monitors or just a specific one.

89

Chapter 5 – Virtual Machine Settings

Graphics Controller specifies the graphics adapter type used by the guest VM and VirtualBox should default to the highest quality setting your host computer will support. *VBoxSVGA* is the default for VMs running Windows 7 and higher.

Remote Display Tab
Earlier in this chapter, I mentioned how you can use the Windows Remote Desktop (RDP) tool to connect to your VMs console. Here is where you can enable this feature if it's not enabled for some reason. RDP uses port 3389 by default so make sure you don't change this number unless you need to, for example to get through your firewall.

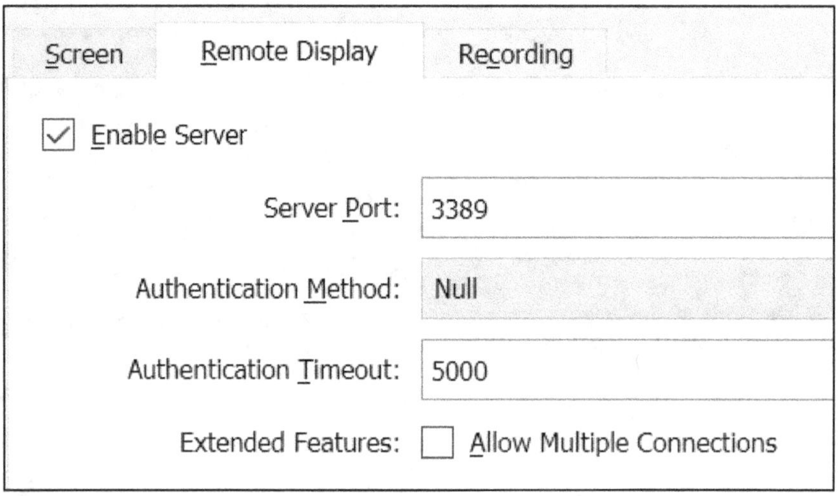

Figure 5.21

Recording Tab
Earlier I discussed how VirtualBox gives you the ability to record the activity that is occurring within your VM and then save it as a video file that you can watch later. The Recording tab is where you can go to enable this feature and also change its settings. Figure 5.22 shows all of the settings that can be changed for this feature.

Chapter 5 – Virtual Machine Settings

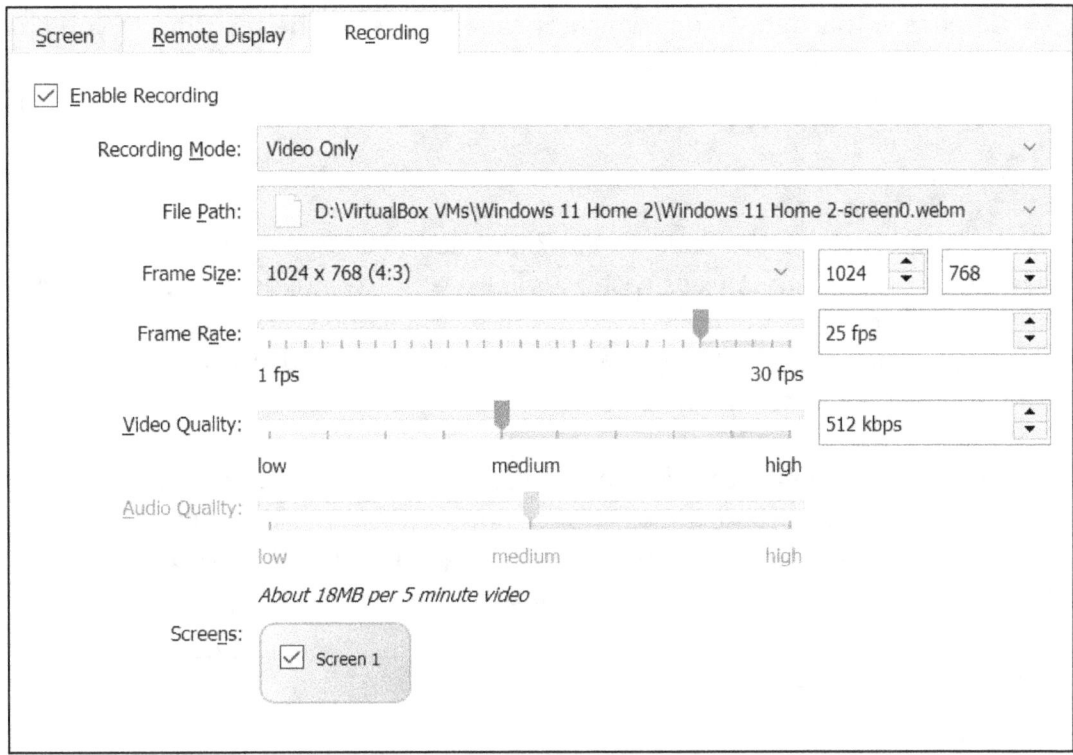

Figure 5.22

There are quite a few settings here so I will now go over each one of them.

- **Recording Mode** – Settings to record video only, audio only or both video and audio.

- **File Path** – The location on the hard drive of the host computer that the videos will be stored at.

- **Frame Size** – This controls how large the recorded video will be in regards to its screen resolution and aspect ratio.

- **Frame Rate** – The frame rate (frames per second) used in the recording. The higher the number, the smoother the video playback will be.

- **Video Quality** – The higher the video quality, the larger the video file will be.

- **Audio Quality** – The higher the audio quality, the larger the video file will be.

Chapter 5 – Virtual Machine Settings

- **Screens** – This determines which of the screens will be recorded if you have more than one monitor enabled.

Storage Settings

The Storage settings are used to view and edit the properties of your storage devices. The *Storage Devices* section will list any storage devices that you have attached to your VM. Figure 5.22 shows that I have one storage controller for my VM with a virtual hard disk (Windows 11 Home.vdi) and the VirtualBox Guest Additions ISO mounted on my Optical drive.

A controller is a device that is used to control various storage devices like hard disks, storage arrays and optical drives and allows them to communicate and work with the operating system. I will be going over how to add additional storage controllers and hard disks in Chapter 7.

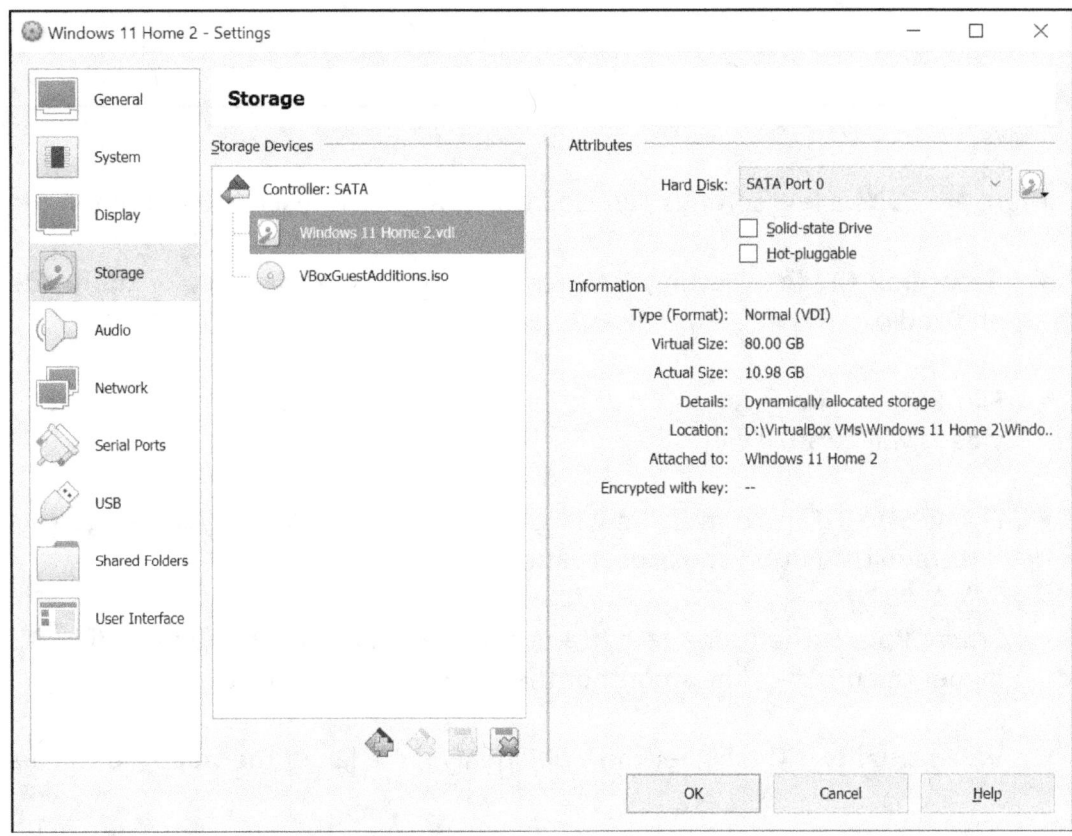

Figure 5.23

Chapter 5 – Virtual Machine Settings

When you click on a particular storage device, it will show its attributes and other information off to the right as seen in figure 5.23. As you can see, my virtual hard disk is using SATA Port 0 (these ports start with the number 0 and go up from there) on my storage controller and has 80 GB of space allocated to it. The *Actual Size* of my hard disk is 10.98 GB because it's a dynamically expanding disk that only takes up the space as needed.

Audio Settings
VirtualBox has the capability to allow sound to transfer from your VM to the speakers used by your host computer and should be on by default. If not then you can come to the Audio Settings section and check the box that says *Enable Audio*.

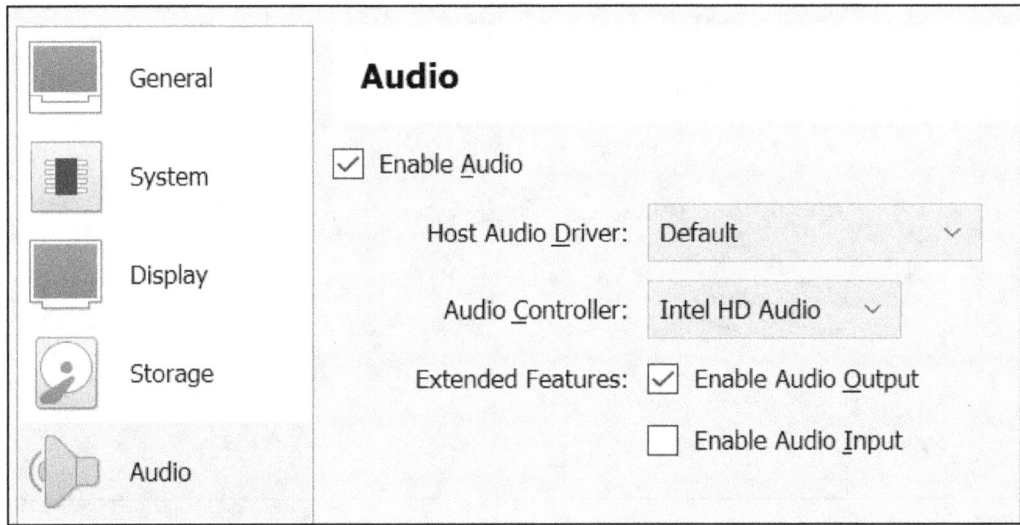

Figure 5.24

The *Host Audio Driver* is the software that is used to enable audio to be heard from your VM. VirtualBox will install its own driver based on the OS used on your VM. The *Audio Controller* is the virtual audio hardware that VirtualBox uses to emulate the sound card for the VM. Once again, VirtualBox will install an audio controller based on the guest OS. It will give you some other options to try in case you are having issues getting sound output from your VM.

Chapter 5 – Virtual Machine Settings

The *Enable Audio Output* allows sound to be sent from your VM to your host computer while *Enable Audio Input* allows you to send audio to your VM from your host.

Serial & USB Ports
Serial ports are a bit outdated now but there are still some uses for them. Normally they are used to attach older, legacy type hardware to your computer such as older modems and printers and console connections to things like network switches. You can enable up to four serial ports from the *Serial Ports* settings.

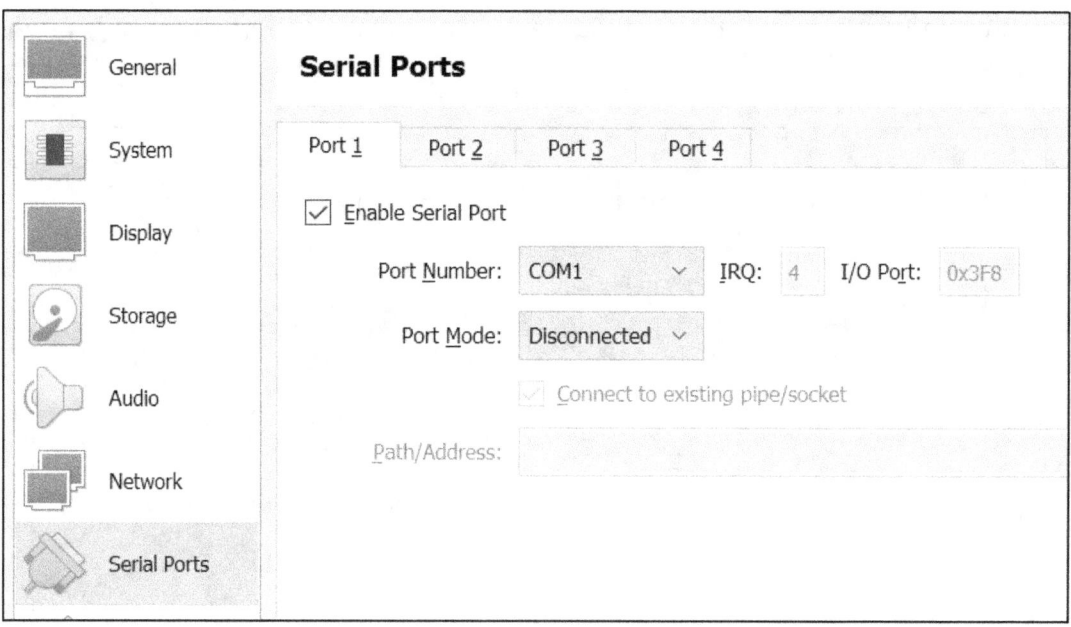

Figure 5.25

Most of us use many USB devices on our computers and it's nice to be able to use those same devices on our virtual machines. Fortunately, VirtualBox makes this possible by giving us the ability to add USB ports to VMs that map to the USB ports on the host. Once you check the *Enable USB Controller* checkbox, you can then add a USB 1.1, 2.0 or 3.0 USB controller to your system and then attach one of the USB devices from your host to your VM.

Chapter 5 – Virtual Machine Settings

Figure 5.26 shows that I am using a USB 3.0 controller and when I click on the *Add New USB* button it shows me a list of devices that it has found on my host computer. I will then click on the *SanDisk U3 Cruzer Micro device* which is a USB flash drive. Figure 5.27 shows the new USB device added to my VM.

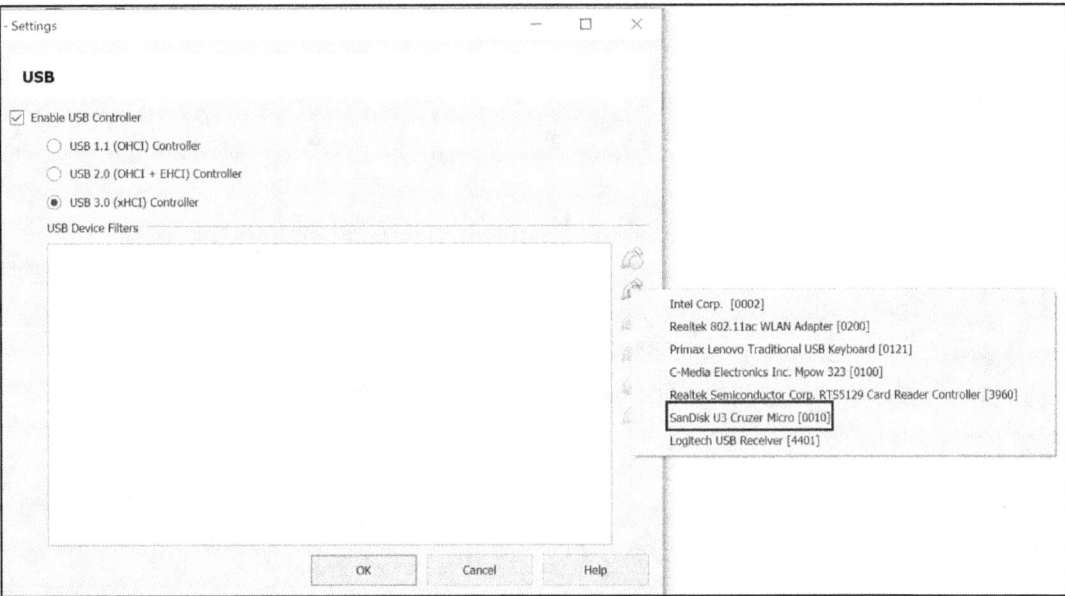

Figure 5.26

Chapter 5 – Virtual Machine Settings

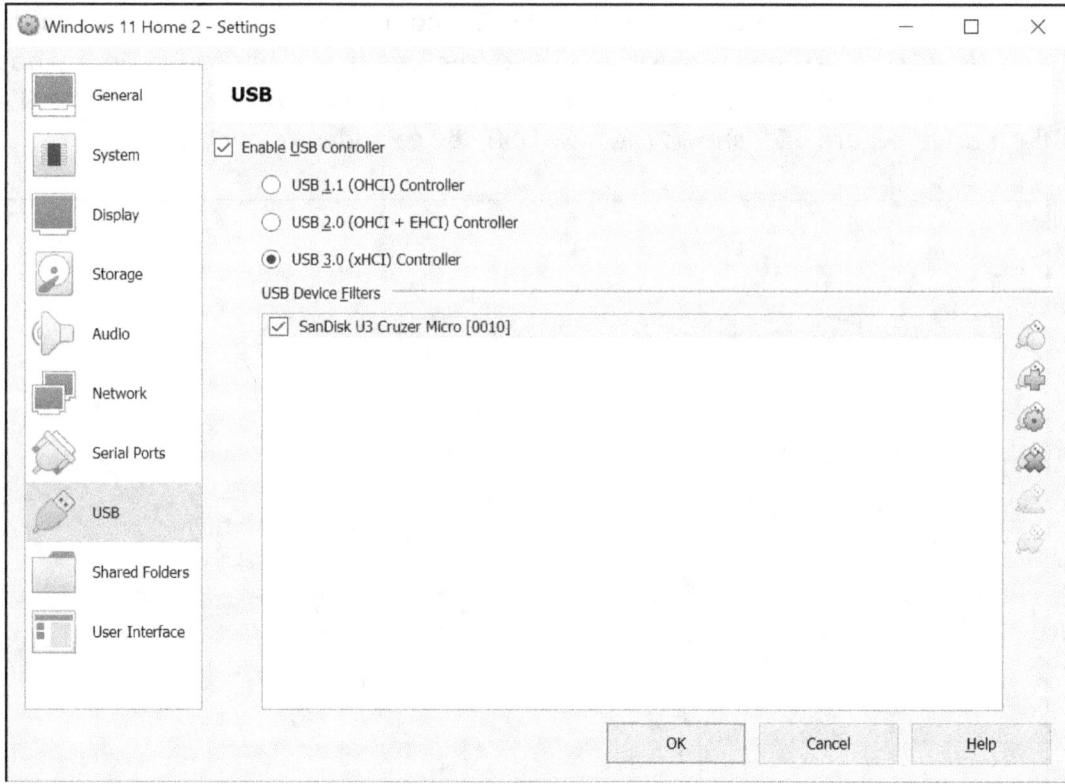

Figure 5.27

If you find that your USB device does not show up in your VM when you boot it up then go to the Devices menu on the VM console itself, then USB and choose your USB device from the available choices.

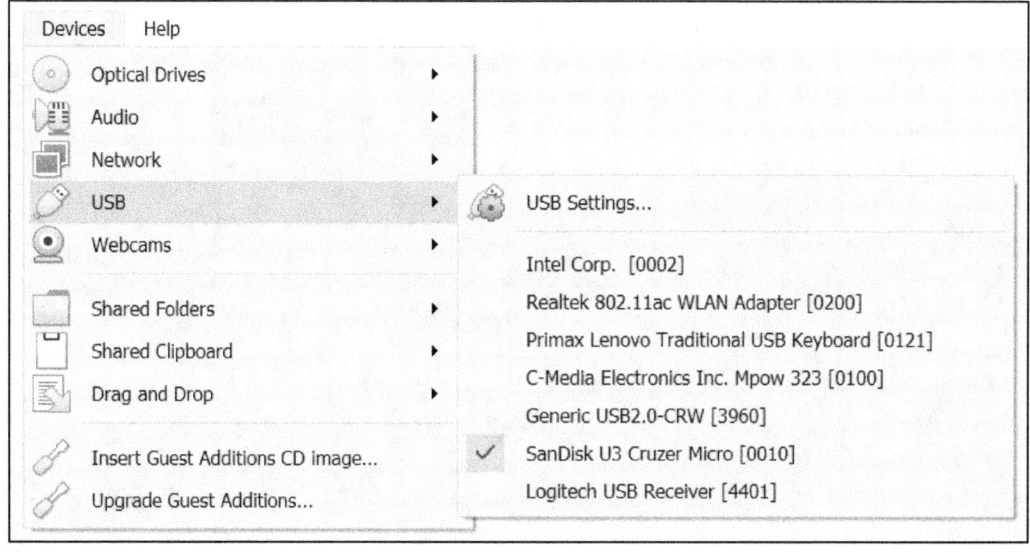

Figure 5.28

Shared Folders

You might remember my discussion on the File Manager feature where you could transfer files to and from your VM right from your host computer. There is another similar feature that allows you to access your host computer's files from within your VM called Shared Folders.

If you have ever worked with network shares then this will look familiar to you because it works in a similar fashion except no network connection is required between the two computers. Once you configure a shared folder on your host, your VM will be able to use that folder as if it were another drive configured within the VM itself.

To set up a shared folder, click the *New Shared folder* icon as seen in figure 5.29 and then fill in the required information. For the *Folder Path,* you can either type in the path to the folder or browse to the folder itself. Then you can give the folder a name and decide if you want it to be read only or if you want to be able to make changes to the content of that folder from within the VM.

The *Auto-mount* feature will make VirtualBox mount the folder in your VM and use the drive letter you assign it under *Mount point* (for Windows). Finally, the *Make Permanent* checkbox can be used to have the shared folder re-mounted every time you start the VM.

Chapter 5 – Virtual Machine Settings

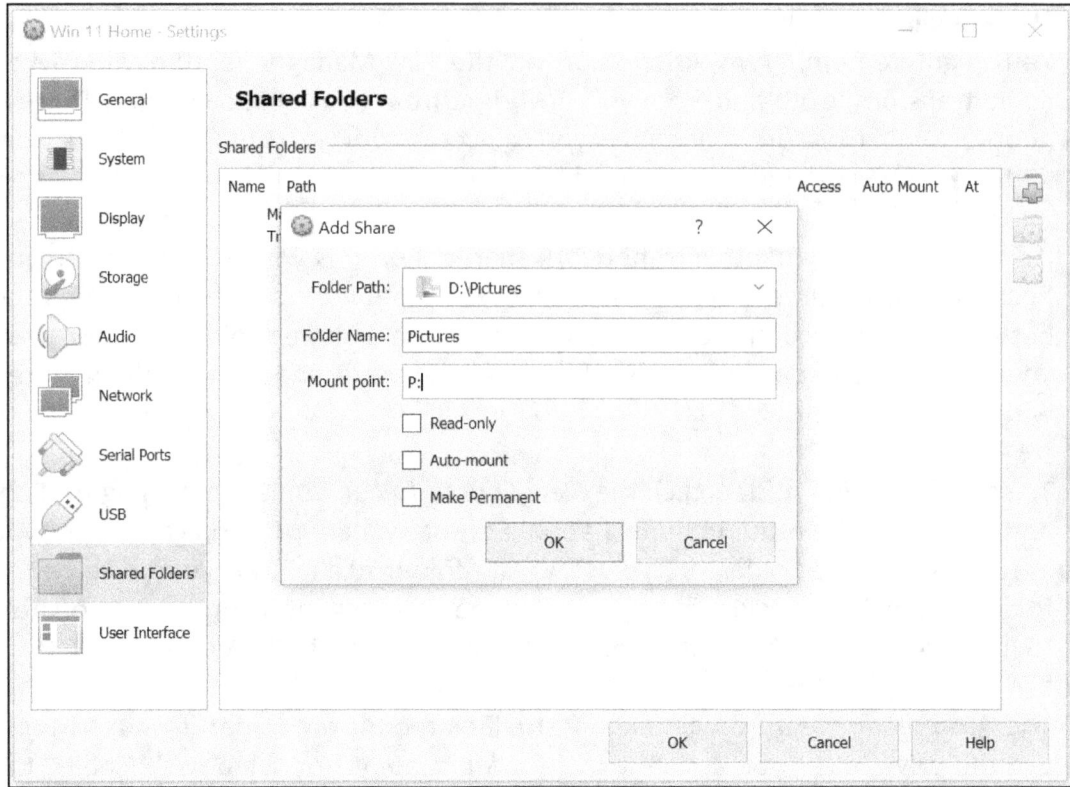

Figure 5.29

Once you click OK you will see the new shared folder with its details listed as shown in figure 5.30.

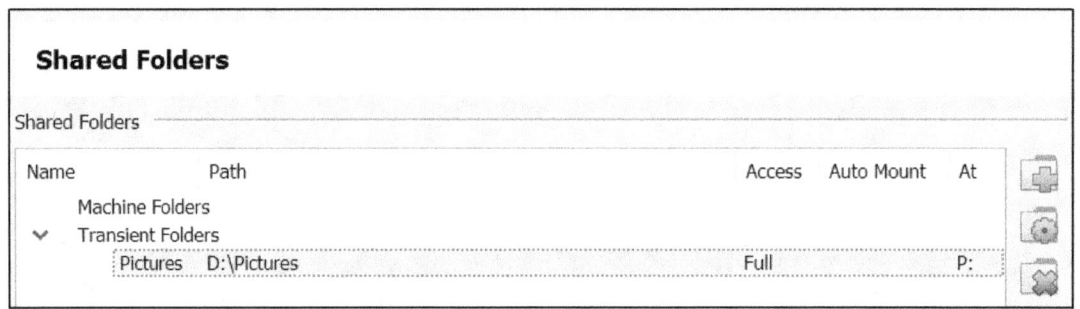

Figure 5.30

When I go to the VM and look at all the drives for this computer I can see that I now have a **P:** drive under *Network locations* mapped to *\\VBoxSrv* even though it's not technically a network drive. When I open that shared location it will actually open the Pictures folder on my host computer.

Chapter 5 – Virtual Machine Settings

User Interface

The last of the settings categories that I will be discussing in this chapter is for the User Interface options (figure 5.31). These options are used to determine what menu items and status icons will be available with your VM console window.

You can select which items from each of the menus will be displayed by checking or unchecking the boxes next to that particular item. By default, all menu items will be shown with the exception of a couple under the Machine menu.

The *Mini Toolbar* options correspond to the small toolbar that floats down from the top of the screen when you are in Full Screen or Seamless mode (figure5.32).

The checkbox at the bottom of the User Interface settings box is used to show or hide the status icons in the VM's console window.

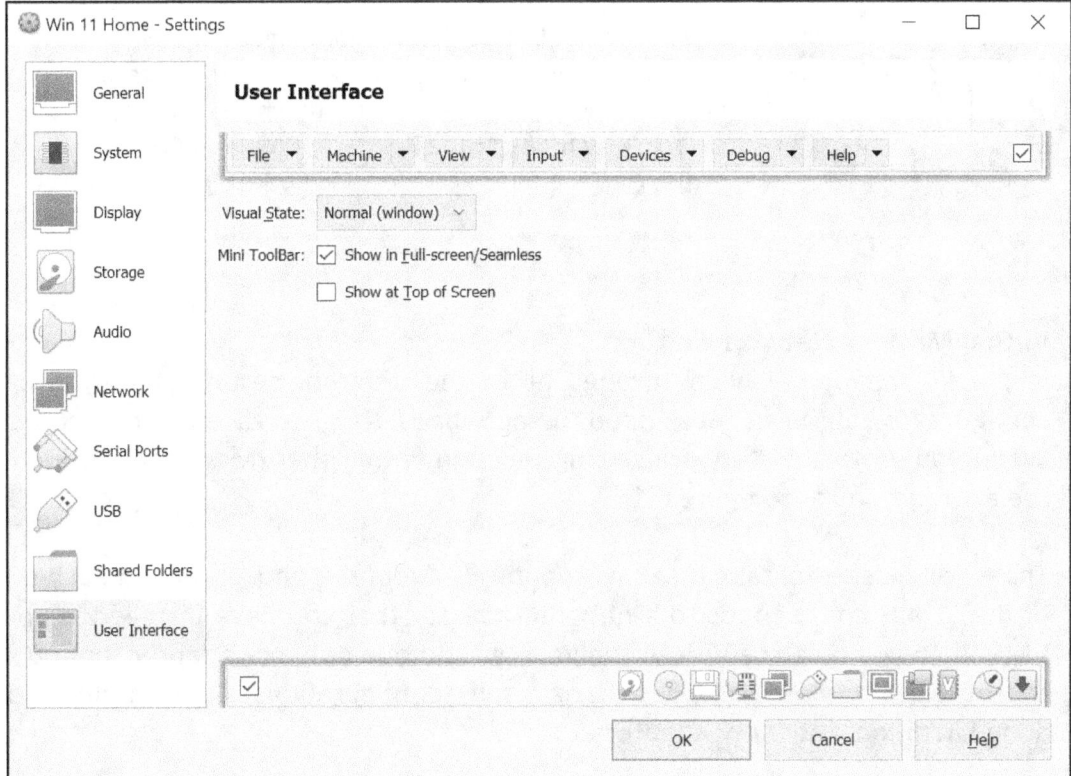

Figure 5.31

Chapter 6 – Networking

If you plan on running more than one virtual machine and want your VMs to be able to communicate with each other then you will need to know a little about how VirtualBox networking works. Fortunately, if you are new to virtualization and networking, VirtualBox will do most of the work for you at least when it comes to getting your VMs on the Internet by sharing the Internet connection that your host computer uses.

If you plan on doing some more advanced networking within your VMs then you are looking at configurations that are outside of VirtualBox and will be more dependent on the operating system of your VMs and what you are planning to do with your network.

If you would like to learn more about networking in general without being worried about getting lost in the process, then you might want to check out my book called **Networking Made Easy - Get Yourself Connected**.
https://www.amazon.com/dp/1720034109

Virtual Machine Network Settings
In the last chapter, I went through all of the different settings that you can configure for your VMs but skipped the network settings to save for this chapter. When you go to the Network settings section within the VMs settings you will see a screen similar to figure 6.1.

There will be several tabs that say *Adapter 1*, *Adapter 2* and so on and each one of these tabs corresponds to a network adapter that you have installed in your VM. When you create a VM, VirtualBox will add one network adapter for you so the other tabs most likely won't have any configurations shown unless you added additional network adapters yourself.

Now I will take some time to go through all of the settings that are shown within the Network settings for the VM. I have clicked on the arrow next to *Advanced* to have all of the additional configurations shown.

Chapter 6 – Networking

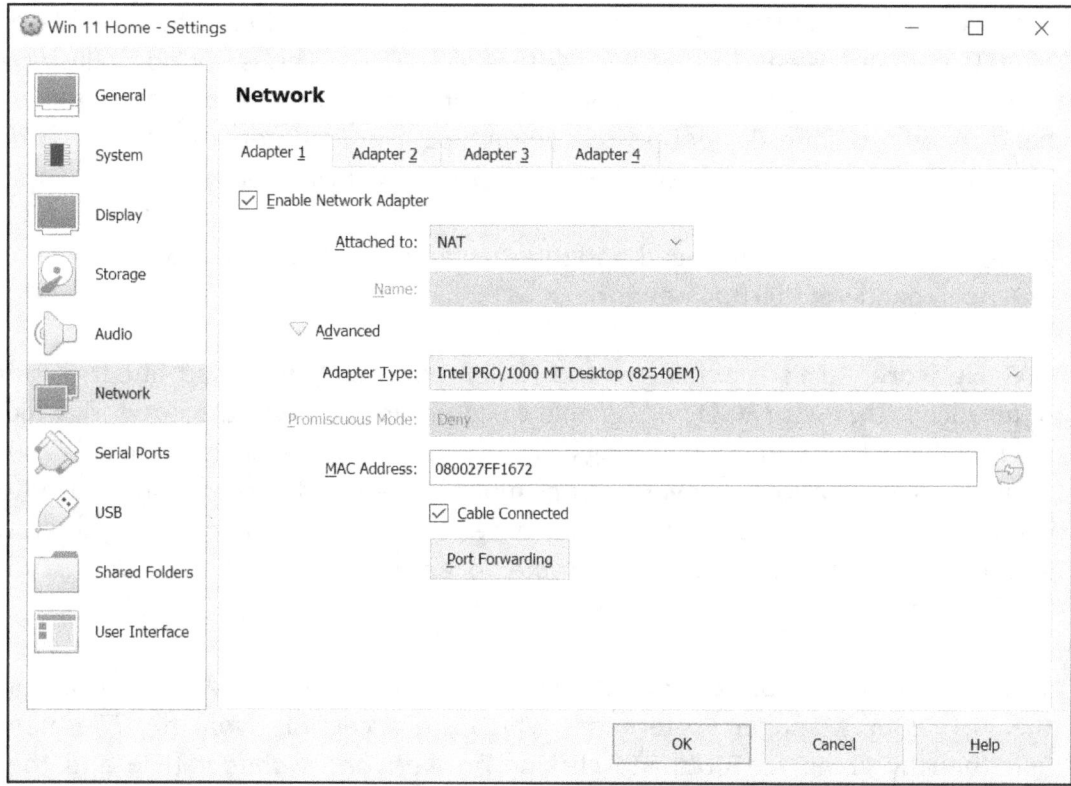

Figure 6.1

It should be obvious that you will need to make sure the box that says *Enable Network Adapter* is checked otherwise you will not be doing any networking whatsoever! Here are what all the other settings are used for.

The *Attached to* section is where you can change how your virtual network adapter uses your host network to communicate. The default setting that will be used for new VMs is **NAT** which stands for Network Address Translation.

For simplicities sake, NAT is the process of sharing one network or Internet connection with multiple devices or in other words, your host computer is sharing its network connection will all of your virtual machines. VirtualBox includes a built in DHCP server (discussed later) and NAT engine that takes care of assigning IP addresses to your VMs and performing any host to guest networking translations.

Using NAT, your VMs can access the Internet through your host computer's network adapter. They can also access outside networks that are connected to your host but the VMs can't communicate with each other.

Chapter 6 – Networking

When using NAT, VirtualBox will assign your VMs an IP address (discussed later) of 10.0.2.15 and use a DHCP server address of 10.0.2.2. This is not normally what you would do in a physical network environment because each computer will need its own unique IP address to communicate on the network, but it works just fine for the communication capabilities that NAT provides.

There are other more advanced options you can play around with when it comes time to expand your virtual network.

NAT Network – This is similar to the NAT mode I just discussed but the main difference is that your VMs will be able to communicate over the network which is crucial if you need to do things like share resources such as files or run networked applications or even set up things like a Windows domain. Your VMs can also access the Internet and other networks attached to your host network adapter but your host will not be able to access the guest VMs unless you configure port forwarding as seen in figure 6.3.

To use the Nat Network option you will need to configure a NAT Network from the VirtualBox Manager Preferences which are accessible from the *File* menu and then by going to *Tools* and clicking on *Network Manager* (File and then Network for VirtualBox 6). To create a new NAT network, click on the *Create* button and the default name will be *New NAT network*. You then edit the name and IP prefix as needed.

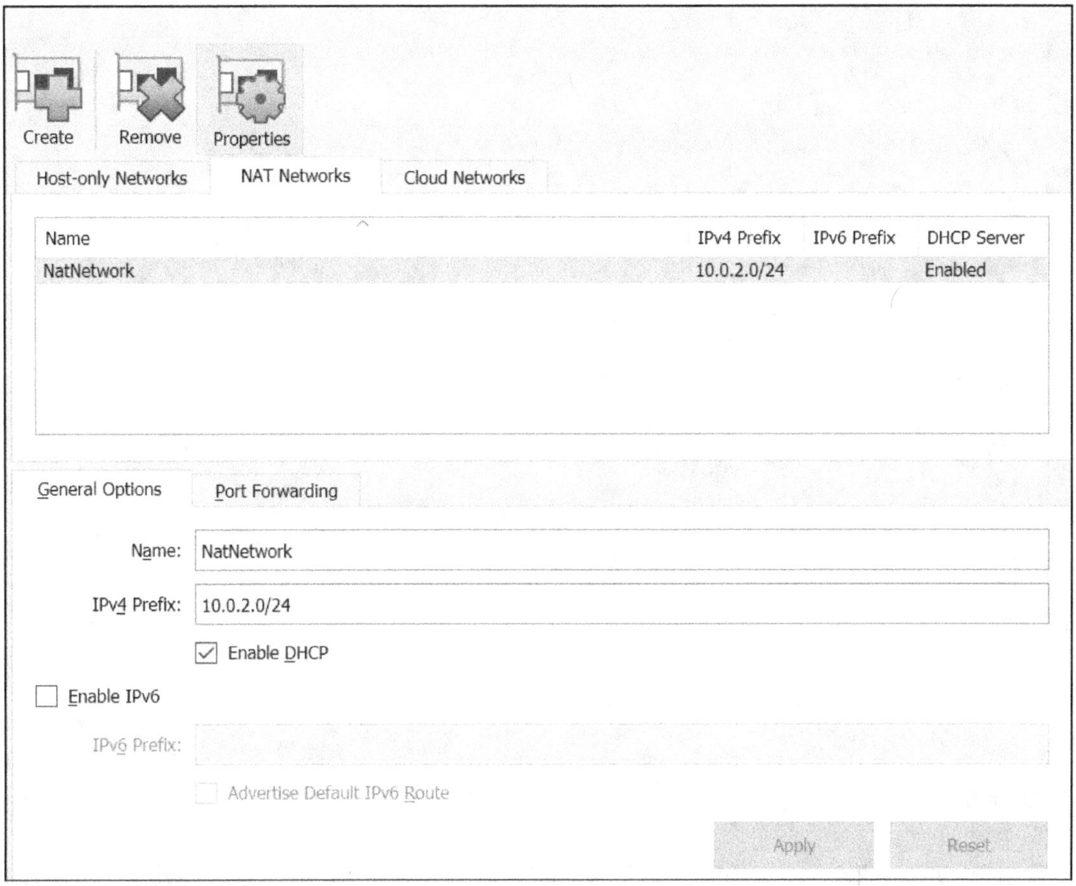

Chapter 6 – Networking

Figure 6.2

After you configure a new Nat Network in the VirtualBox preferences you can go back to your VM settings and change the network type in your VMs to NAT Network and then choose your new NAT network name that you just configured.

Chapter 6 – Networking

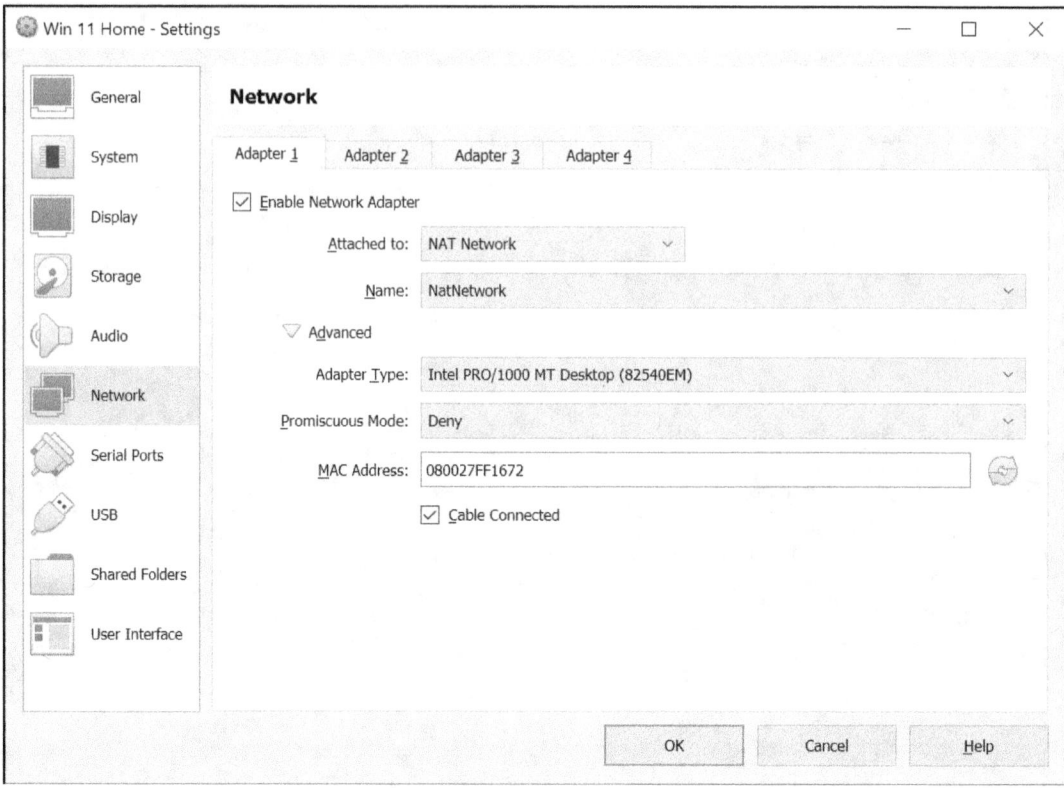

Figure 6.3

Then if your VMs are using DHCP which they probably are, they will get new IP addresses that are different from each other and will now be able to communicate with each other.

Bridged Adapter – This method is used to connect a VM to the physical network to which your host computer is attached to by using its physical network adapter as a "bridge" to make the connection. VirtualBox will do its own filtering of data

Chapter 6 – Networking

coming through the host's physical network adapter so that only the data that is designated for the VM will reach the VM.

To use this feature you will also need to select the host's network adapter that is used to connect to the network. For example, if you have a wireless adapter and an Ethernet adapter (wired) then you would need to choose the appropriate one from the *Adapter Type* dropdown menu.

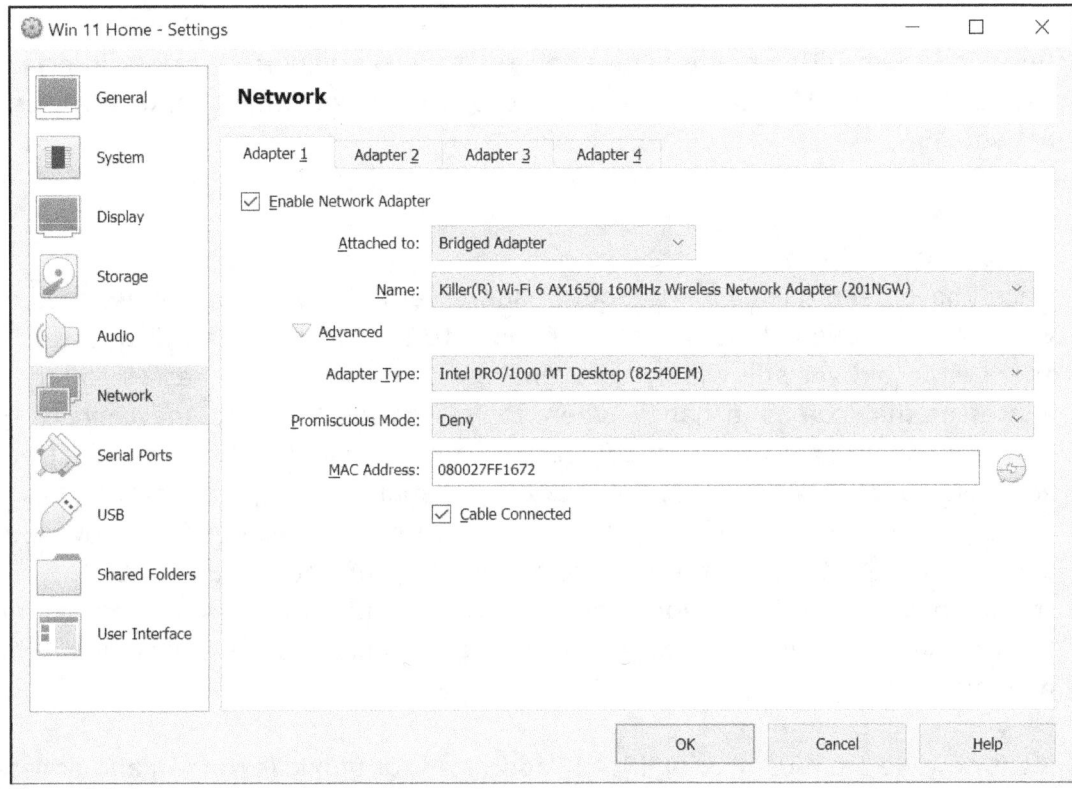

Figure 6.4

When you use a Bridged Adapter, you have three choices for *Promiscuous Mode* which tells the adapter what types of traffic to allow or deny.

- *Deny* – This is the default option and it will deny any traffic that is not intended for the VM.

- *Allow VMs* – All network traffic will be hidden from the VM except the traffic transmitted to and from other VMs.

- *Allow* All – This mode does not place any restrictions on traffic. A VM can see all incoming and outgoing traffic.

Chapter 6 – Networking

SInternal Network – This mode allows any VMs that are also configured with this mode to communicate with each other but cannot communicate with the VirtualBox host or any networks connected to that host.

Host-only Network – This is similar to the Internal Network option but also allows communication with the VirtualBox host. You will need to have a host only adapter configured to use this option. This adapter type will be covered in the section on the *Host Network Manager* later in this chapter.

Generic Driver – This mode allows you to share the generic network interface between your VMs and its used more for development and advanced networking.

What is an IP Address?
Since I have been talking a bit about IP addresses and how they are assigned to your VMs, I thought I would take a minute to go over what an IP address is. There is an old yet still widely used analogy comparing IP addresses to street addresses that comes in handy when you're first getting into the concept of network addressing where you compare computer IP addresses to house street addresses and packets (data) to packages or mail. If the postal carrier has a package that needs to be delivered to your house, they will need to know your address in order to get it there. And, of course, your address is unique to your street, so you can think of your house as your computer and your street as the network segment, with your computer having a unique address of its own on the network.

Right now we are mostly using IPv4 IP addresses for public (external) and private (internal) addressing. IPv4 addresses are 32 bit binary numbers that have four octets which can contain values from 0-255. An example of a common, privately used address is 192.168.1.20. You might see something like this assigned to your home computer from your broadband modem or wireless router. These types of IP addresses can be reasonably easy to remember depending on how many you have. If your network devices are on the same network or subnet, then each device will have a similar address, such as 192.168.1.30 and 192.168.1.32, so you only need to memorize the last number (octet) for each device for this type of IP address.

Chapter 6 – Networking

Finding Your IP Address
It's generally pretty easy to find the IP address of your computer or other device, and the method will vary depending on what device you are trying to find it on. Since Microsoft Windows is a very popular operating system, I will show you how to find your IP address on a Windows computer.

One very common way to find your IP address is from a command prompt. Command prompts are used to type in command line requests to the operating system in order to perform tasks or obtain information. It's similar to the old days of typing DOS commands. To open a command prompt, simply click on your Start button and type in **cmd** in the run or search box and press enter or click on the Command Prompt or cmd.exe icon from the search results. You can also type this in the Cortana search box for Windows 10 computers.

If you just want to find the basic IP address information you can type in **ipconfig** and press enter. You will get a listing similar to figure 6.5. If you have more than one network (Ethernet) adapter or a wireless connection, then you will get the same type of information for all of your connections.

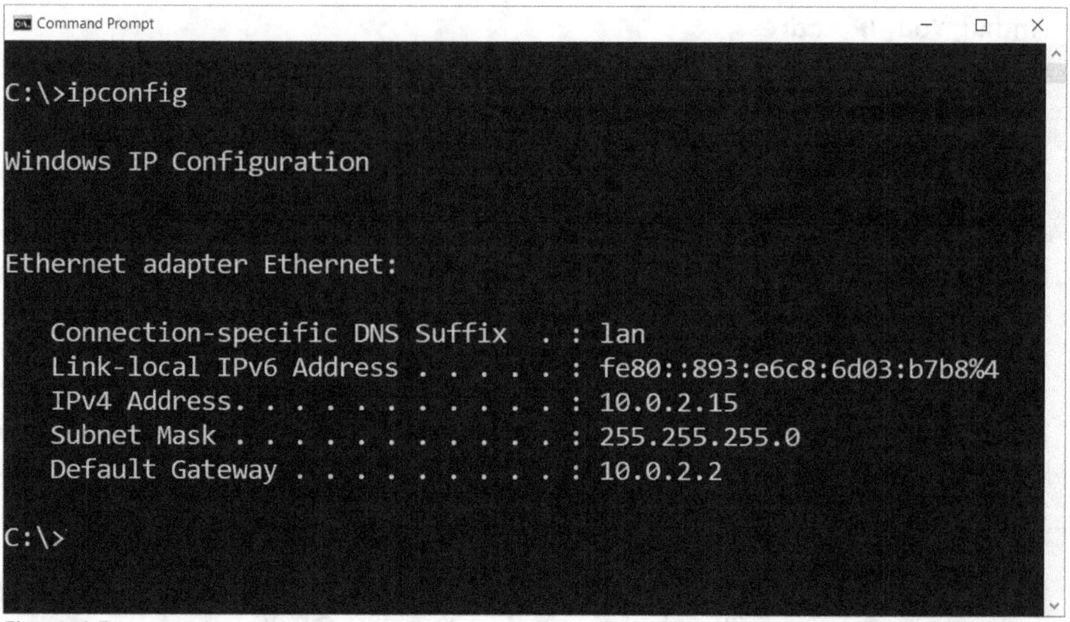

Chapter 6 – Networking

```
C:\>ipconfig

Windows IP Configuration


Ethernet adapter Ethernet:

   Connection-specific DNS Suffix  . : lan
   Link-local IPv6 Address . . . . . : fe80::893:e6c8:6d03:b7b8%4
   IPv4 Address. . . . . . . . . . . : 10.0.2.15
   Subnet Mask . . . . . . . . . . . : 255.255.255.0
   Default Gateway . . . . . . . . . : 10.0.2.2

C:\>
```
Figure 6.5

As you can see in my example, my IP address is 10.0.2.15 and my subnet mask is 255.255.255.0. If you want to get more detailed information, including your default gateway address, computer's hostname, DHCP server address, etc., then use the same command but add the /all switch to the end so it looks like **ipconfig /all.** As you can see from figure 6.6, you get much more detailed information with the command.

Chapter 6 – Networking

```
C:\>ipconfig /all

Windows IP Configuration

   Host Name . . . . . . . . . . . . : DESKTOP-IPCF9IB
   Primary Dns Suffix  . . . . . . . :
   Node Type . . . . . . . . . . . . : Hybrid
   IP Routing Enabled. . . . . . . . : No
   WINS Proxy Enabled. . . . . . . . : No
   DNS Suffix Search List. . . . . . : lan

Ethernet adapter Ethernet:

   Connection-specific DNS Suffix  . : lan
   Description . . . . . . . . . . . : Intel(R) PRO/1000 MT Desktop Adapter
   Physical Address. . . . . . . . . : 08-00-27-1B-22-D8
   DHCP Enabled. . . . . . . . . . . : Yes
   Autoconfiguration Enabled . . . . : Yes
   Link-local IPv6 Address . . . . . : fe80::893:e6c8:6d03:b7b8%4(Preferred)
   IPv4 Address. . . . . . . . . . . : 10.0.2.15(Preferred)
   Subnet Mask . . . . . . . . . . . : 255.255.255.0
   Lease Obtained. . . . . . . . . . : Tuesday, January 10, 2023 6:42:16 PM
   Lease Expires . . . . . . . . . . : Wednesday, January 11, 2023 6:42:15 PM
   Default Gateway . . . . . . . . . : 10.0.2.2
   DHCP Server . . . . . . . . . . . : 10.0.2.2
   DHCPv6 IAID . . . . . . . . . . . : 101187623
   DHCPv6 Client DUID. . . . . . . . : 00-01-00-01-29-FB-38-88-08-00-27-1B-22-D8
   DNS Servers . . . . . . . . . . . : 192.168.1.1
   NetBIOS over Tcpip. . . . . . . . : Enabled
```

Figure 6.6

You can also find your IP address using the GUI (graphical user interface), but the command prompt method is much faster. For other operating systems you can use their associated commands. For example, Linux and Apple computers use the **ifconfig** command rather than the ipconfig command.

DHCP

Since I have mentioned DHCP a few times in this chapter I figure now is a good time to go into a little more detail about what it is and how it works because your network will most likely be using DHCP whether it's a large network or a small one.

DHCP stands for *Dynamic Host Configuration Protocol*, and it was designed to simplify the management of IP address configuration by automating this configuration for network clients. All computers that participate on TCP/IP networks or the Internet need to have IP addresses assigned to them and have other IP information configured.

Some of the additional information needed by network clients may include a subnet mask, default gateway, and DNS server information. This information is needed in order for the computer to do things such as send data outside the network and resolve hostnames to IP addresses. Rather than manually inputting all of this information on each client, DHCP can do this for you automatically once it's set up on the DHCP server.

In order for DHCP to work, you need to have a device acting as a DCHP server. This device can be a computer, router or another type of network device. In our case, the VirtualBox software is acting as the DHCP server. The DHCP server is configured with a range or ranges of IP addresses that can be used to give to clients that request one. It can also be configured with other network parameters, as stated earlier.

For a client to be able to obtain information from a DHCP server, it must be DHCP enabled. When it is configured this way, then it will look for a DHCP server when it starts up. This process will vary depending on what implementation of DHCP is in use. For example, the Microsoft implementation of DHCP works as follows:

- The client sends out a DHCPDiscover packet the first time the client attempts to log on to the network.

- Then the DHCP server that receives the DHCPDiscover packet responds with a DHCPOffer packet which contains an un-leased IP address and any additional TCP/IP configuration information.

- When a DHCP client receives a DHCPOffer packet, it then responds by broadcasting a DHCPRequest packet that contains the offered IP address, and shows acceptance of the offered IP address.

- The selected DHCP server acknowledges the client DHCPRequest for the IP address by sending a DHCPAck packet and then the client can access the network.

- DHCP clients try to renew their lease when fifty percent of the lease time has expired by sending a DHCPRequest message to the DHCP server. They also send this message when they restart to try and get the same IP configuration back.

The amount of time a client keeps its lease on its IP address varies depending on how it is setup. The default Microsoft duration is eight days, and most computers end up with the same IP address they had before when it comes time to renew.

If the client computer is set up to use DHCP to obtain its IP address and cannot find a DHCP server, then it will most likely use an *APIPA* (Automatic Private IP Addressing) address instead. When using APIPA, DHCP clients can automatically self-configure an IP address and subnet mask for themselves when a DHCP server is not available. The IP address range used by APIPA is 169.254.0.1 through 169.254.255.254 with a subnet mask of 255.255.0.0. The client will use this self-configured IP address until a DHCP server becomes available. So, if you are trying to configure your new computer at home and notice your IP address is 169.254.x.x when running the ipconfig command, then it's most likely because it can't get an IP address from the router.

With DHCP, you can also do things like reserve an IP address for a specific computer or exclude a range of IP addresses so they will not be given out to DHCP clients. Plus there are special settings called *options* where you configure things such as your DNS and gateway (router) configurations so they are given to clients along with the IP address settings.

Host Network Manager
When discussing the Host-only Network configuration earlier in this chapter, I mentioned that you need to have a host only adapter set up in order to use this option. When you install VirtualBox it should configure this adapter for you and to check your settings you can go to the *Tools* option in the VirtualBox Manager and then select *Network*. From there you should see something similar to figure 6.7.

The IP address range that you have will depend on what IP address range your physical network and your host computer are using. As you can see my IP address is 192.168.56.1 for my host only adapter.

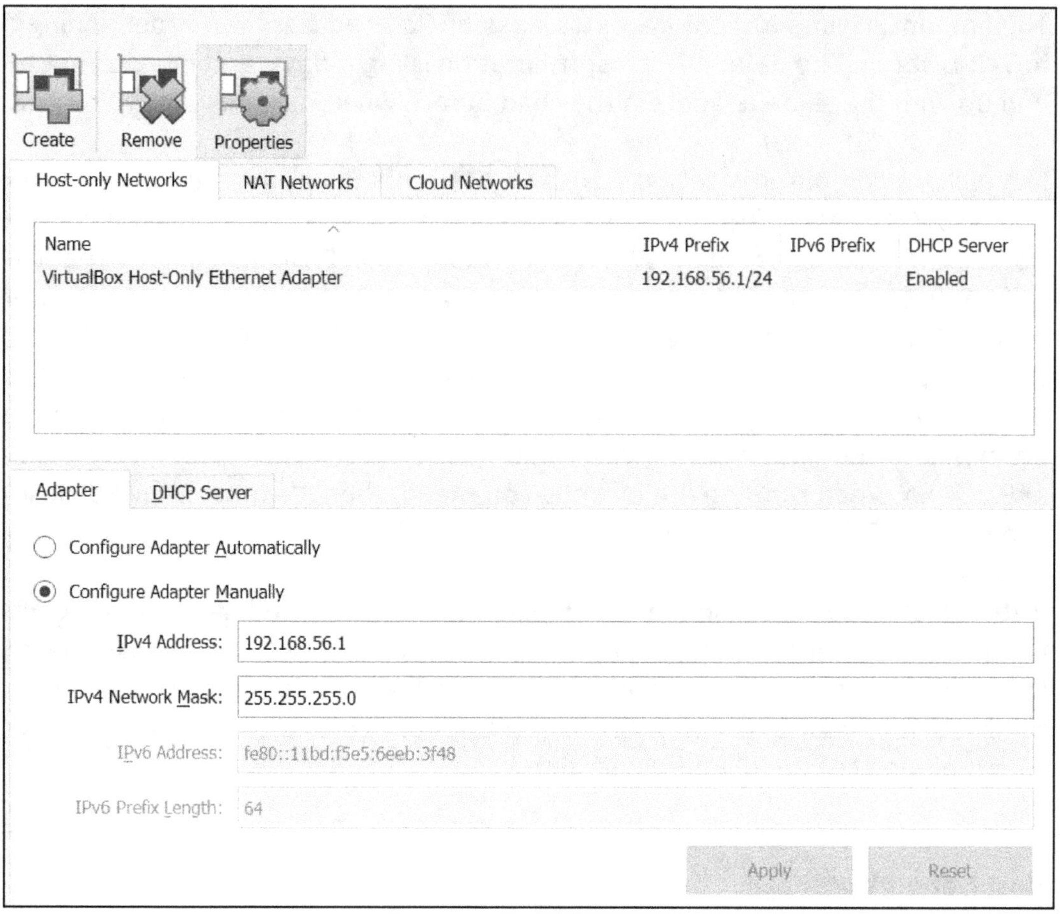

Chapter 6 – Networking

Figure 6.7

Figure 6.8 shows my DHCP server settings that were also automatically configured by VirtualBox.

Chapter 6 – Networking

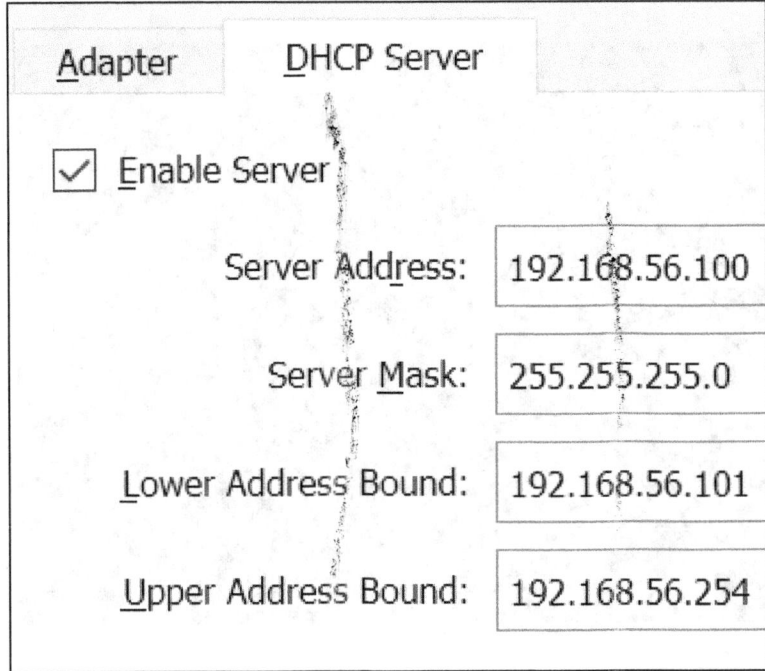

Figure 6.8

If you don't have anything listed here then you can click on the *Create* button and VirtualBox will create a new Host-Only Ethernet Adapter for you.

Figure 6.9 shows the IP configuration for my host computer. I have a physical Ethernet network adapter address of **192.168.1.141** and that address came from the DHCP server built into my router.

I also have another Ethernet adapter IP address of **192.168.56.1** which is more of a virtual IP address and was configured by VirtualBox when I installed it on my computer. This is used to communicate with virtual machines within my environment when they are using the Host-only Adapter.

```
Command Prompt
Windows IP Configuration


Wireless LAN adapter Wi-Fi:

   Connection-specific DNS Suffix  . : lan
   IPv6 Address. . . . . . . . . . . : 2603:8000:fc01:24cb::13ee
   IPv6 Address. . . . . . . . . . . : 2603:8000:fc01:24cb:3dcd:6de8:f81a:bd3a
   Temporary IPv6 Address. . . . . . : 2603:8000:fc01:24cb:f930:f799:8392:1154
   Link-local IPv6 Address . . . . . : fe80::80ad:b0b9:cfe2:4dd9%7
   IPv4 Address. . . . . . . . . . . : 192.168.1.141
   Subnet Mask . . . . . . . . . . . : 255.255.255.0
   Default Gateway . . . . . . . . . : fe80::faaa:3fff:feeb:6490%7
                                       192.168.1.1

Ethernet adapter Ethernet 2:

   Connection-specific DNS Suffix  . :
   Link-local IPv6 Address . . . . . : fe80::11bd:f5e5:6eeb:3f48%4
   IPv4 Address. . . . . . . . . . . : 192.168.56.1
   Subnet Mask . . . . . . . . . . . : 255.255.255.0
   Default Gateway . . . . . . . . . :
```

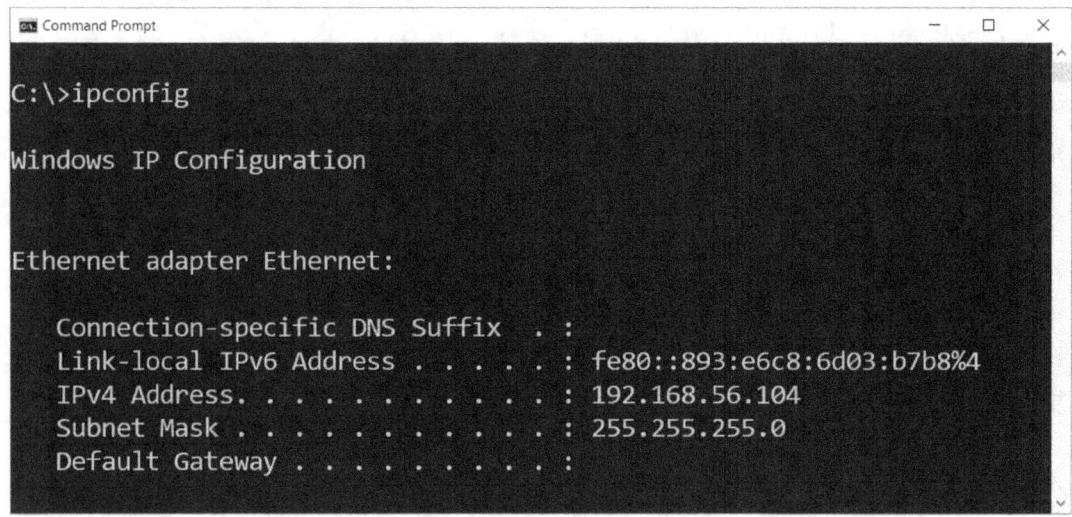

Figure 69

Figure 6.10 shows the IP configuration on a VM that is using the Host-only Adapter setting. Notice how its IP address of **192.168.56.104** is on the same network as my host computer's second Ethernet network adapter address? By being on the same network, my host and the VM can communicate with each other.

```
Command Prompt

C:\>ipconfig

Windows IP Configuration


Ethernet adapter Ethernet:

   Connection-specific DNS Suffix  . :
   Link-local IPv6 Address . . . . . : fe80::893:e6c8:6d03:b7b8%4
   IPv4 Address. . . . . . . . . . . : 192.168.56.104
   Subnet Mask . . . . . . . . . . . : 255.255.255.0
   Default Gateway . . . . . . . . . :
```

Figure 6.10

Chapter 7 – Preferences and Additional Features

Now that you know how to get your virtual machines configured and running on your network, it's time to go over some of the other features of VirtualBox that I feel you should know about. Like I mentioned before, VirtualBox is not a super complicated virtualization platform so mastering how it works should not be a real difficult task.

In this chapter, I will be discussing the changes you can make to the VirtualBox Manager as well as going over other topics such as adding additional virtual hardware to your VMs and using snapshots to save the state of a VM at a given time.

VirtualBox Manager Preferences
In the last chapter, I went over all the settings related to Virtual Machines which are specific to the VM that you are changing them on. VirtualBox has its own settings, or preferences as they are called that apply to the entire VirtualBox environment itself rather than the virtual machines.

For the most part, the default settings should be ok for most users, especially those new to VirtualBox, but later on you might find yourself wanting to check out these preferences to see if there is anything you would like to change to make things a little easier on yourself. The preferences are broken down into categories just like the VM settings are and in this section, I will go over each one of these categories.

General
Here you will see the default folder on your host that is used to store virtual machines. You might remember that I changed my VM folder when I created new VMs. If you don't want to have to manually change the folder each time you create a VM, you can simply change the *Default Virtual Machine* folder path here.

The *VRDP Authentication Library* setting is the location of the library containing authentication credentials for remote desktop clients.

Chapter 7 – Preferences and Additional Features

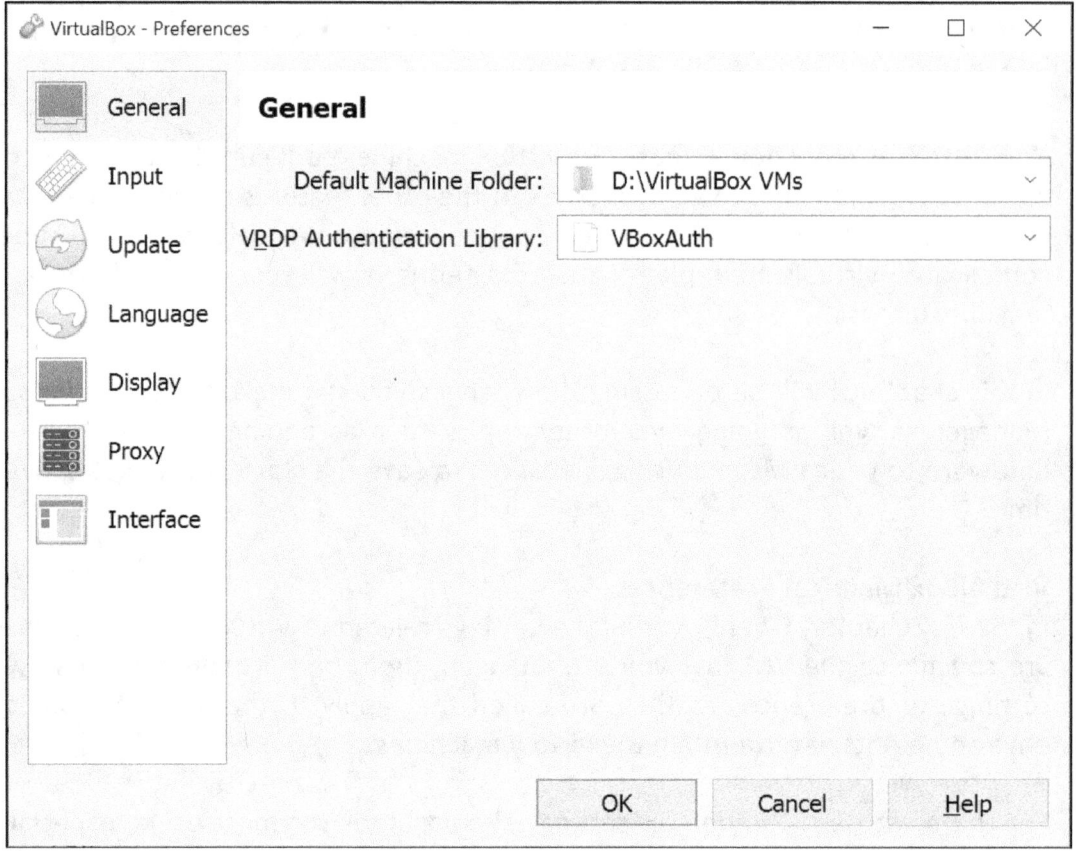

Figure 7.1

Input
If you are the type who likes to use keyboard shortcuts to perform certain tasks then you can edit the default VirtualBox keyboard shortcuts or create your own for the VirtualBox Manager as well as for virtual machines.

Keyboard shortcuts consist of a combination of keys that you press on your keyboard. For example, you might use the popular Windows keyboard shortcuts Ctrl-C to copy text and Ctrl-V to paste text in your documents or email etc.

Chapter 7 – Preferences and Additional Features

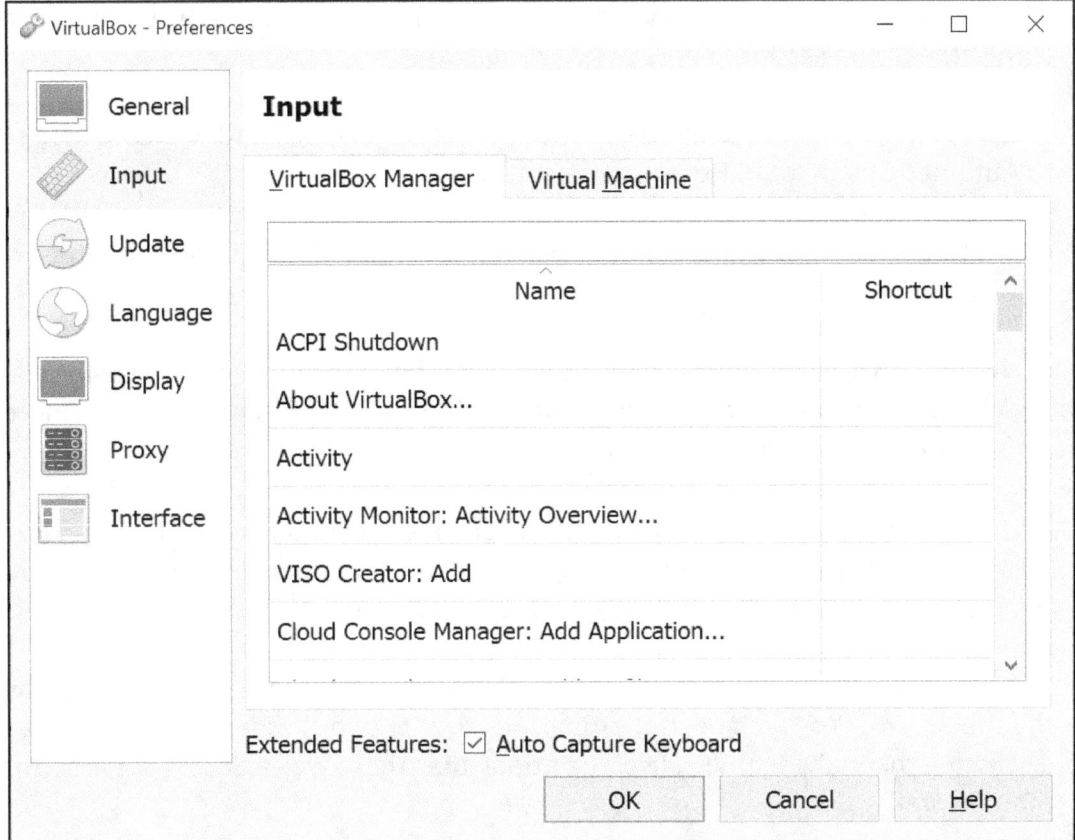

Figure 7.2

Update
Just like with most operating systems and software, there will be updates that are periodically released that contain new features, bug fixes, security patches and so on. VirtualBox comes out with its own updates and new versions from time to time so here is where you can tell VirtualBox how often to check for these updates and also what types of updates you want it to check for.

Language
Here you can change the language that VirtualBox uses for its interface if you don't want to use the one that was configured when it was installed.

Display
You might have noticed that when you create a VM it has a low video resolution. Then after you install the Guest Additions software and reboot you have some higher resolution settings you can choose from. VirtualBox has some universal display settings as well that apply to all of your VMs and if you are having issues

Chapter 7 – Preferences and Additional Features

with getting your display to look the way you like then you might want to play with some of the settings here.

The Maximum Guest Screen Size section has three choices and is most likely set to Automatic by default. Here is what each setting will do.

- **Automatic** – This will suggest a maximum screen size to your VM after you install the Guest Addition Tools.

- **None** – This will not put any restrictions on the maximum screen size for your VM, but you will need to have enough video memory assigned to your VM to support higher screen resolutions.

- **Hint** – Using this option you can enter in a maximum resolution for your virtual machines by typing the height and width numbers in the boxes below. This will only apply if you have the Guest Addition Tools installed.

The *Scale Factor* will set the virtual machine scale sizing on a global level rather than per VM. You might remember in the previous chapter when I was discussing the individual VM display options that there was a Scale Factor setting there as well.

When checked, the *Raise Window Under Mouse* checkbox will move a window to the front when you hover your mouse over that particular window.

Proxy
If for some reason you use a proxy server to gain access to the Internet then you can enter the settings for your proxy server here. Otherwise, the default setting of *Auto-Detect Host Proxy Settings* should work for most situations.

Extensions
Extensions are software packages that can be installed in your VirtualBox environment to add additional functionality to VirtualBox. I mentioned how you can install the VirtualBox Extension Pack back in Chapter 2 and for the most part that will be the only extension you will be adding to VirtualBox.

Interface
This can be used to change how the VirtualBox Manager appears in regards to using a light or dark theme.

Chapter 7 – Preferences and Additional Features

Snapshots
One of the great things about using virtual machines compared to physical computers is that you can use what they call snapshots to take a point in time backup of the state of your VM. Once you have this snapshot in place you can always "roll back" to it at any given time in case you have an issue with your VM or if you want to undo some changes that were made to the VM.

This feature comes in very handy when testing out new software other operating system patches because if you seriously mess up your VM, you can revert back to the previous state of the VM with just a few clicks.

One thing to keep in mind when using snapshots is that when you revert back to a particular snapshot, everything you have done to that VM since the snapshot was taken will be gone, including any files that were added to the hard disk.

Snapshots can be taken when the VM is powered on or powered off and are taken on a per VM basis. You can also have multiple snapshots for a VM, each one with a different date and time allowing you to revert back to various points in time.

To take a snapshot of a VM you need to have that VM selected in the VirtualBox Manager and then go to the menu bar to the right of the VM name and click on *Snapshots*. Then click on the *Take* camera icon button to have the snapshot taken.

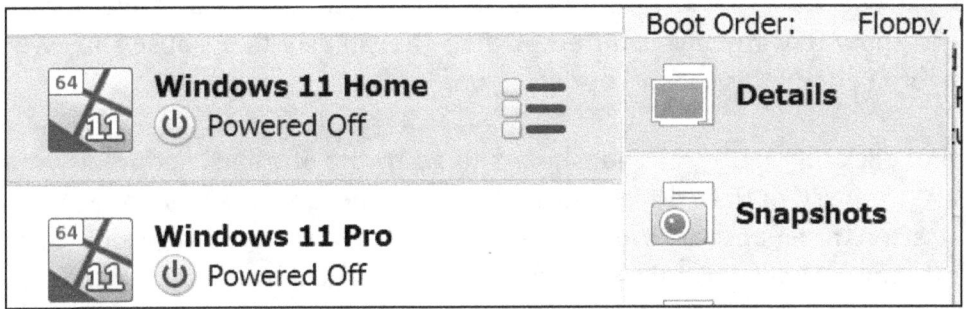

Figure 7.3

Next, you will need to give your snapshot a name or you can stick with the default name given to you by VirtualBox. You can also add a description if you like as seen in figure 7.4. I will take this snapshot and then take another snapshot after installing the Windows patches and name it accordingly.

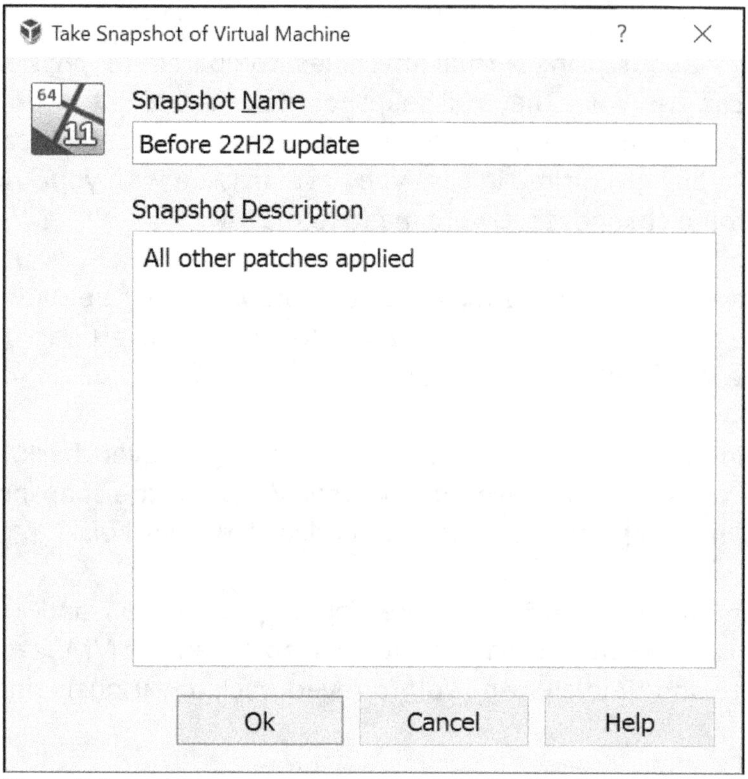

Chapter 7 – Preferences and Additional Features

Figure 7.4

I will then add a second optical drive to my VM to show you how that affects the state of the snapshots. Figure 7.5 shows both snapshots as well as the current state of my virtual machine. But you might have noticed how it says *changed* next to *Current State*. This is because I added a second optical drive and it's letting me know that my VM is different than the snapshots because they were taken before I added this second optical drive.

If I were to click on one of my snapshots and go to the Storage section, it would show just the first optical drive and not the second one that I added since I added it after the snapshots were taken. Then if I were to restore one of my snapshots, my VM would only have the original optical drive that was in the snapshot since it reverts the VM exactly to how it was when the snapshot was taken.

Chapter 7 – Preferences and Additional Features

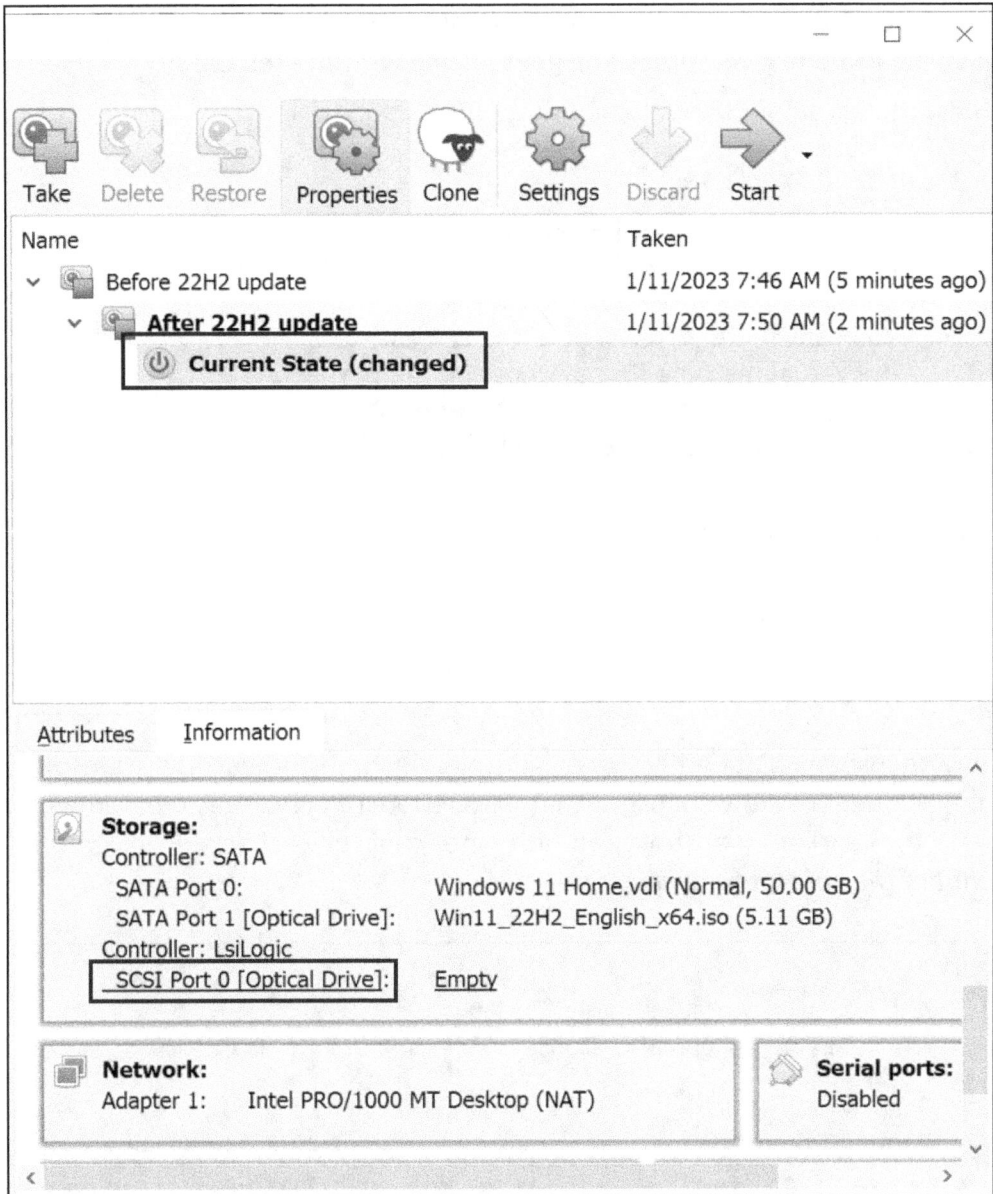

Figure 7.5

Now let's say that my VM was acting funny after I installed some Windows patches and I want to revert it back to the state it was in before I installed the patches. To do this I just have to click on the snapshot that says *Before 22H2 update* from figure 7.5 and then click on the *Restore* button. You will then be prompted to decide if you wish to create a snapshot of the current state of the virtual machine before restoring the snapshot (figure 7.6). This is up to you to decide because once you restore a snapshot then that will become the current version of your VM. If you choose to have another snapshot created then you will have a backup in case something goes wrong with the restore.

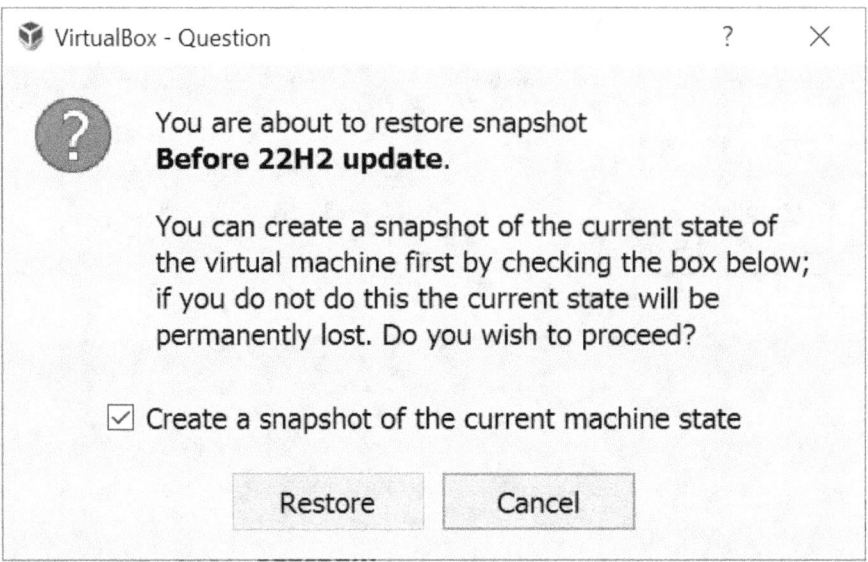

Figure 7.6

Now my snapshot has been restored and has become the current state of the virtual machine. The new snapshot that is called *Just in case* was created when I restored the earlier snapshot and left the checkbox checked to *Create a snapshot of the current machine state*.

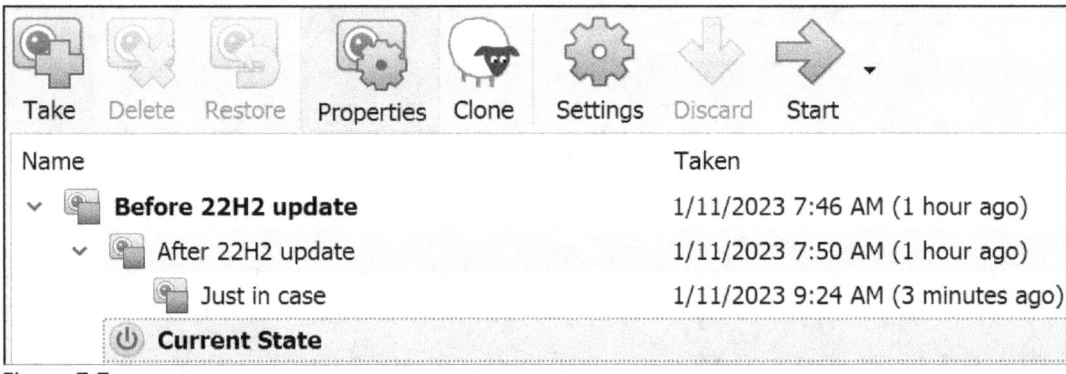

Figure 7.7

Since I have restored the snapshot that was created before I added my second optical drive, that new optical drive is no longer a part of my currently running VM (figure 7.8).

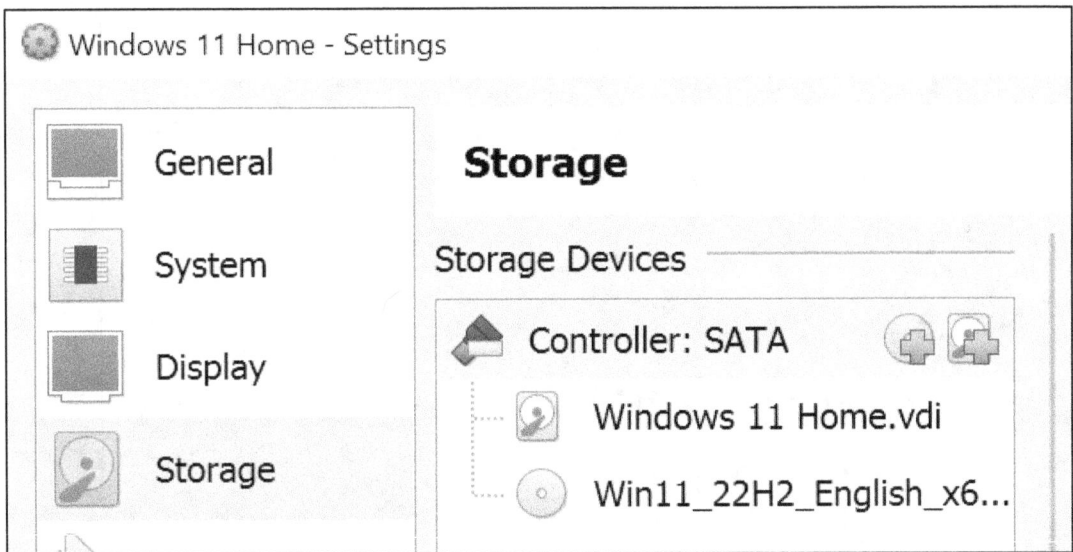
Figure 7.8

After running my VM after it has been restored I have realized that things are looking good and I don't need to keep that snapshot that is called Just in case. Now I will now remove that snapshot by clicking on it and then clicking on the *Delete* button.

I will then get a message telling me that the state of the VM in this snapshot will be lost and that the VM files will be merged together into one file which is normal.

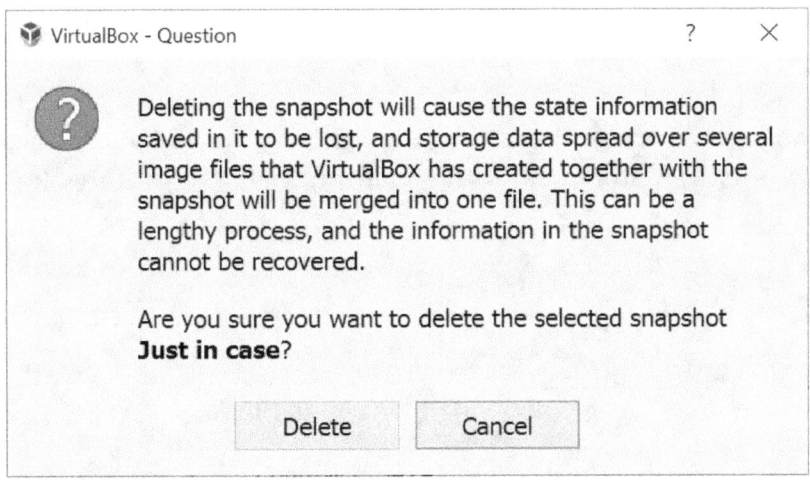
Figure 7.9

I am now left with my previous two snapshots that I created originally plus the current state of my virtual machine as shown in figure 7.10.

Chapter 7 – Preferences and Additional Features

Figure 7.10

 When restoring and deleting virtual machine snapshots you might want to backup any important data you might have on the VM just in case you remove or restore the wrong version or if something goes wrong with the process to avoid any potential data loss.

If you look at your host in the folder that stores the files for your VM you will see a folder called Snapshots that stores all of the snapshot files for your VM (one file per snapshot).

Chapter 7 – Preferences and Additional Features

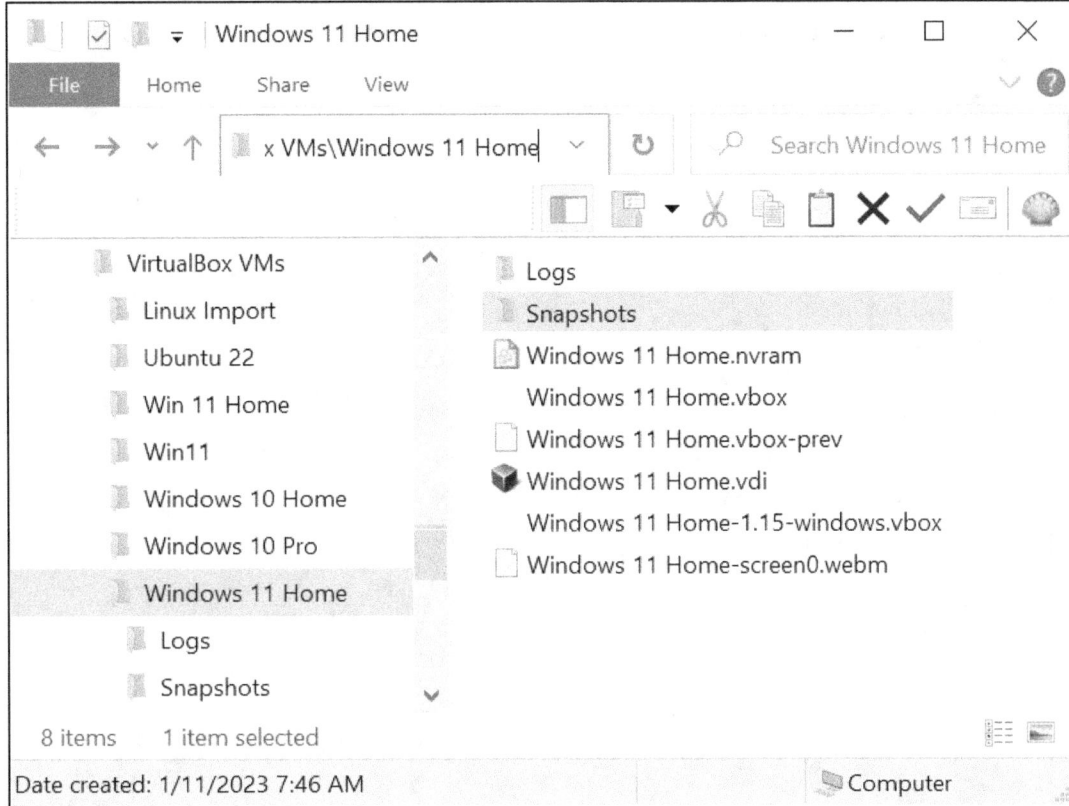
Figure 7.11

Snapshot files will have a file extension of *.vdi* and depending on how large your virtual machines are and how many snapshots you are taking, you might find yourself taking up a lot of space on the hard drive of your host.

Chapter 7 – Preferences and Additional Features

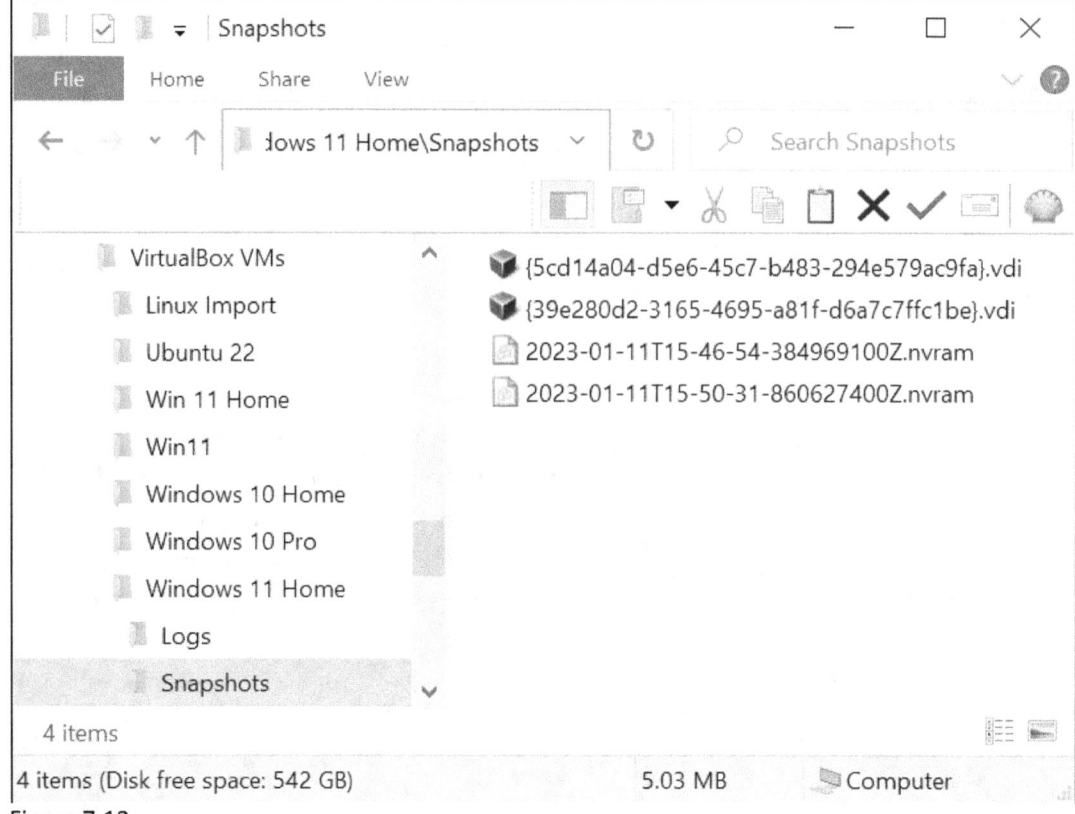

Figure 7.12

One last thing I want to point out when it comes to snapshots is that you can't restore a snapshot on a running VM, but you can create and delete snapshots while a VM is running.

Cloning a Virtual Machine
Another great feature of using virtual machines in your environment is having the ability to clone or make copies of them. This comes in handy if you want to have a duplicate VM to run some tests on and not have to worry about messing up your main VM or having to take snapshots to revert back to when things go wrong.

One thing that many people do is create a "golden image" of a VM with a fresh operating system installed with all the latest patches and then clone this VM to make additional virtual machines that are all ready to go rather than having to do the OS installation and patching procedure multiple times.

Chapter 7 – Preferences and Additional Features

To create a VM clone you will go to the same area where you create snapshots, but this time click on the *Clone* button. If your VM is powered on then this button will be greyed out so make sure it's shut down first.

There will be a few choices that you need to make when cloning a VM as seen in figure 7.13.

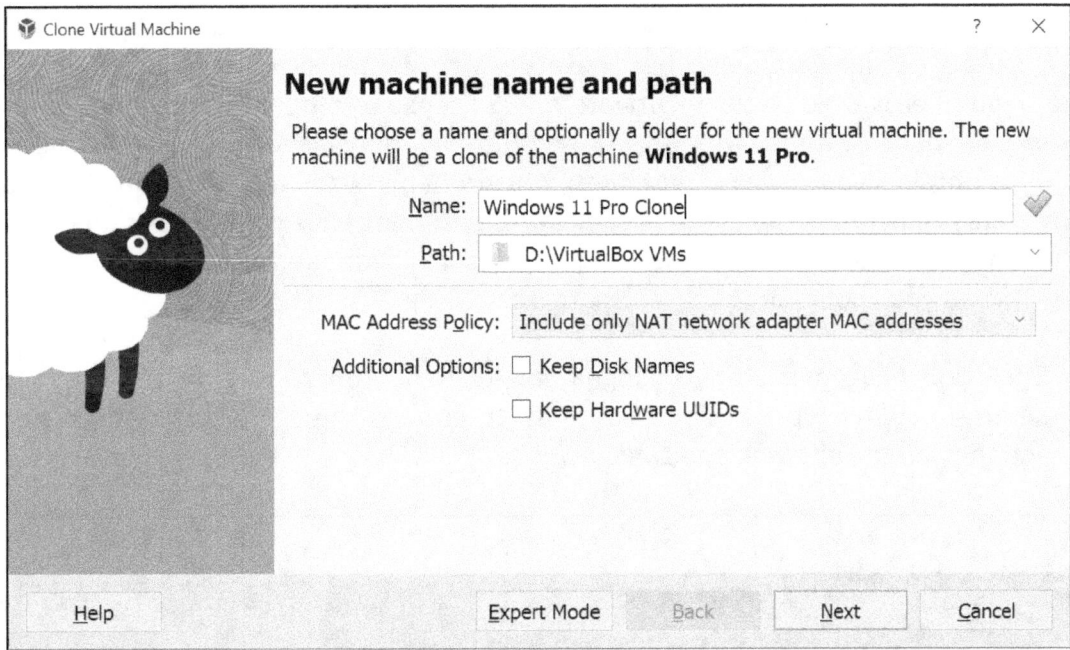

Figure 7.13

I will now go over each one of these options.

- **Name** – By default, VirtualBox will just add the word *Clone* to the end of your existing VM name but you can name your clone whatever you like.

- **Path** – This is the location that the clone will be created in so you might want to make sure it's stored with your other VMs if you want to keep everything in one place.

- **MAC Address Policy** – MAC addresses are unique hardware addresses assigned to network cards and if you want to have the original VM and the clone communicate on the same network then you should choose the *Generate new MAC addresses for all network adapters* choice. If the clone will be running by itself and is meant to be an identical configuration to the original then you can use one of the other options depending on what type of networking you will be doing.

- **Keep Disk Names** – By default, VirtualBox will name the virtual disks after the name of the VM so if you want your disk files to have the same name as the original VM then you would check this box.

- **Keep Hardware UUIDs** – A UUID (Universally Unique Identifier) is a number used to identify unique hardware on a computer system. Many times this number is used to tie a software or OS license to a particular computer so it can only be used with that computer. If you plan on using your clones alongside your original VM then you probably want to make sure this box stays unchecked. If your clone will be running software that is tied to a hardware address and you need to be sure it functions properly for testing then you should probably check this box.

Once you have made any changes you will click on *Next* and then need to determine what type of clone you wish to create. There are two options here and they are a *Full clone* and *Linked clone*.

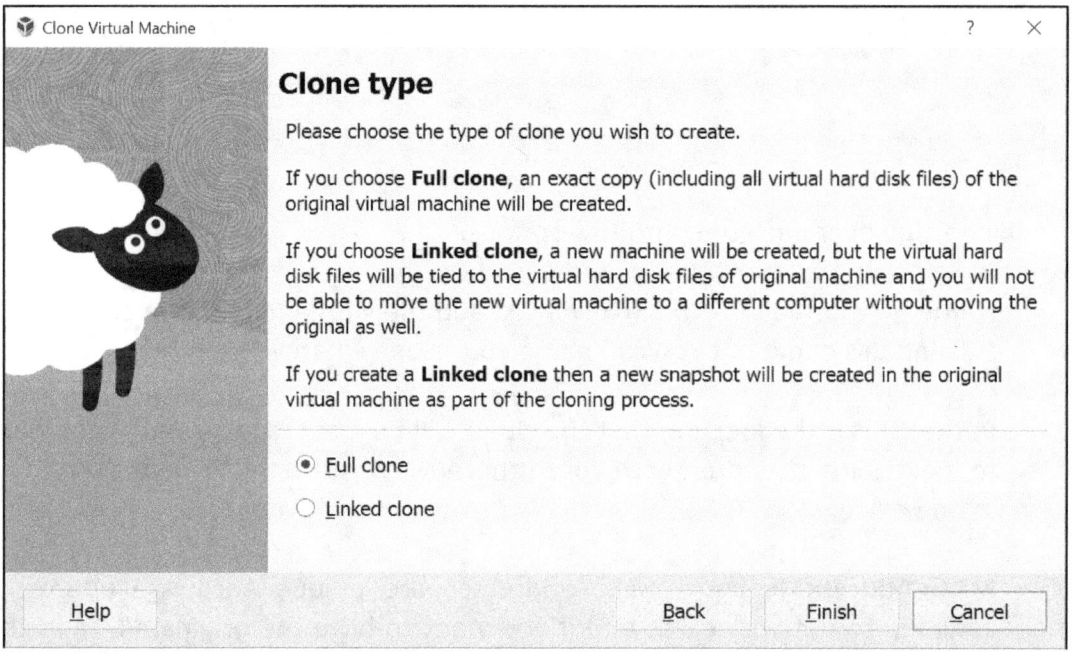

Figure 7.14

For the most part, you will most likely be using the Full clone method because that creates an actual clone of the VM including the virtual disk files and this way

Chapter 7 – Preferences and Additional Features

you end up with an independent virtual machine that does not rely on the original VM to run.

Linked clones are tied to the original VM and use what are called differencing disk images which means that it shares the virtual hard disk data with the source VM and requires a connection to that source VM in order to run. One advantage of Linked clones is that you can create multiple clones that share the disk which allows you to save on storage space. Linked clones do not have the same level of performance as Full clones for this reason.

I will now choose the Full clone option and then click the *Finish* button. The cloning process with take some time and the larger your virtual machine's hard disk, the longer it will take.

Figure 7.15

After the cloning process is complete I will see both of my VMs in the VirtualBox Manager (figure 7.16). Also when I go to the location on my host where I keep my virtual machine files, I will have a new folder for this newly created clone (figure 7.17).

When I power on my cloned VM, it will look and feel just like the original or source VM did and since it's a Full clone, any changes I make to it will not affect the original VM.

Chapter 7 – Preferences and Additional Features

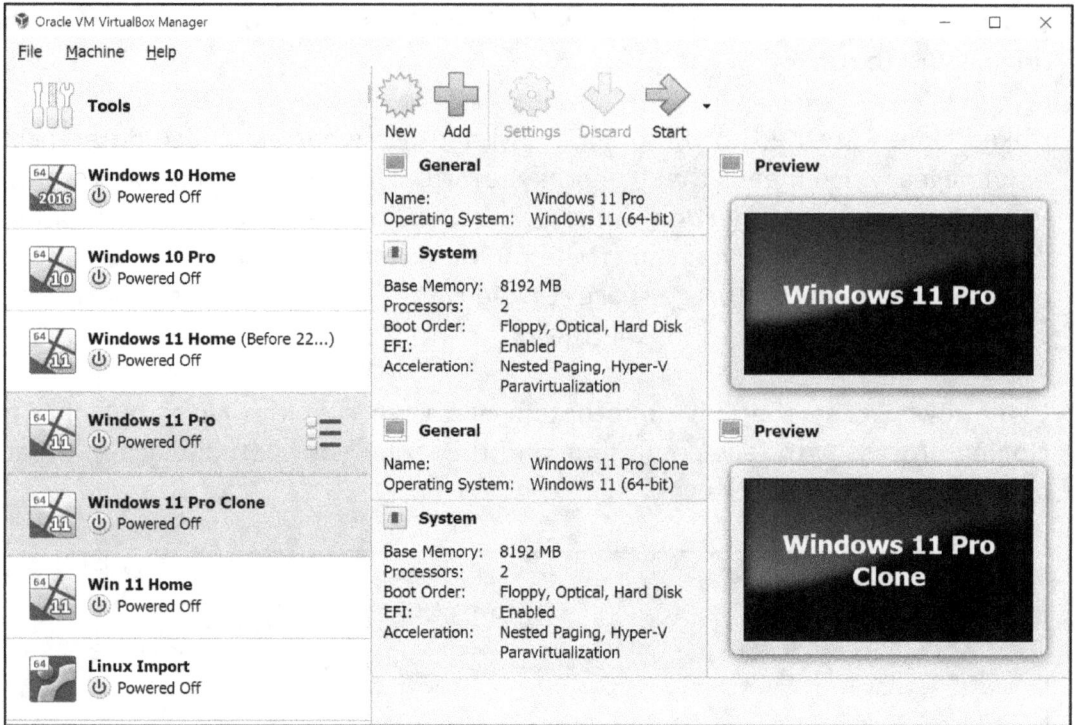

Figure 7.16

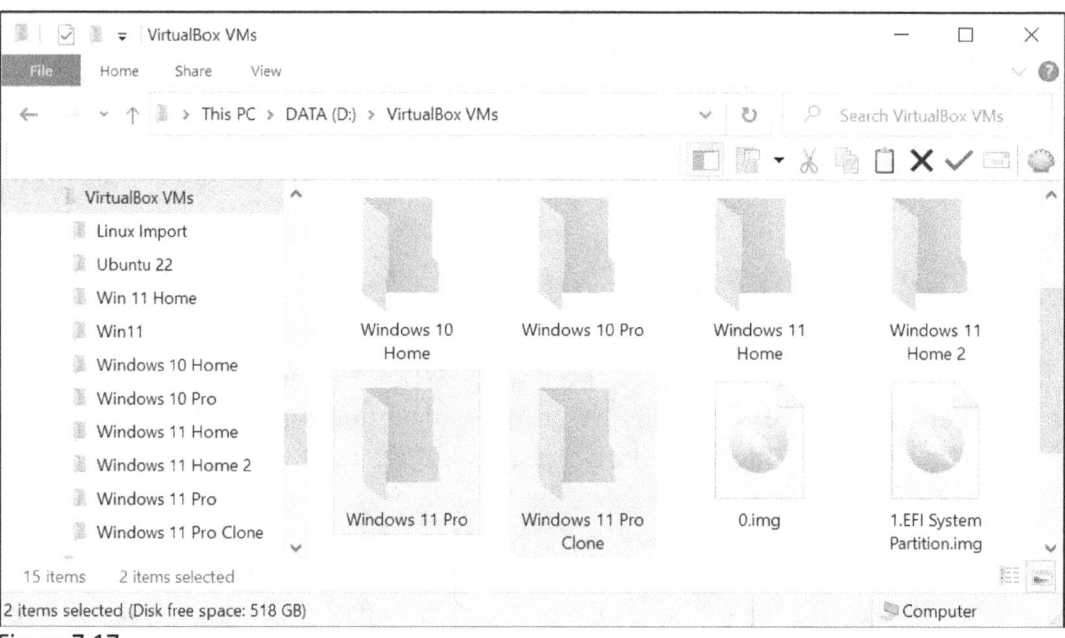

Figure 7.17

Chapter 7 – Preferences and Additional Features

Adding an Additional Storage Controller or Hard Disk to a VM

If you end up using VirtualBox on a regular basis then you most likely will run into a situation where you need more hard disk space for a VM. If you run out of space on a physical computer, you will need to make a trip to the electronics store and buy a new hard drive to install on your computer.

Fortunately, adding more space to a virtual machine is a lot easier than with a physical computer. But the main thing you need to keep in mind is that you will need to have the available space on your host (physical) computer to allocate to your VM.

For this example, I will be using my *Windows 10 NEW* virtual machine and adding another hard disk and then configuring the new hard disk within Windows. The process for configuring a new hard disk in Linux is different but usually Linux users are more on the techy side and should already know how to configure their new disks.

To begin with I will go to the settings for my VM and then to the *Storage* section. To be able to add a new hard disk I will first need to click on the installed Controller as shown in figure 7.18.

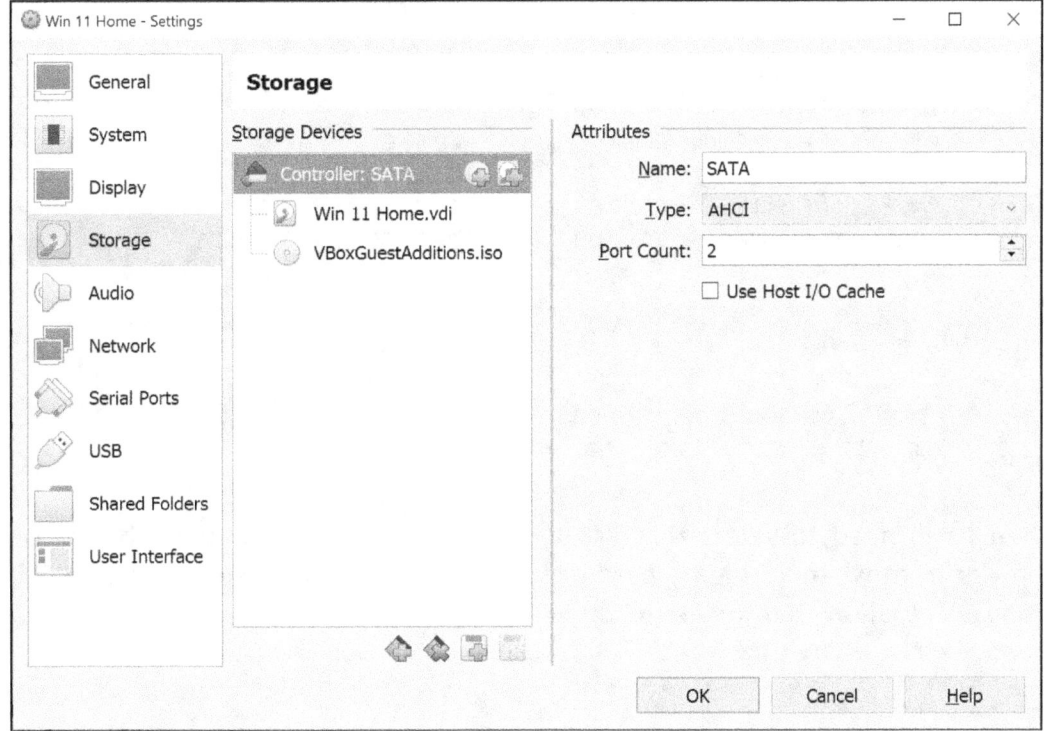

Figure 7.18

Chapter 7 – Preferences and Additional Features

If I were to click on the virtual hard disk or optical drive I would only have the option to remove that device or add a new\additional controller. Since a hard disk needs to be attached to a controller, it makes sense that I need to select the controller first.

Next, I will click on the button next to the controller that looks like a hard drive with a + sign next to it to add a new hard disk. I will then be taken to the *Medium Selector* where I can see the virtual disks that are used for my virtual machines as well as any other disks that I might have configured and not attached to a VM. If I have a disk that is not in use by another virtual machine, I can attach it from here but since I want to create a new hard disk, I will click on the *Create* button.

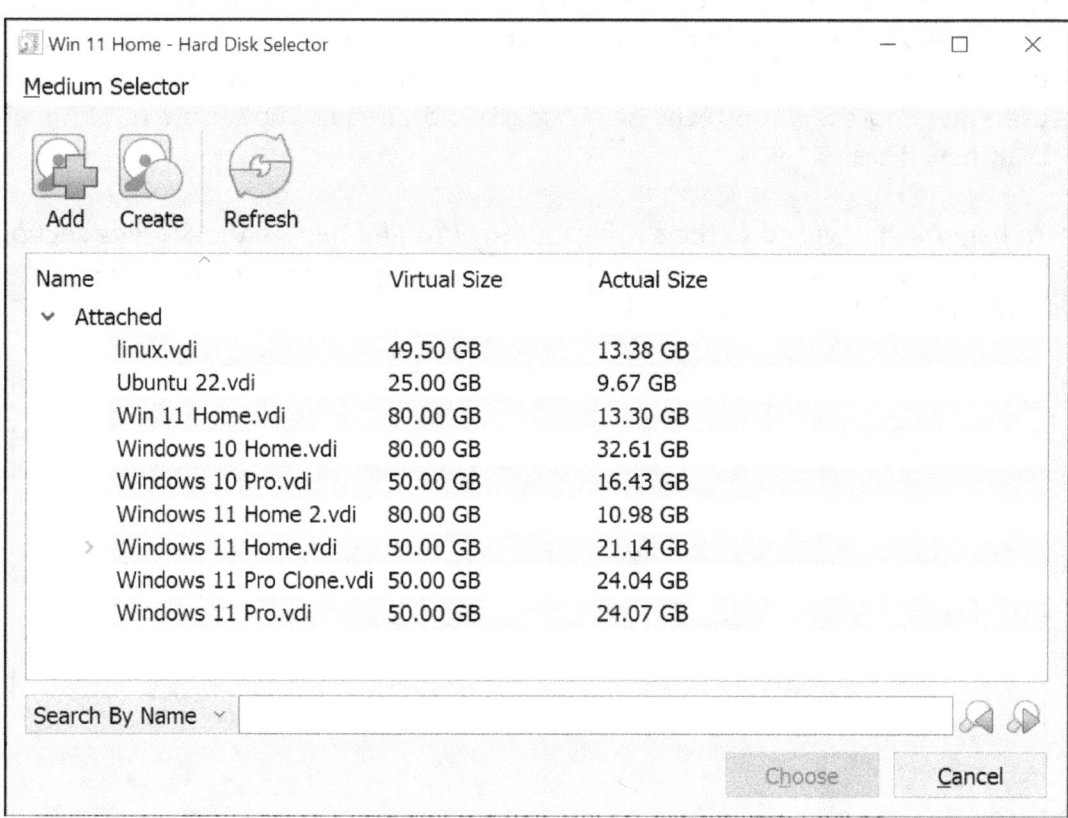

Figure 7.19

Then I will need to select the disk type I want to use. This part should look familiar from when I added a hard disk to a new VM. For this example, I will be using a VirtualBox Disk Image (VDI).

Chapter 7 – Preferences and Additional Features

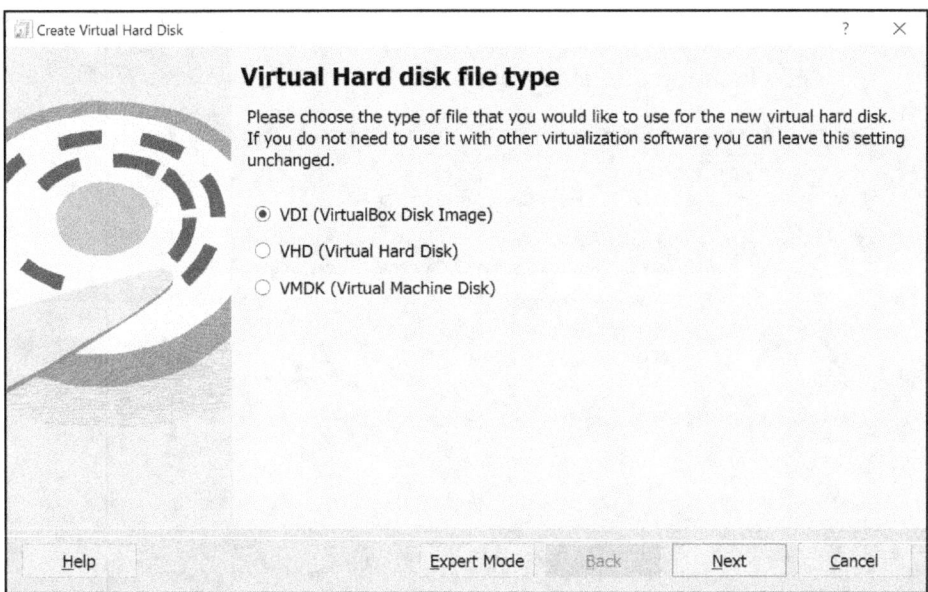

Figure 7.20

I will once again be using a dynamically allocated disk to save space on my host's hard drive so I will not check the *Pre-allocate Full Size* box.

Figure 7.21

For the disk size, I will only be allocating 10 GB of space to my VM.

133

Chapter 7 – Preferences and Additional Features

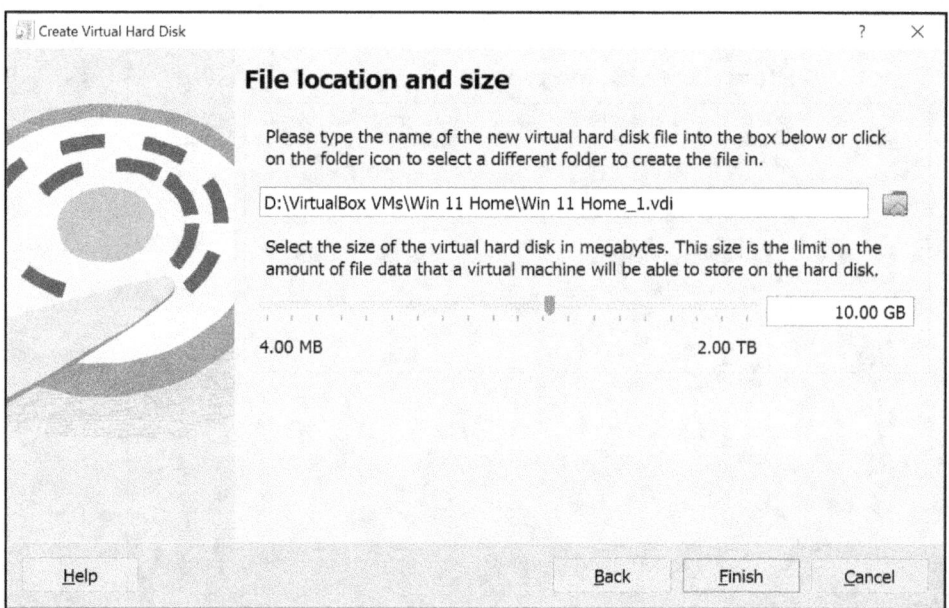

Figure 7.22

After I click on the Finish button, my new virtual disk is created and will show in the Medium Selector under the *Not Attached* section. Then I can simply click the *Choose* button to have it attached to my VM.

Chapter 7 – Preferences and Additional Features

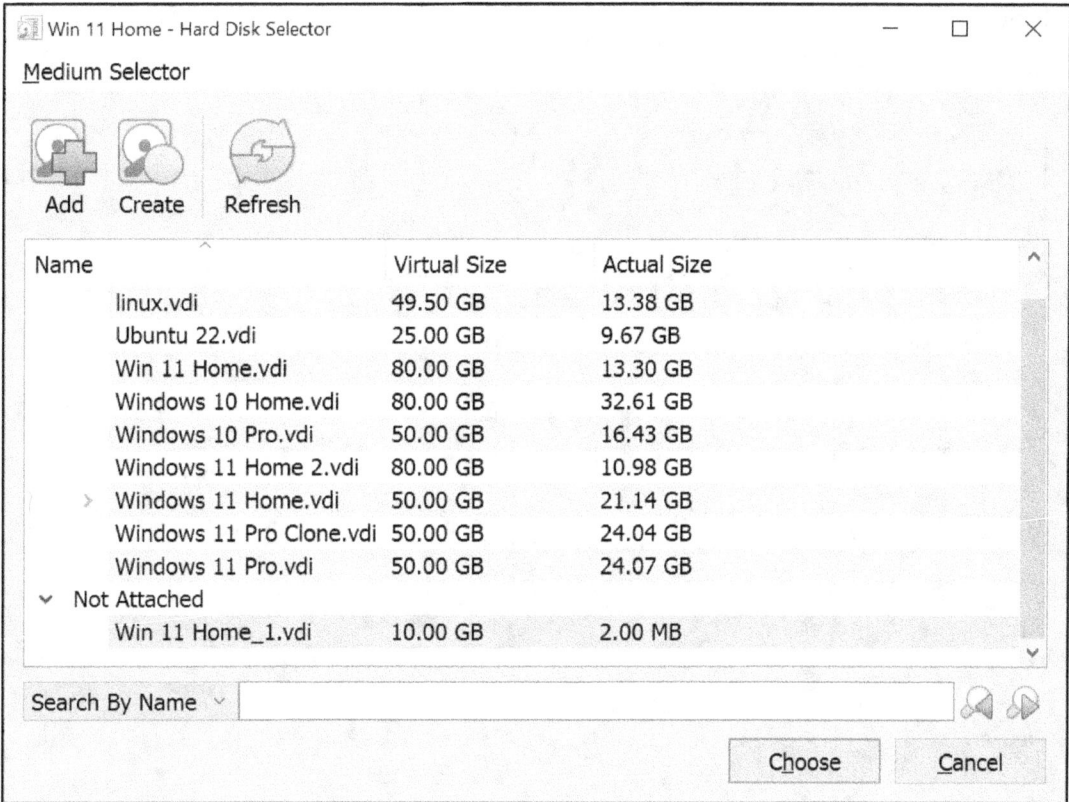

Figure 7.23

Chapter 7 – Preferences and Additional Features

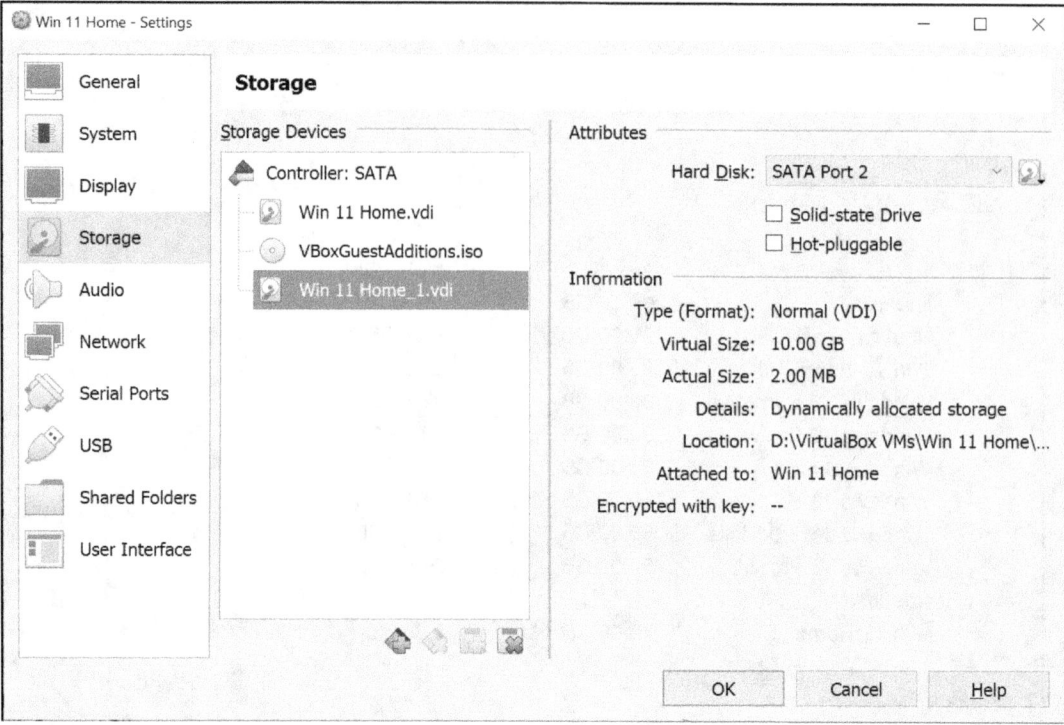

Figure 7.24

To configure this new hard disk for use in Windows I will need to go to the *Disk Management* utility that is built into Windows and used for managing hard drives and DVD drives. The easiest way to get to this tool is to type disk management in the search box and then open the console.

Many times when you run the Disk Management utility after connecting a new hard disk to your computer, it will find it and prompt you to initialize the disk and decide if you want to use the MBR or GPT partition style for your disk. GPT is the newer standard and if you are running newer versions of Windows you will be fine using that. Or you can stick with MBR if you are worried about compatibility problems. Since this is just for demonstration purposes, I will stick with the MBR default.

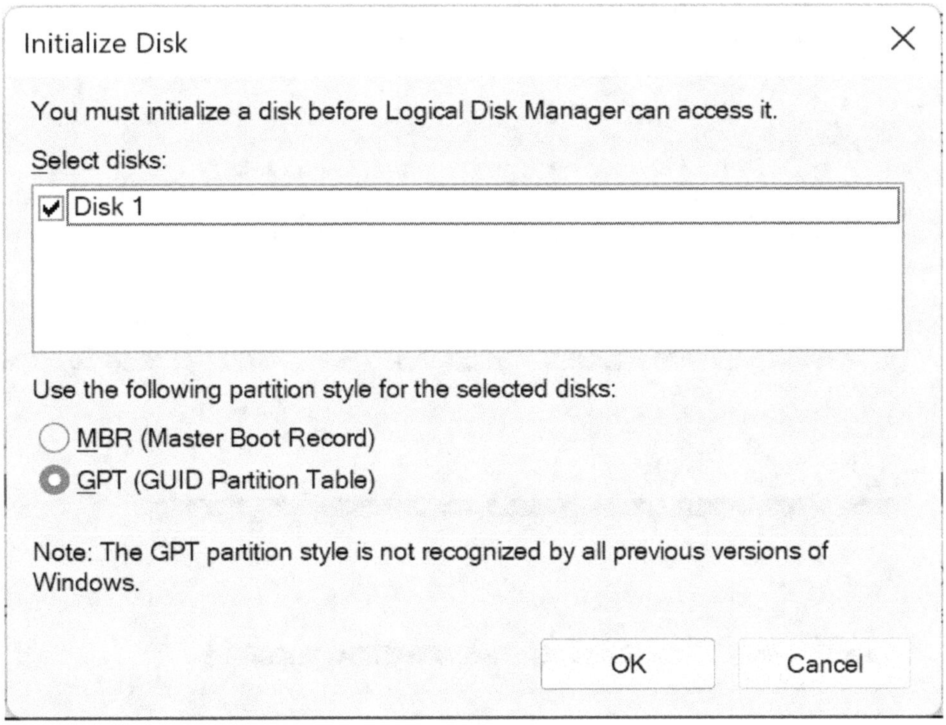

Chapter 7 – Preferences and Additional Features

![Initialize Disk dialog box showing Disk 1 selected with GPT (GUID Partition Table) option chosen]

Figure 7.25

Figure 7.26 shows my new 10 GB hard disk listed in Disk Management along with my 64 GB C: drive and my CDROM with the Windows 11 ISO mounted. The new hard disk says *Unallocated* meaning there has not been any volumes created on the disk that can be used to store data. I can then right click on the drive and choose *New simple volume* to create one.

Chapter 7 – Preferences and Additional Features

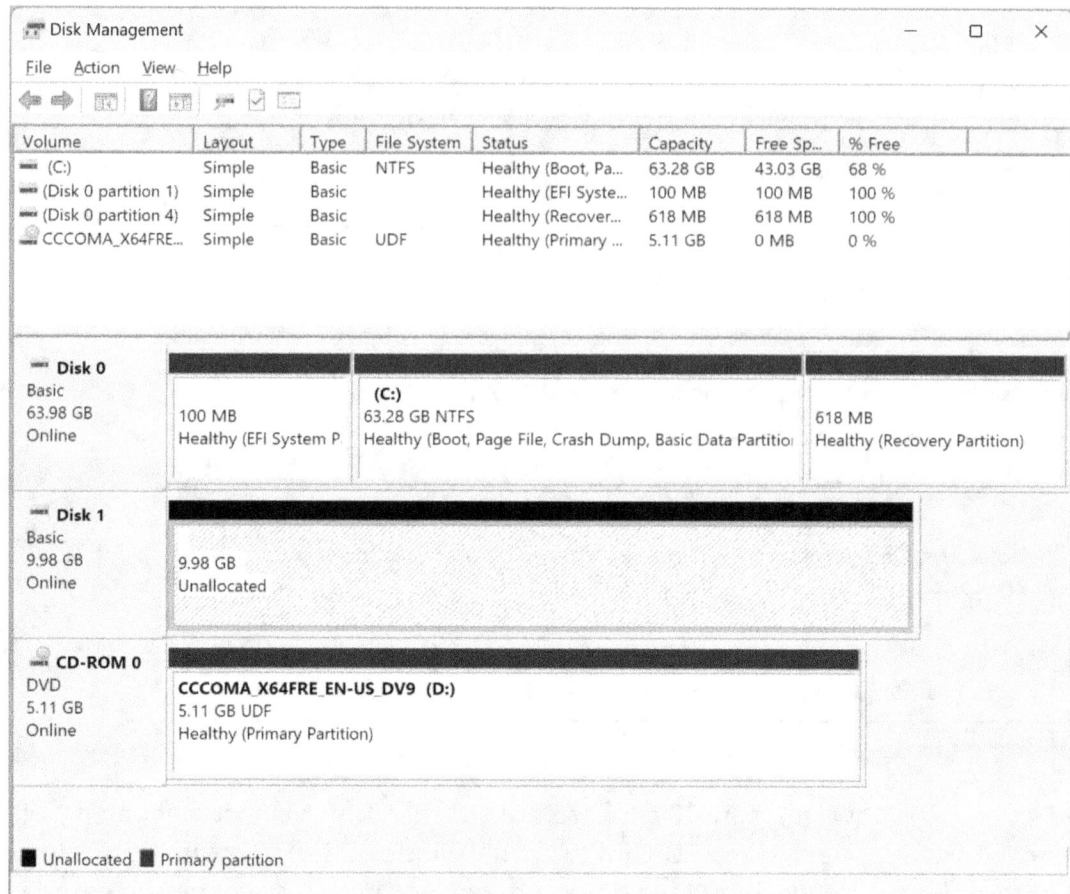

Figure 7.26

Then I can go through the wizard to create the new volume on my new disk. For the volume size, I can either use the entire 10 GB or use part of it now and then the other part later if I want to create an additional volume on this hard disk. I will go ahead and use the entire drive which is the default and click on Next.

Chapter 7 – Preferences and Additional Features

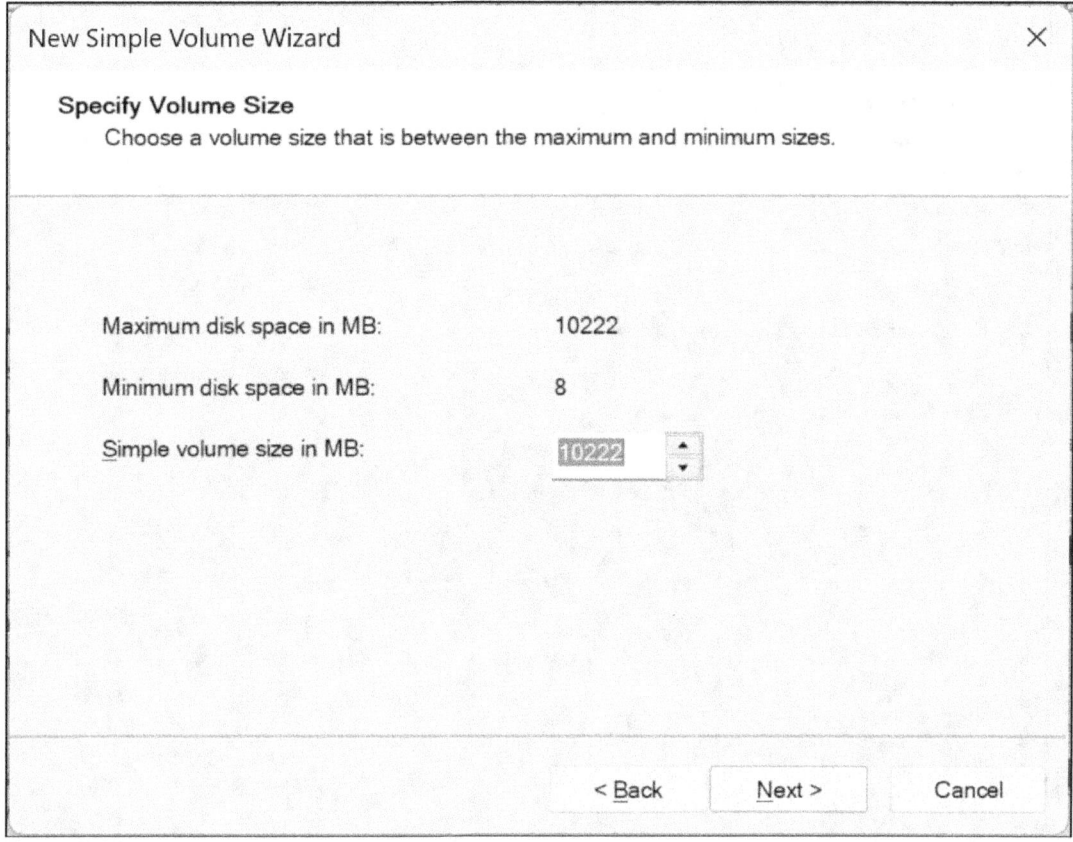

Figure 7.27

Next, I will need to assign it a drive letter so Windows will be able to use the new volume for things such as installing software and storing files. I will choose V for VirtualBox just for fun, but you can choose any letter you like as long as it's not already in use like my C and D drive letters are as you can see back in figure 7.26.

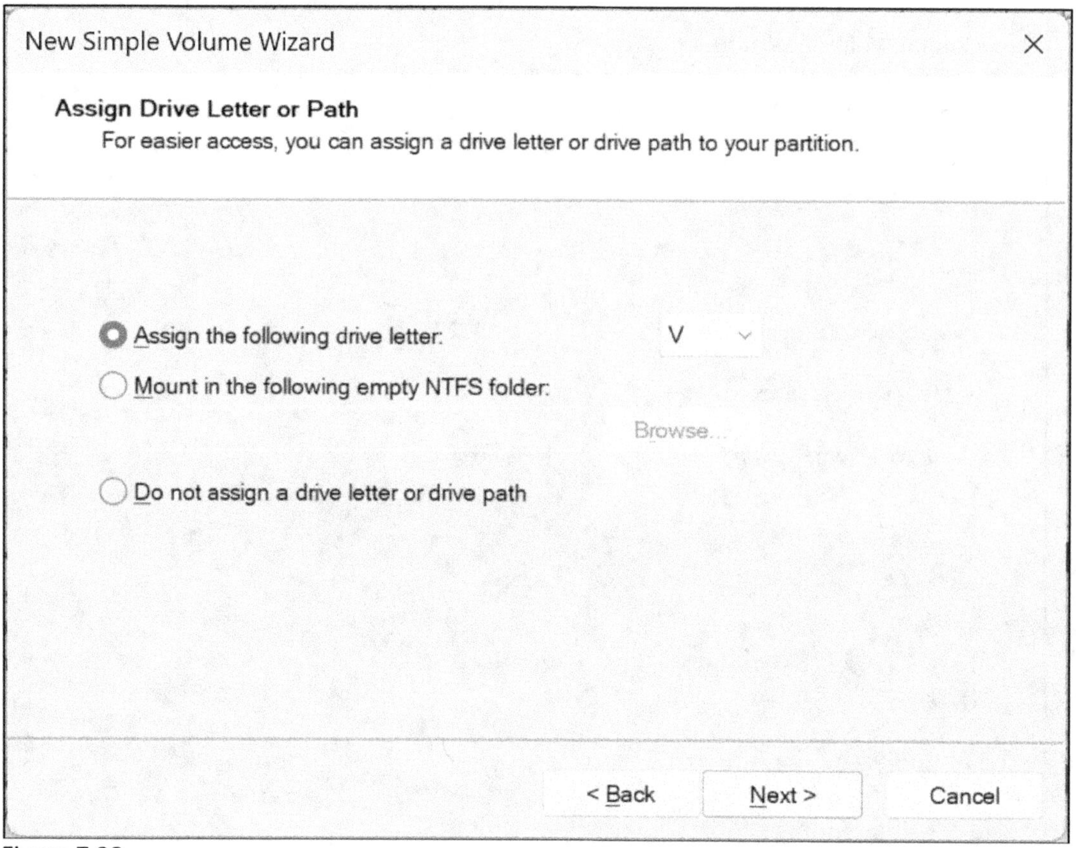

Chapter 7 – Preferences and Additional Features

![New Simple Volume Wizard - Assign Drive Letter or Path dialog, with "Assign the following drive letter: V" selected]

Figure 7.28

I will then format my drive by choosing the *quick format* option and change the volume label to say *Virtual Drive*. For the most part, you are ok doing a quick format, especially on a new hard disk since its less likely to have any errors that might be found and fixed when doing a normal format. The Volume label that you give the disk will be shown when viewing the new drive in Windows Explorer.

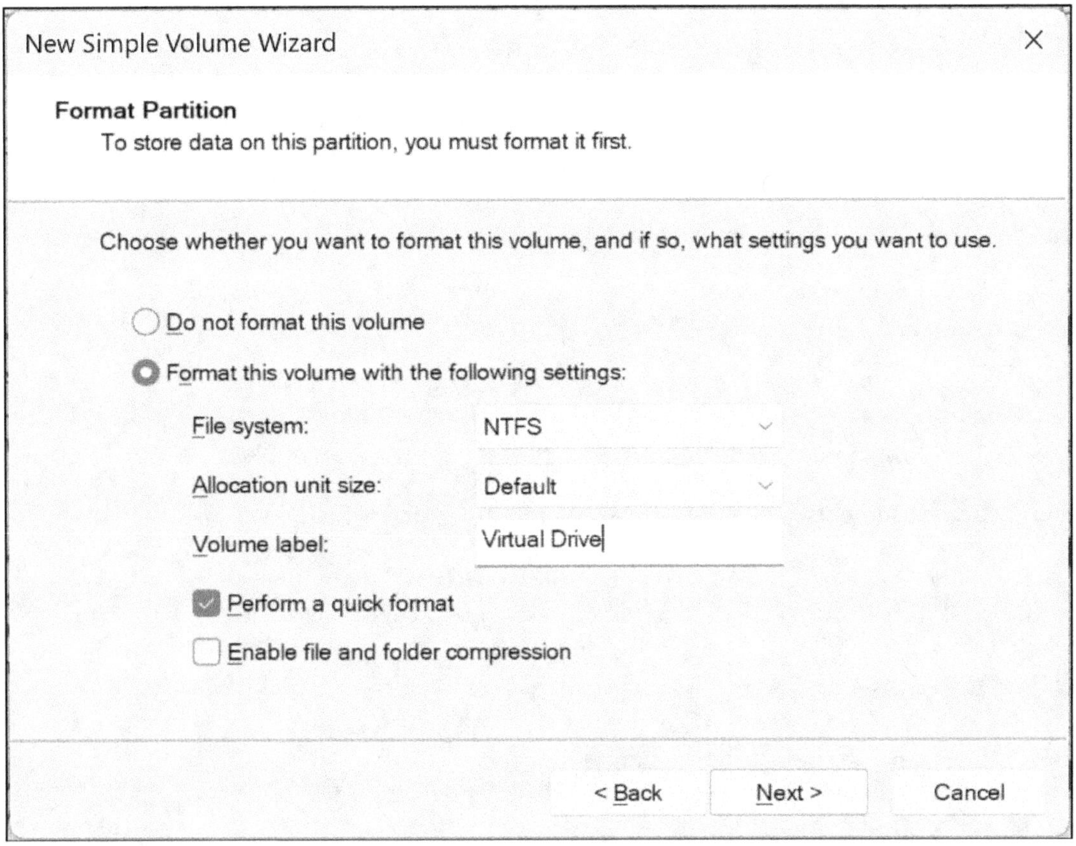

Chapter 7 – Preferences and Additional Features

Figure 7.29

After I click *Next* and then *Finish*, my new hard disk will be ready to use in Windows and will show up with the other drives belonging to the computer.

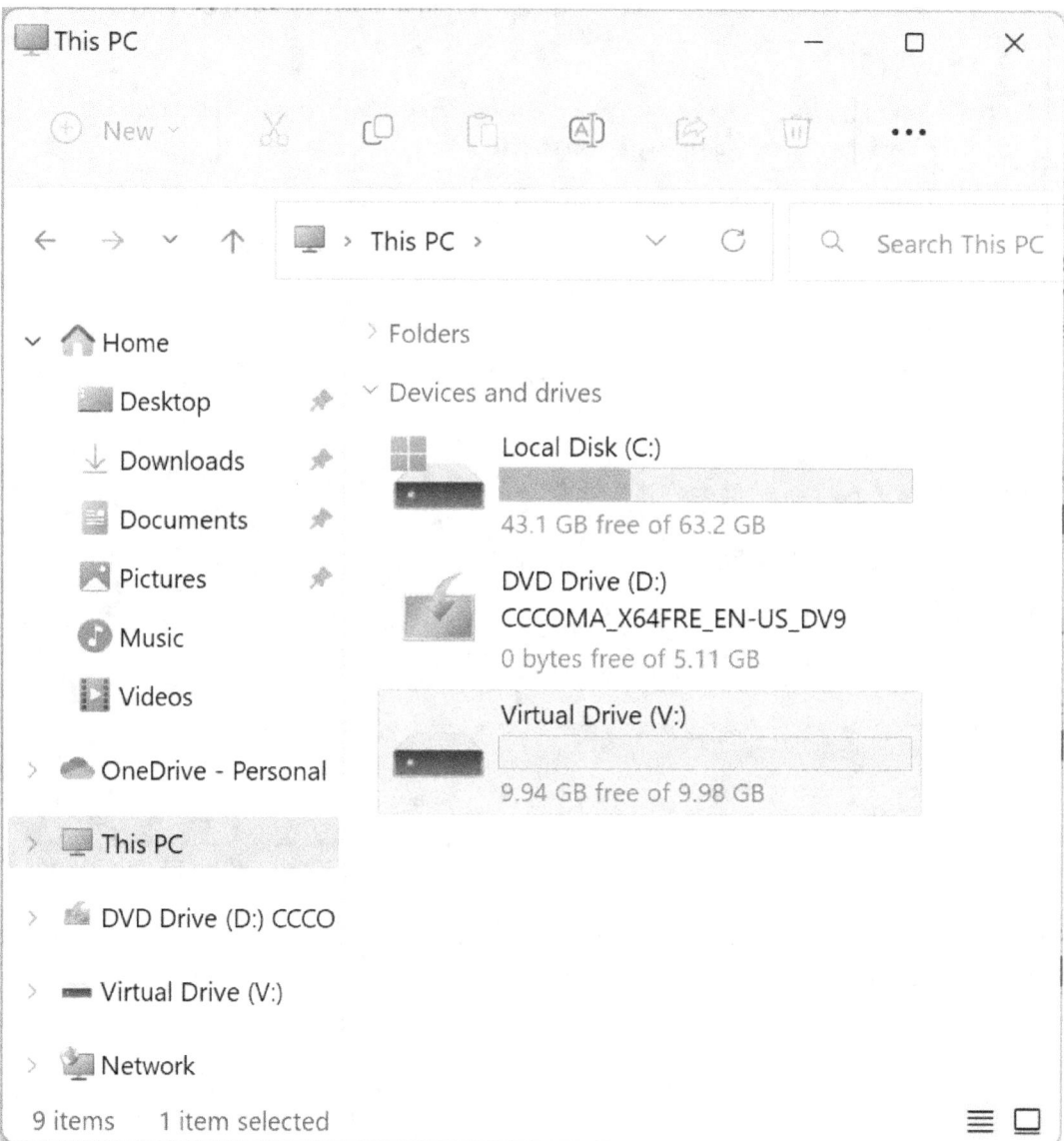

Figure 7.30

Later in the chapter, I will go over how to extend the size of a hard disk and then how to extend the size of the volume in Windows, so it uses this additional space.

Adding Other Hardware to Your VMs

I just went over how to add an additional hard disk to your VM, but hard disks are not the only virtual hardware that you can add to your virtual machines. It's possible to add a wide variety of additional devices to your virtual machines to enhance their functionality.

Chapter 7 – Preferences and Additional Features

In this section, I will show you what other types of hardware you can add to your VMs and where you need to go to do so. If you are not able to change a particular setting and notice that the option is greyed out, it's most likely because the VM is running and you can't make the changes until you shut it down.

RAM (Random Access Memory)
Adjusting RAM is one of the most commonly changed hardware configurations you will be performing with your virtual machines. Since your VMs use your host's RAM, you want to make sure not to assign them too much otherwise your host computer's performance might suffer.

You can change the amount of RAM for your virtual machines from the *System* setting and then the *Motherboard* tab.

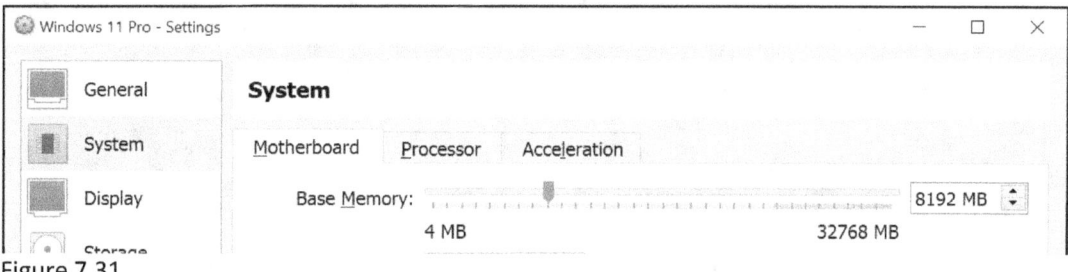
Figure 7.31

CPU\Processor
When you create a VM with the default settings, it will give it just one virtual processor and normally you will be fine with just the one. But if you need to add an additional CPU then you can do so from the *System* section and then the Processor tab in the VM settings.

The number of virtual processors you can add will depend on what physical processor or processors you have in your host computer. In my case, I can add up to 16 processors as shown in figure 7.32.

Chapter 7 – Preferences and Additional Features

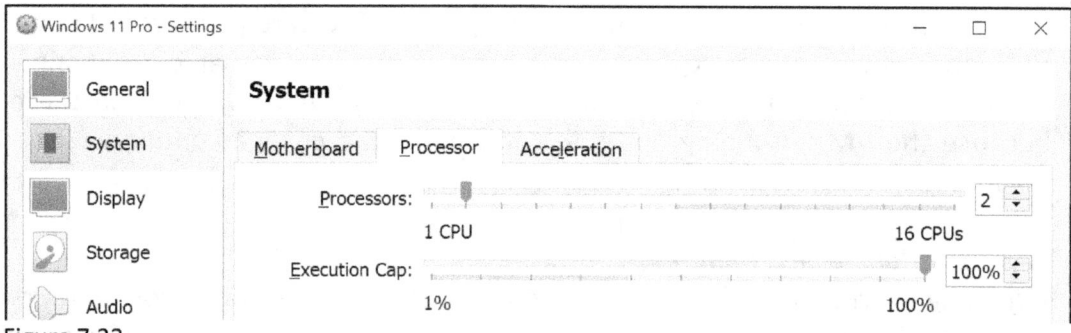
Figure 7.32

Monitors

If you are the type who works in multiple programs at the same time then having more than one monitor comes in very handy. To add additional monitors to your VM you will need to go to the *Display* settings and change the *Monitor Count*.

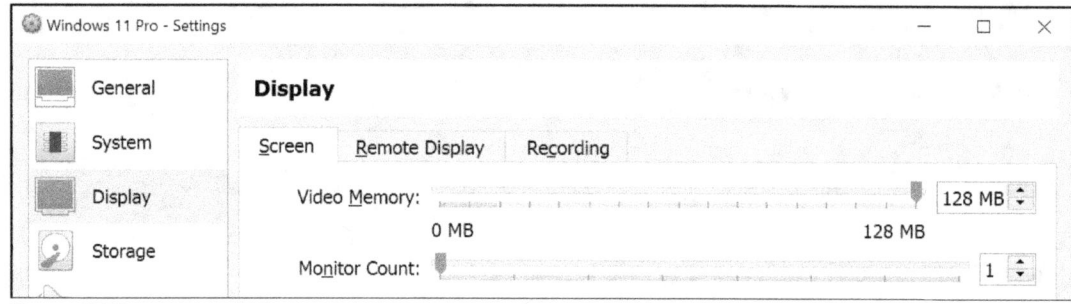
Figure 7.33

Optical Drive (CD\DVD)

Adding a new optical drive is similar to adding a new hard disk and is done from the same place (Storage) where I added the new hard disk from in the previous section.

To add a new optical drive you need to have your storage controller highlighted since the optical drive is attached to the controller. Then you will click on the plus sign CD icon as shown in figure 7.34 to add the new optical drive.

Chapter 7 – Preferences and Additional Features

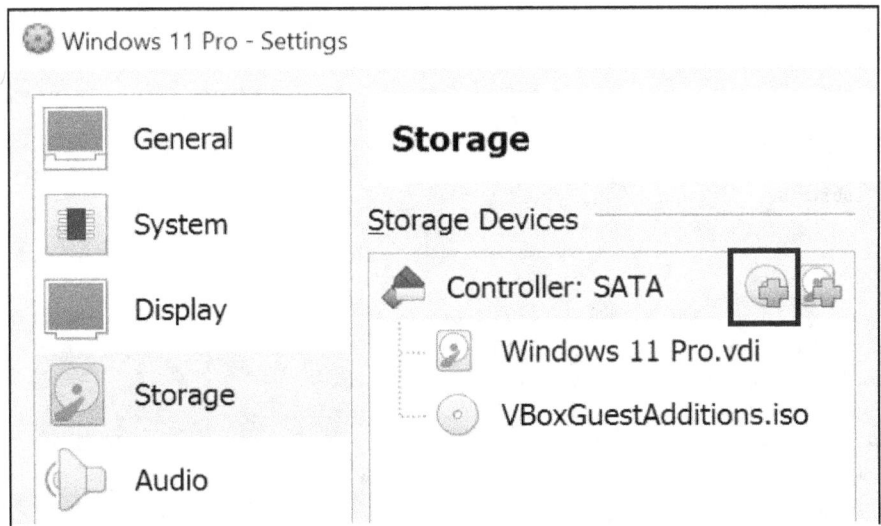

Figure 7.34

You will then be prompted to either add the drive with an attached CD\DVD or ISO file, or you can leave the drive empty and add your attached disk later by clicking the *Leave Empty* button.

The items with the exclamation points next to them indicate ISO files that are no longer accessible. This can happen if the ISO files have been moved or deleted. The *Attached* section shows drives\ISO files that are currently attached to VMs.

Chapter 7 – Preferences and Additional Features

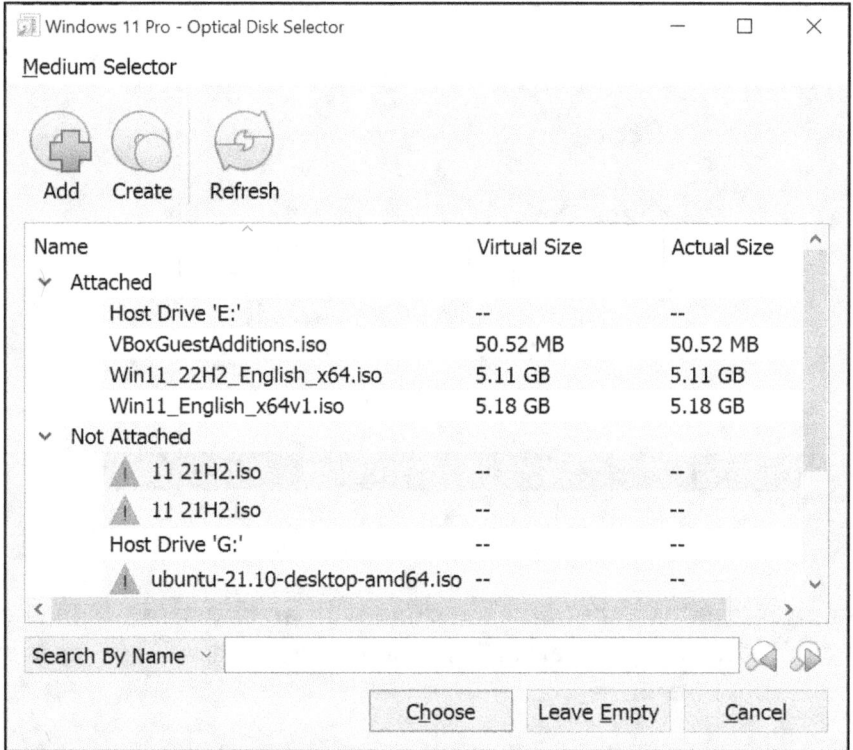

Figure 7.35

Network Adapter

There might come a time when you need to add another network adapter to your VM to do things such as connect your VM to two different networks if you were using it as a firewall for example.

To add another network adapter you need to go to the Network settings for the VM and then click on one of the other unused network adapter tabs and check the box that says *Enable Network Adapter*. Then you will be able to select what type of connection you want to use with this new adapter as well as which physical network adapter from your host that you want to use, assuming you have more than one.

Chapter 7 – Preferences and Additional Features

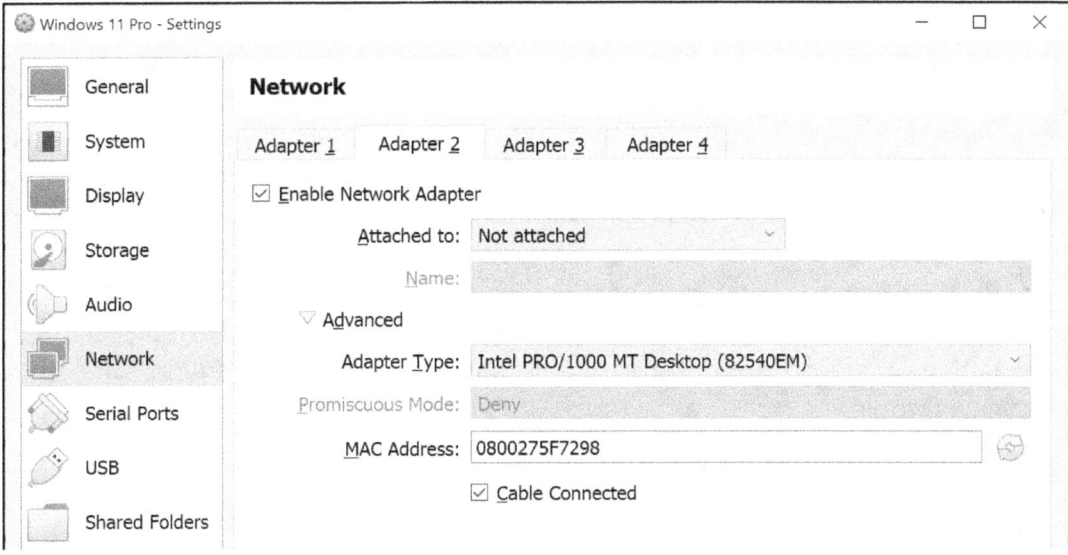

Figure 7.36

Serial Ports

I mentioned serial ports back in Chapter 5 and your VM will not have one configured by default. If you do need to add one you will do so from the Serial Ports section. You can add up to four serial ports to your virtual machine.

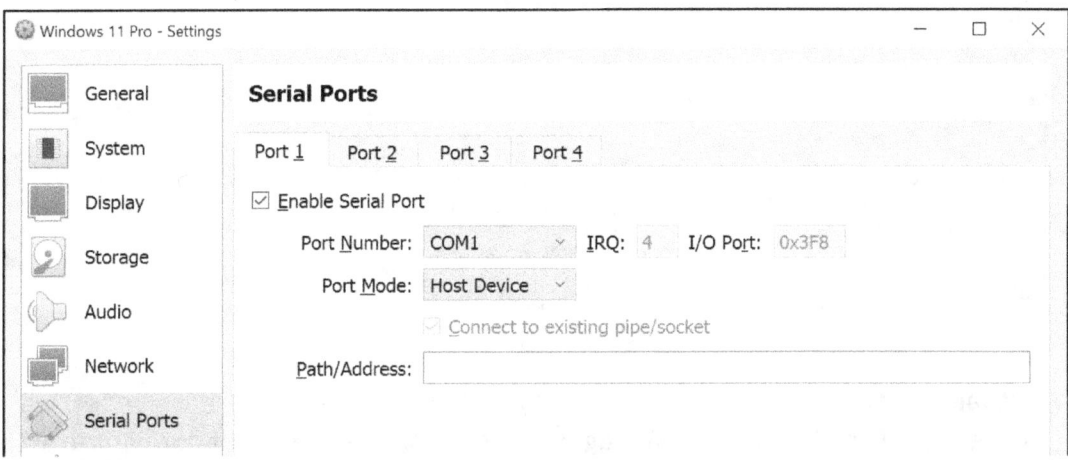

Figure 7.37

When configuring serial ports you will need to know what settings are required for your ports to make them work properly. For example, the *Host Device* Port Mode will connect the virtual serial port to a physical serial port on your host computer while the *Raw File* Port Mode will send the virtual serial port output to a file to capture diagnostic data etc.

Chapter 7 – Preferences and Additional Features

USB Devices

I went over how to add a USB device in Chapter 5 but to refresh your memory, you can add devices from the USB section in the VM settings by checking the box that says Enable USB controller and then choosing which version of USB you would like to use. If your computer is a little older and you don't know if you have USB 3.0 ports then you might want to use the USB 2.0 option.

To add a USB device from your host you can click on the USB icon with the + sign on it and then choose one of the devices from your computer. If you click on the icon above that you can enter in the details for a custom USB filter which is an advanced topic.

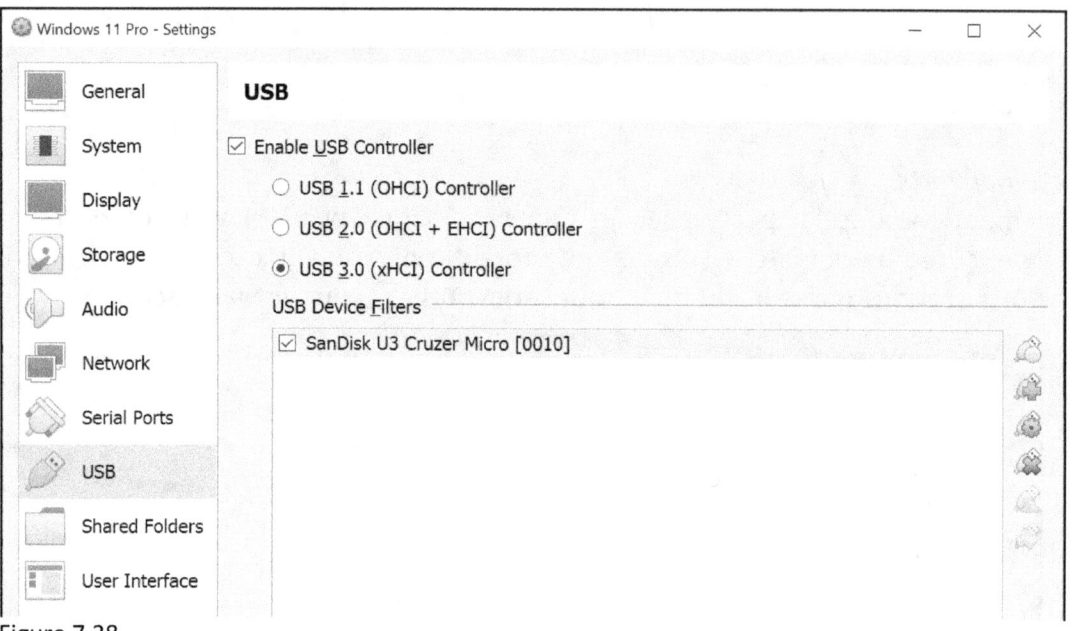
Figure 7.38

VirtualBox Manager Tools

At the top of the VirtualBox Manager window, above the list of configured VMs, there is an icon that says Tools which gives you six choices and each one of these choices contains some potentially useful information.

Chapter 7 – Preferences and Additional Features

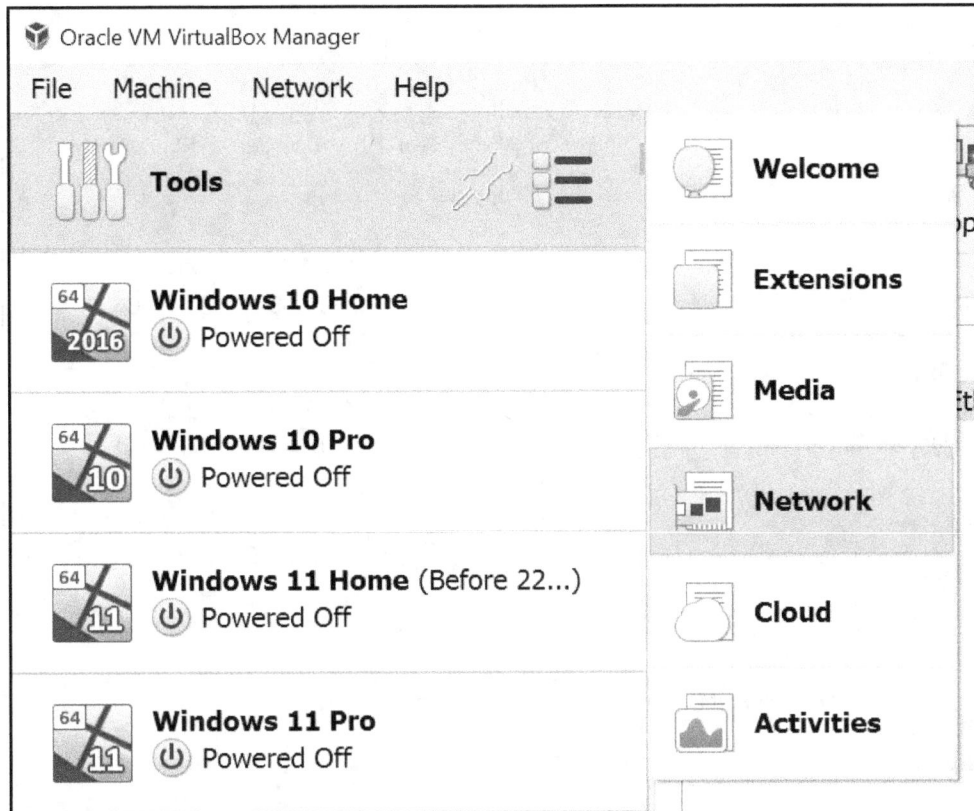

Figure 7.39

Welcome
The first option on the list is the Welcome screen. There is not a whole lot here but from here you have quick access to do things such as view the VirtualBox Manager preferences and create a new virtual machine.

Extensions
Here is where you can go to see your installed VirtualBox Extension Pack as well as install an updated version or remove the current version.

Media
The Media section or *Virtual Media Manager* as it's also called, will show you a listing of all of the hard disks, optical disks and floppy disks you have in your entire VirtualBox environment. It will also show you the virtual and actual size of these disks. The *Virtual Size* is the space allocated for storage while the *Actual Size* is how much space is actually being used on the disk by the VM. Then below this list you can see various information about each disk such as its location and type.

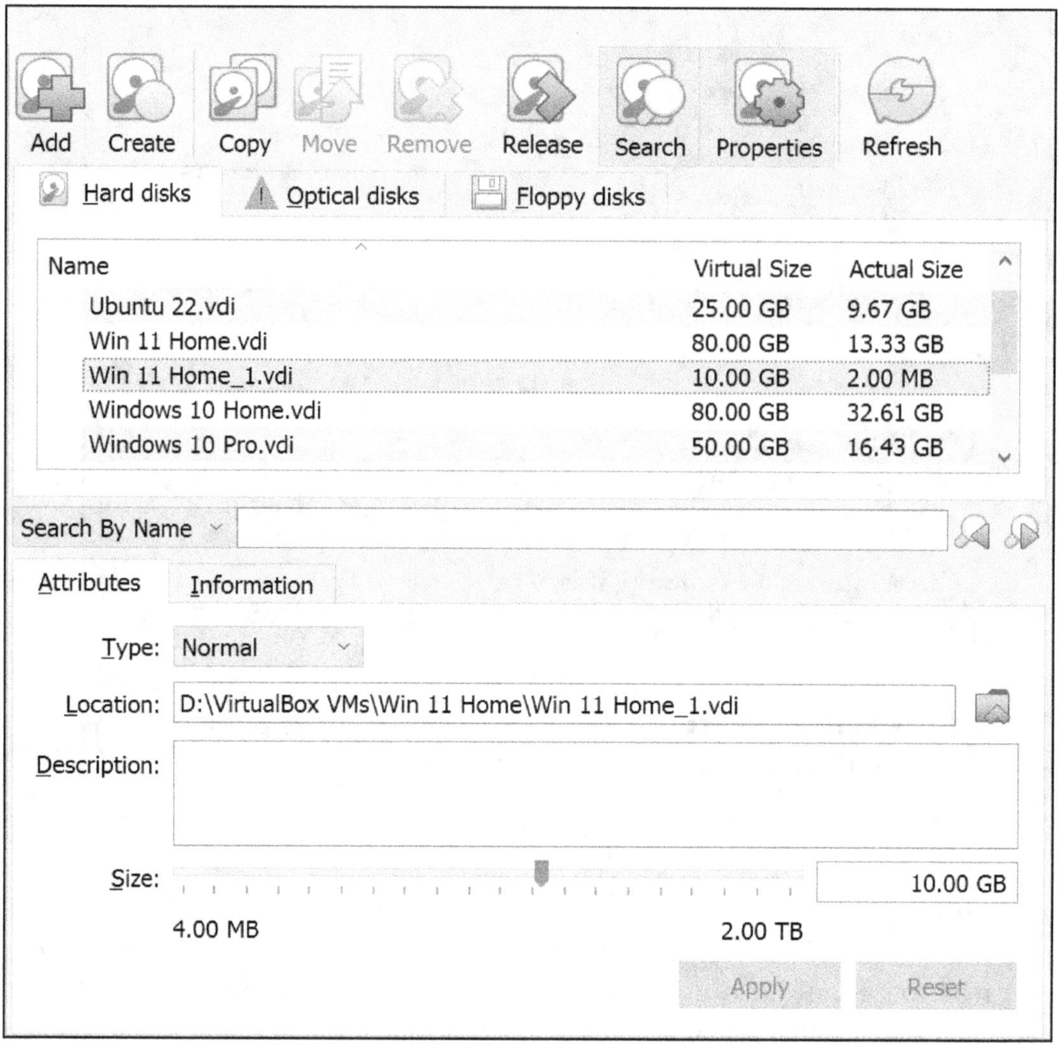

Chapter 7 – Preferences and Additional Features

Figure 7.40

If you have any issues with your disks, it will be indicated by a yellow exclamation point next to the disk name as you can see in figure 7.41 for the Ubuntu ISO image file. If I click on this disk and go to the Information tab, it tells me that the disk is not attached to any VM.

Chapter 7 – Preferences and Additional Features

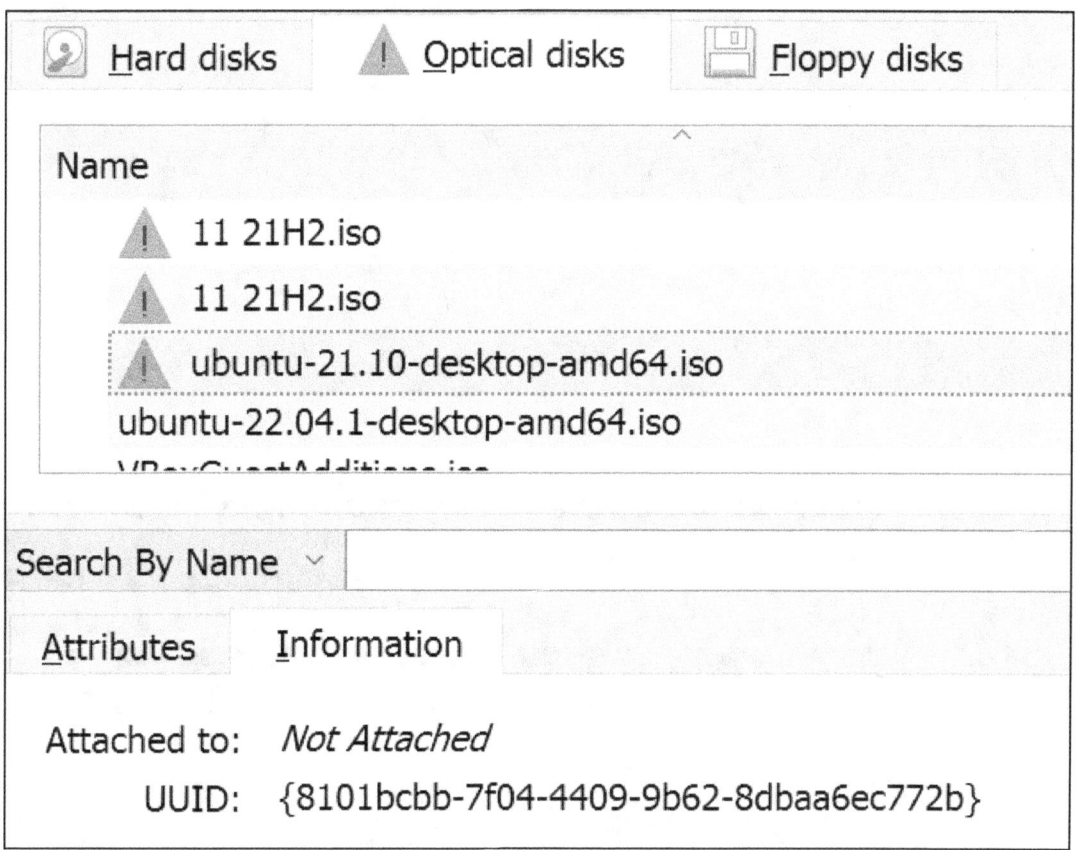

Figure 7.41

If you take a look back and figure 7.40 you will see there is a slider that will allow you to increase the size of an existing virtual disk. So if you need more space in one of your VMs you can increase the size of the disk rather than add a new one. Just be sure to back up your data first before doing this in case something goes wrong.

For example, I will increase the size of the hard disk that I added in the previous section on adding a new hard disk from 10 GB to 20 GB using the slider. Then I will boot up the VM and go back to Disk Management and I will see that I now have 10 GB of unallocated space as seen in figure 7.42.

Chapter 7 – Preferences and Additional Features

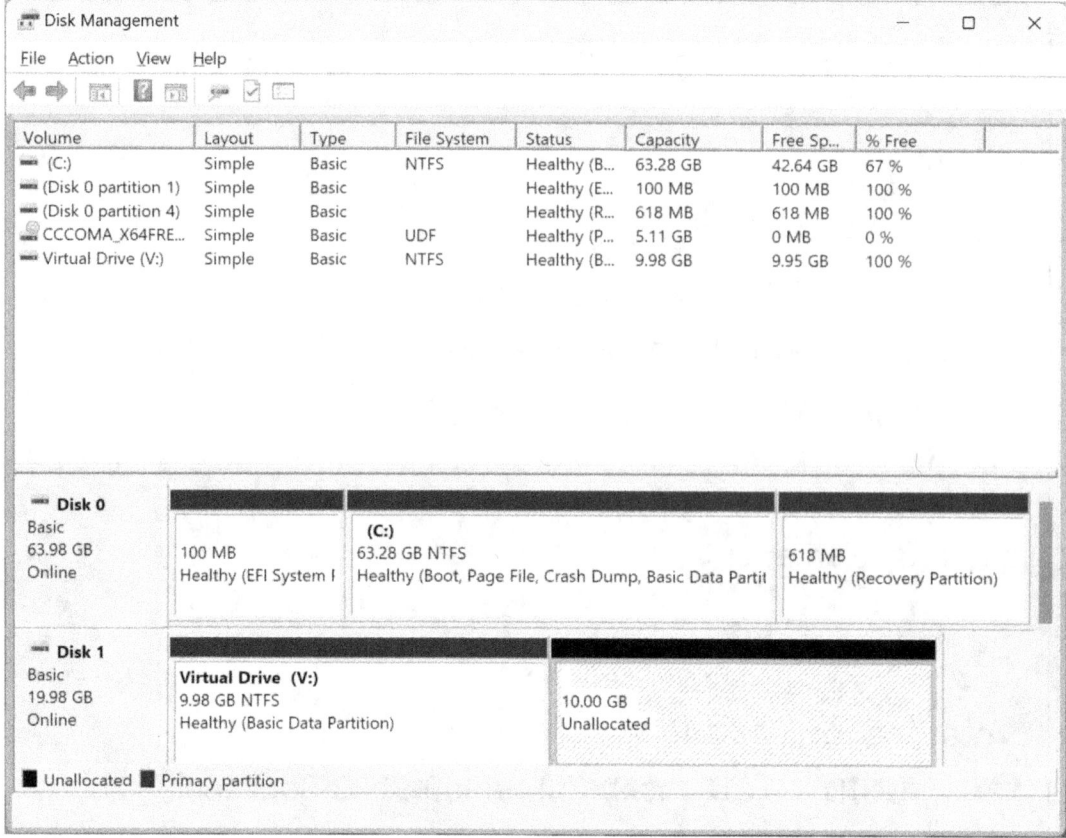

Figure 7.42

From here I can either make a new volume and give it a new drive letter or I can right click on my Virtual Drive (V:) volume and choose the *Extend Volume* option. Windows will then automatically add this new free space to my existing volume and show me the before and after size as seen in figure 7.43.

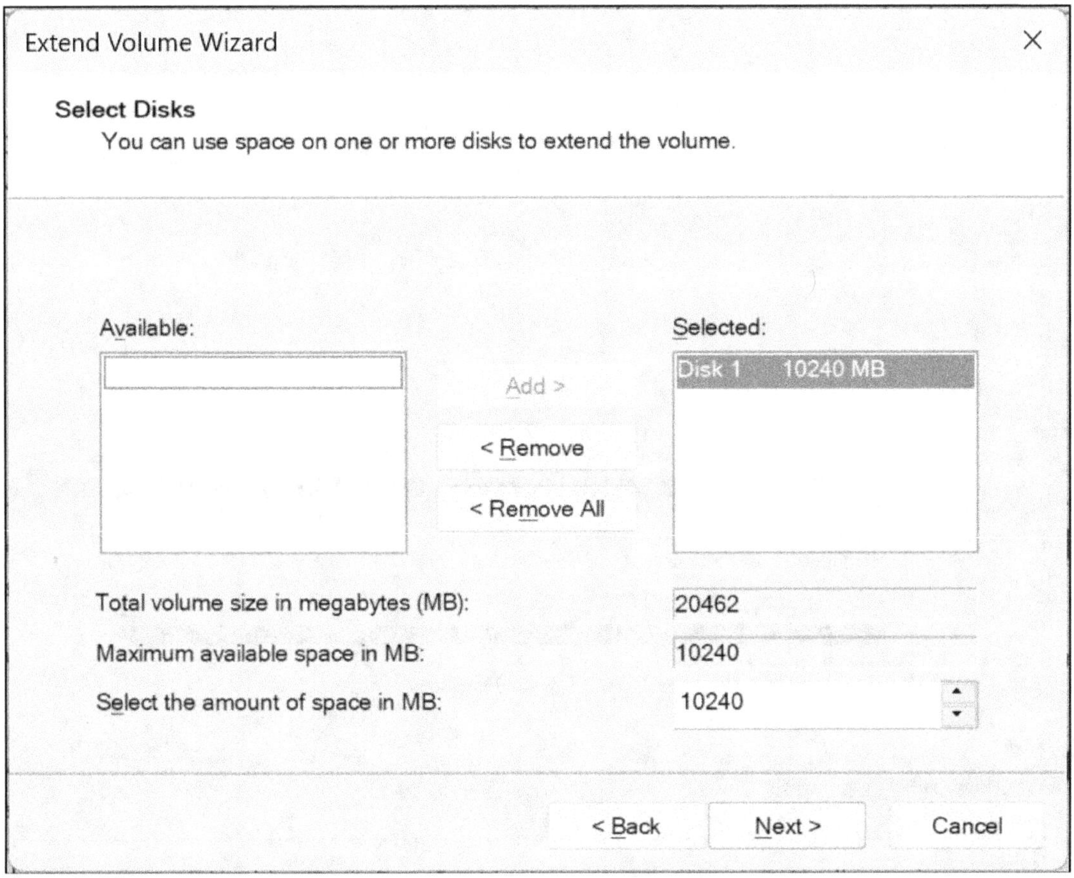

Chapter 7 – Preferences and Additional Features

![Extend Volume Wizard dialog showing Select Disks page with Disk 1 10240 MB selected, Total volume size 20462, Maximum available space 10240, Select the amount of space 10240]

Figure 7.43

After I finish the wizard, I will then have a hard disk that went from 10 GB to 20 GB as seen in figure 7.44 (V: drive).

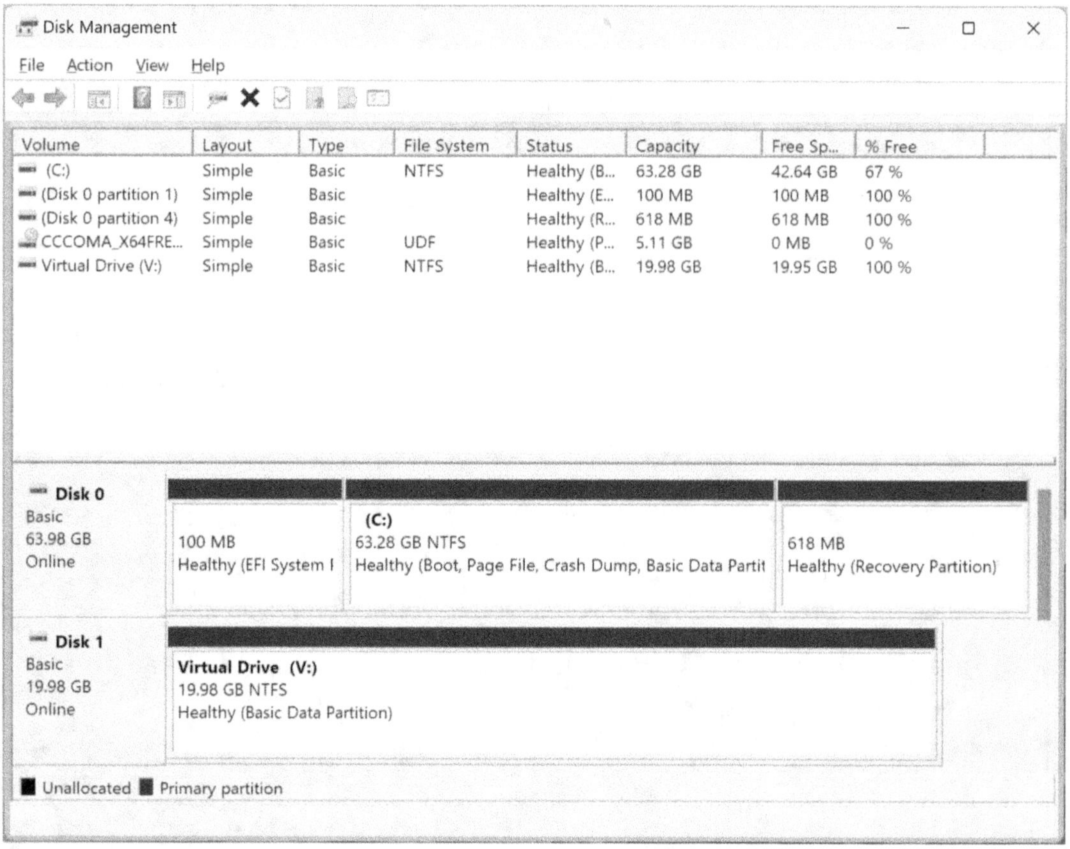

Chapter 7 – Preferences and Additional Features

![Disk Management screenshot]

Figure 7.44

 Extending the hard drive size of a drive is easy but if you want to increase the size of the system drive where your OS is installed then you really need to be careful because there is a greater chance of messing things up and ending up with a computer that won't even boot up.

Network

Back to our discussion on the VirtualBox Manager Tools section, next we have the Network settings which will show you the IP address assigned to your host computer for the VirtualBox network as shown in figure 7.45. You might have noticed under *Adapter* that it is set to *Configure Adapter Manually* even though VirtualBox configured this for me automatically so don't get confused if you see the same thing on your computer.

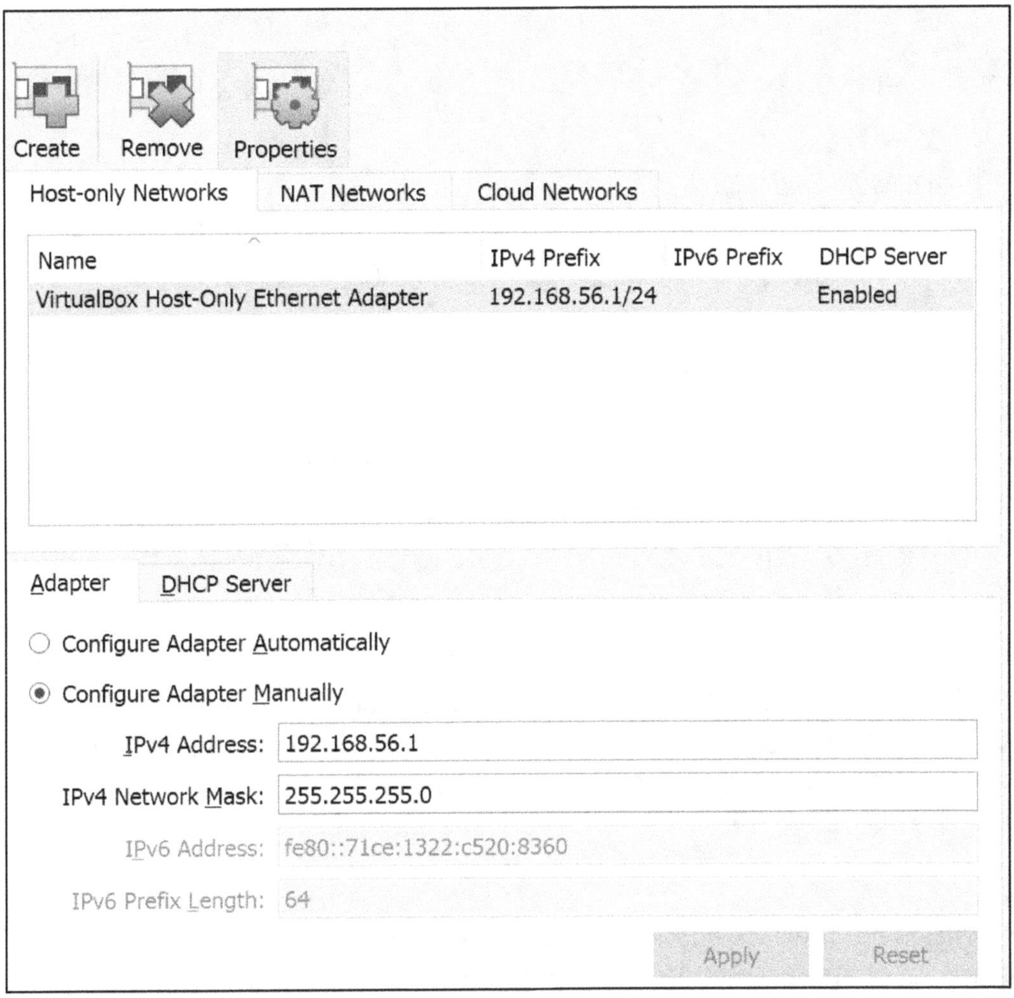

Chapter 7 – Preferences and Additional Features

Figure 7.45

Clicking on the *DHCP Server* tab will show you the IP address assigned to the internal VirtualBox DHCP server The *Lower Address Bound* and *Upper Address Bound* IP addresses shows the range of IP addresses that VirtualBox will assign to your VMs as needed when they boot up.

Chapter 7 – Preferences and Additional Features

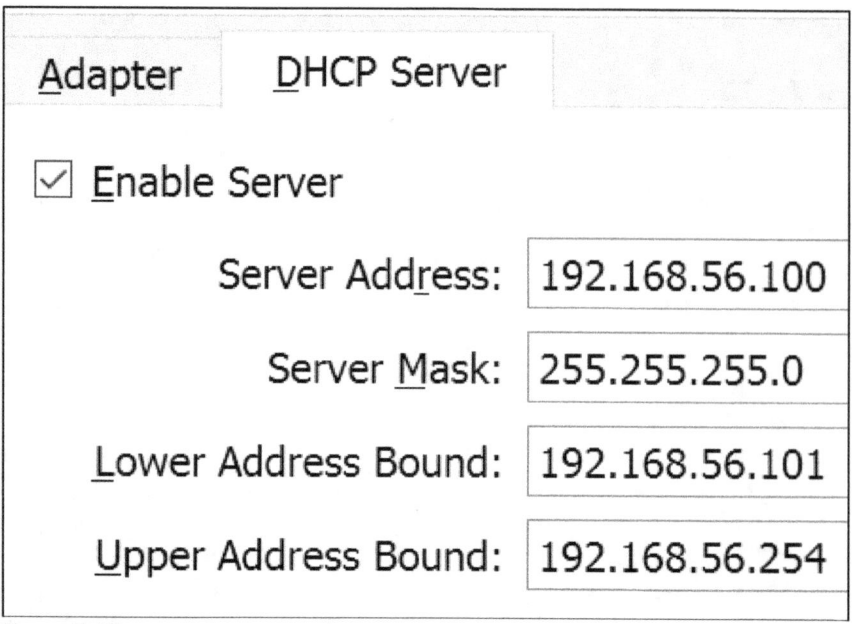

Figure 7.46

With this configuration, VirtualBox can assign IP addresses to up to 153 virtual machines. You can change this range if you like but just make sure not to use the IP address assigned to your host (192.168.56.1 in my case) and don't go any higher than 192.168.56.**254**.

Cloud
The Oracle Cloud Infrastructure is an advanced topic but what it boils down to is that it's a cloud based infrastructure where you can run your virtualized environment on Oracles servers online and use their resources for your virtual machines rather than rely on the resources of your host computer.

Figure 7.47

To use this service you will need to do some additional configuration to your VirtualBox environment and also be prepared to pay a monthly fee. If you click on the *Try* button you will be taken to the signup page where you can begin the trial.

Chapter 7 – Preferences and Additional Features

Exporting and Importing Virtual Machines
VirtualBox has the capabilities to export your virtual machines so they can be imported into another instance of VirtualBox running on a different host. The process is fairly simple and is done from the *File* menu by clicking on *Export Appliance*.

When you choose this option, you will be prompted to select which one of your VMs you want to export. For my example, I will export my Windows 11 Pro VM for this example. If you take a look at figure 7.83 you will notice that there is an Expert Mode for this procedure as well but for now, I will just stick with using the Guided Mode.

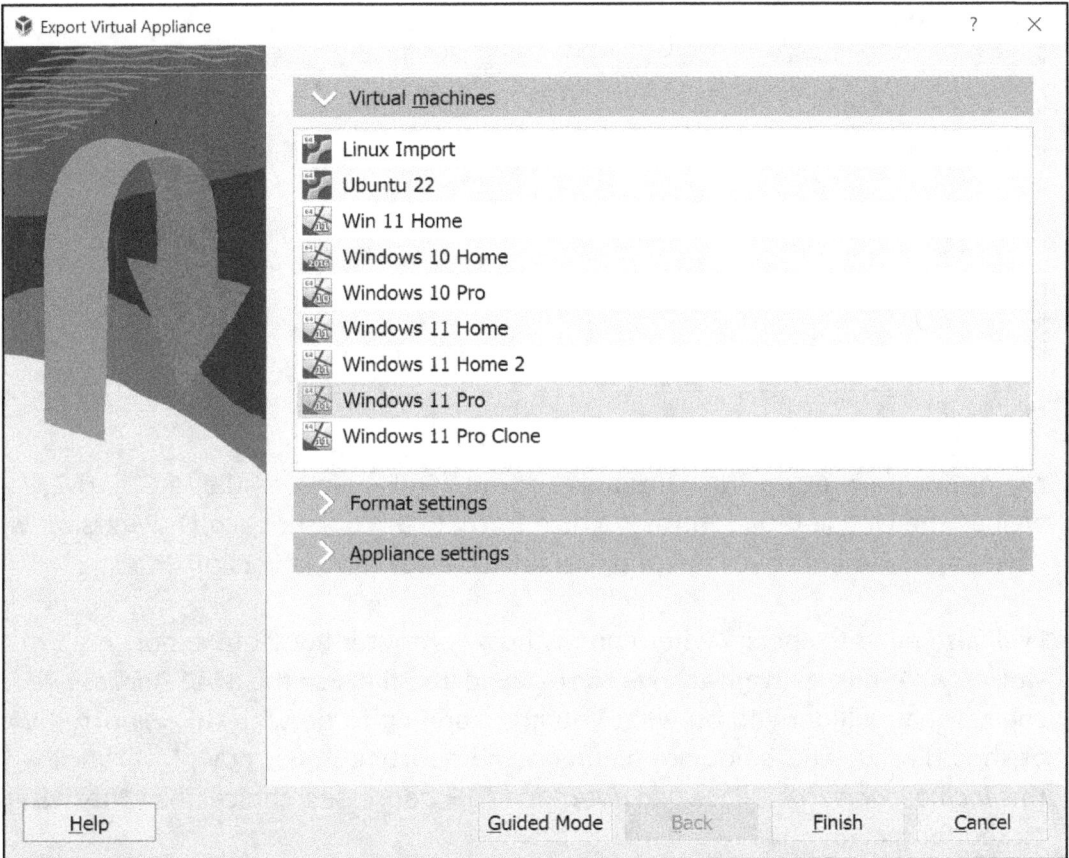

Figure 7.48

I will then need to choose the format that I wish to export my VM in.

Chapter 7 – Preferences and Additional Features

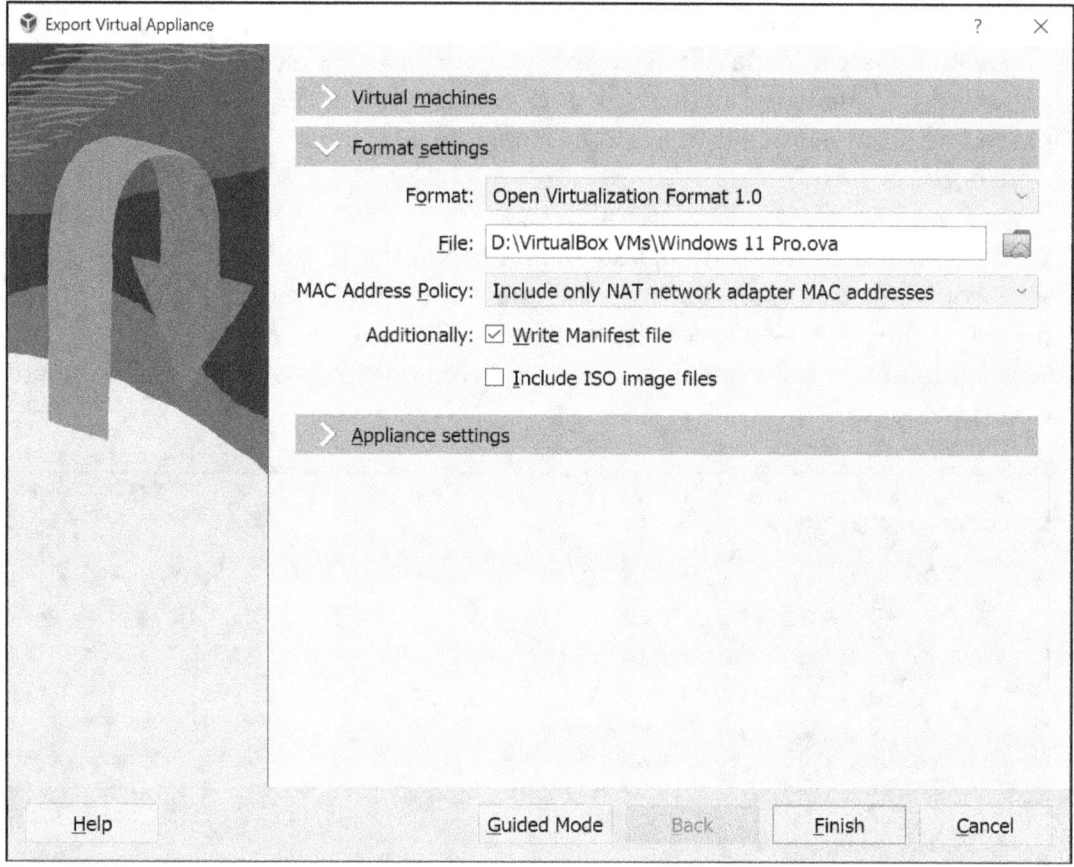

Figure 7.49

My options are Open Virtualization Format (OVF) versions 0.9, 1.0 and 2.0 as well as the Oracle Cloud Infrastructure format. Of course, each OVF version will have improvements over the prior version so I will choose version 2.0.

I will also need to specify where on my host computer I want to export my VM as well as what name I want to give to the exported file. For the *MAC Address Policy* choice, that will depend on what you are planning to do with this exported VM, or should I say, where you are planning on importing it. For now, I will stick with the *Include only NAT network adapter MAC addresses* choice that the wizard picked for me.

The *Write Manifest file* option is used to add control information to your OVF in order to prevent you from importing a damaged file to your new destination.

The *Include ISO Image File* option will include any attached ISO files that you are using with your VMs optical drive in the export. That way you will have them available for use when you import your VM at its new destination.

Chapter 7 – Preferences and Additional Features

Next, I will be prompted to add any information I might find useful to store with my exported VM or I can just leave the fields blank.

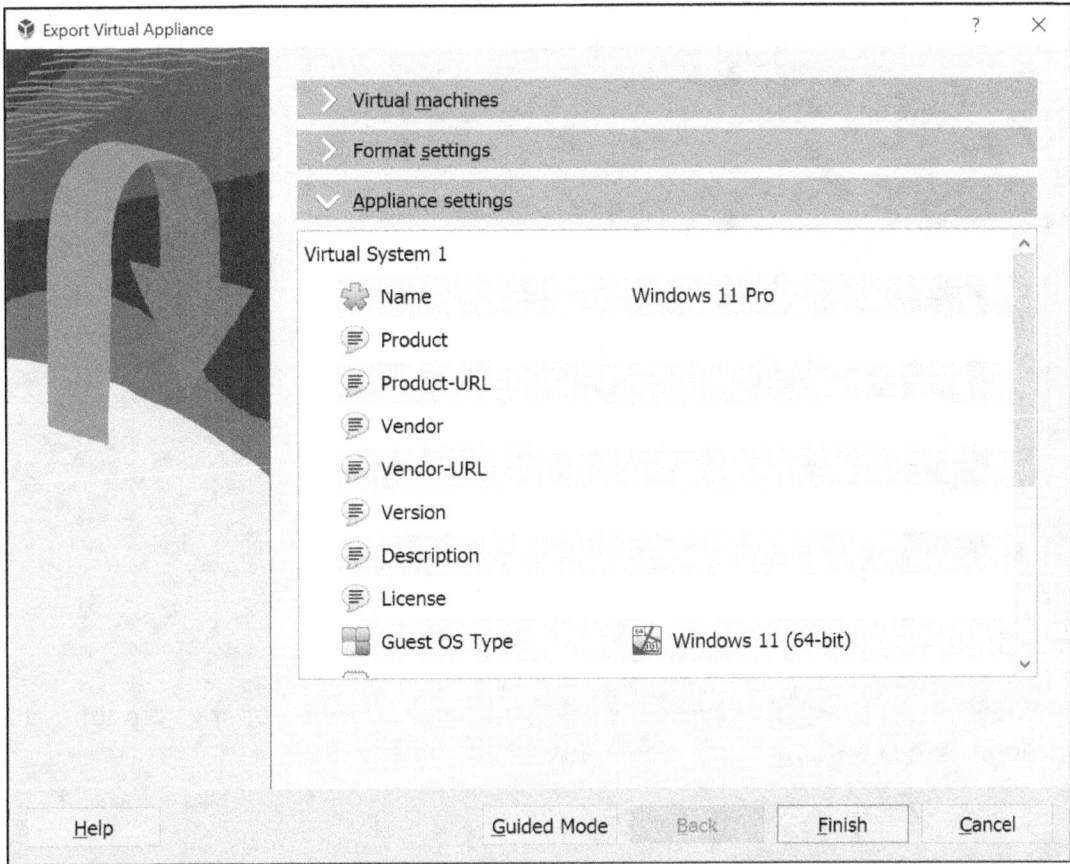

Figure 7.50

When I click on the *Finish* button, the process will begin and will take a little time based on how large your VM is in regard to hard disk size and any attached ISO files that you chose to export.

Chapter 7 – Preferences and Additional Features

Figure 7.51

When the process is complete, I will have a single OVA file on my computer that contains the contents of the entire virtual machine.

Figure 7.52

Chapter 7 – Preferences and Additional Features

Importing a VM is just as easy as exporting one and is kind of like doing the export process, only backward. Once I click the *Import* button I will need to browse to the location of the OVA file I have stored on my computer, DVD, flash drive, network location etc. and click on Next.

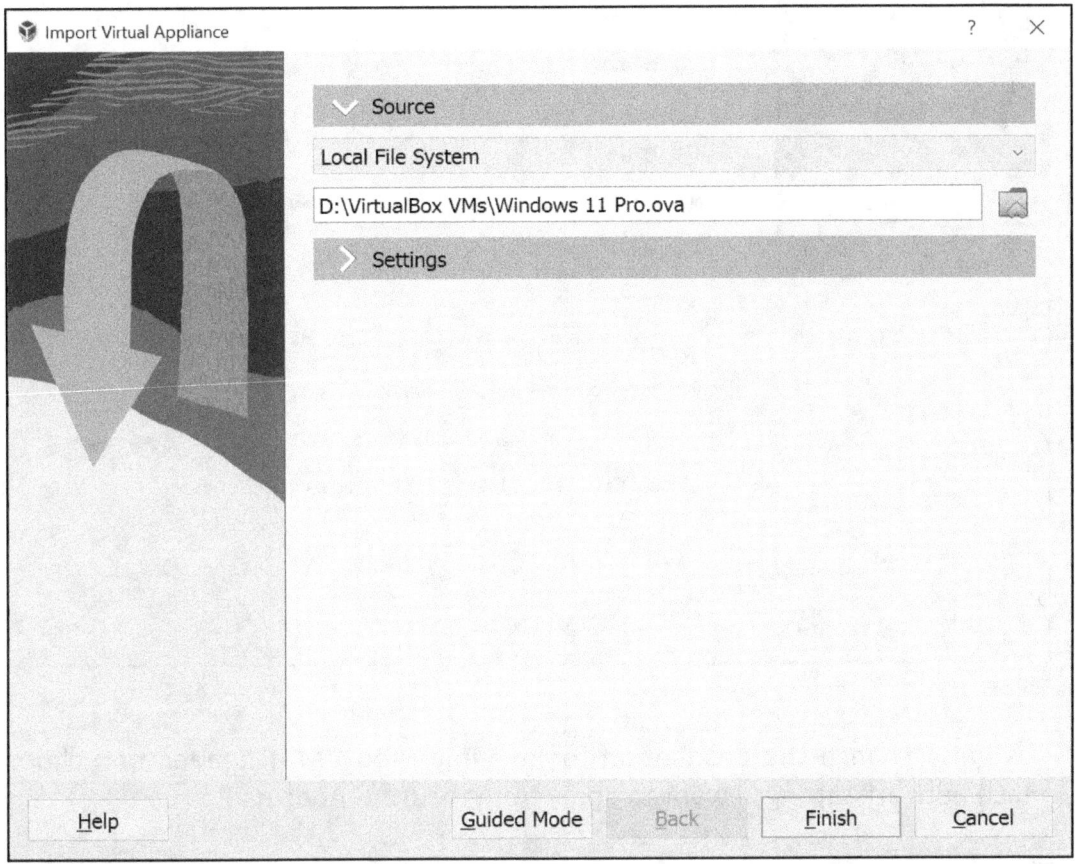

Figure 7.53

As you can see in figure 7.54, all of the details about my VM are summarized and it also includes the information I added from figure 7.50. If needed, I can remove certain devices such as the DVD drive, USB controller, sound card and network adapter by unchecking the appropriate boxes.

Chapter 7 – Preferences and Additional Features

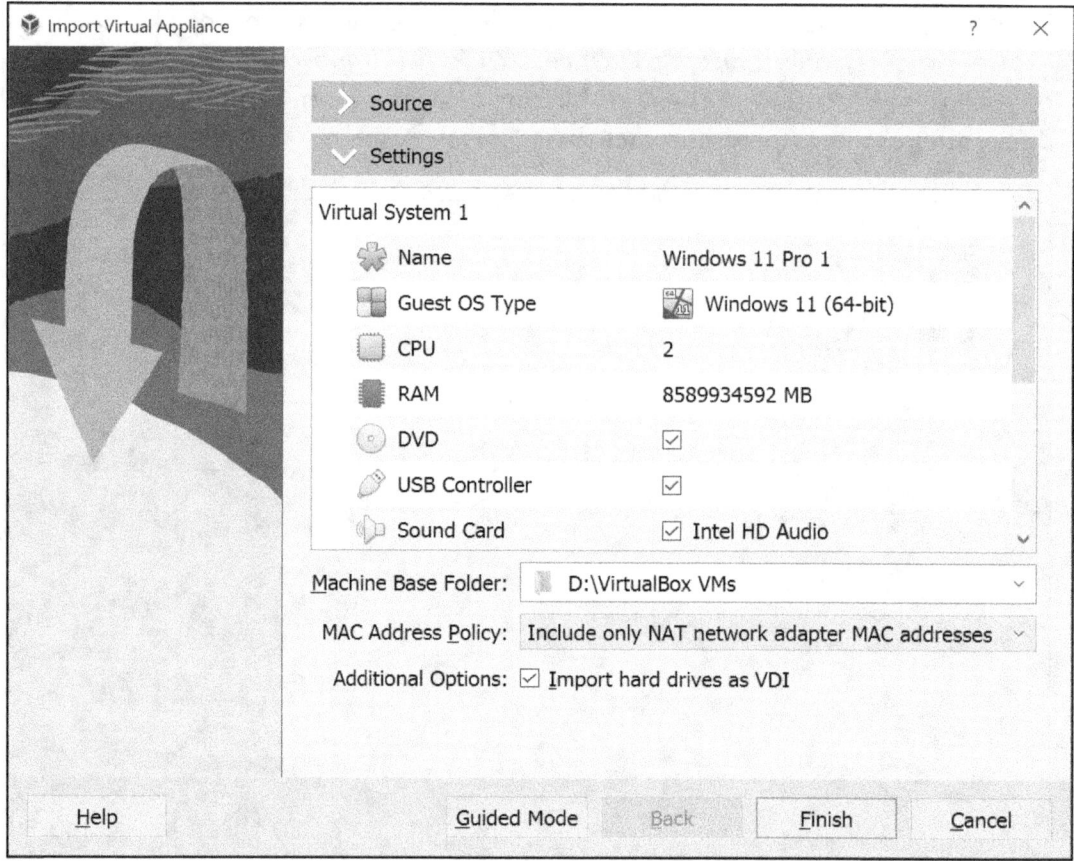

Figure 7.54

I can also change the destination for this imported VM if needed and choose which network settings I want to apply from the MAC Address Policy.

The import process will look very similar to the export process and can also take a bit of time.

Chapter 7 – Preferences and Additional Features

Figure 7.55

After the import is complete, I will have my new VM listed with all my other virtual machines in the VirtualBox Manager and you will notice that its named Windows 11 Pro **Clone**.

Chapter 7 – Preferences and Additional Features

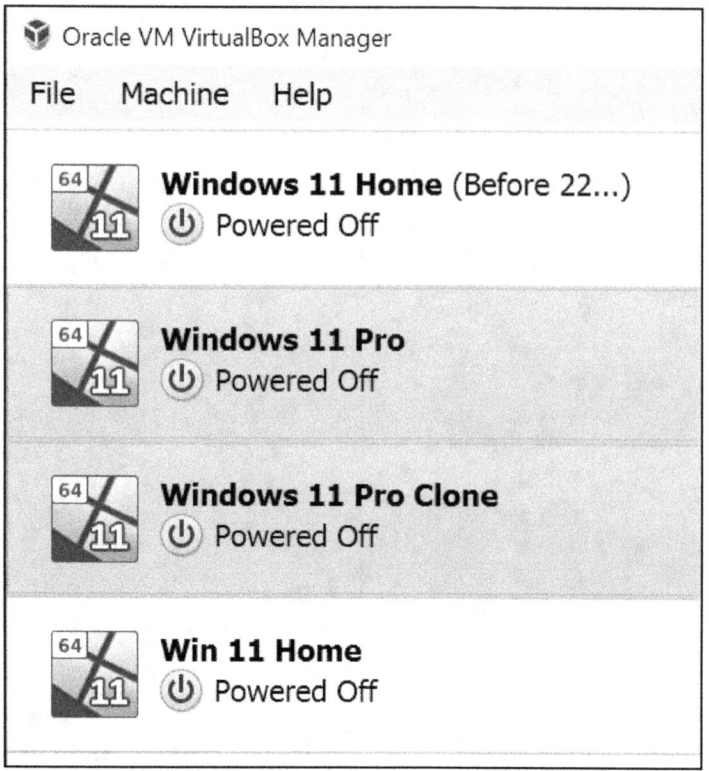

Figure 7.56

Now that you know how to create and manage virtual machines using VirtualBox it's time for you to get started creating your own virtual environment to use for training, testing or just for fun. The more you use VirtualBox, the easier it gets!

What's Next?

Now that you have read through this book and learned how to create virtual machines and get them working together, you might be wondering what you should do next. Well, that depends on where you want to go. Are you happy with what you have learned, or do you want to further your knowledge on virtualization or even take the next step and learn about enterprise level software such as VMware vSphere or Microsoft Hyper-V?

If you do want to expand your knowledge, then you can look for some more advanced books on virtualization or focus on a specific technology such as cloud platforms, if that's the path you choose to follow. Focus on mastering the basics, and then apply what you have learned when going to more advanced material.

There are many great video resources as well, such as Pluralsight or CBT Nuggets, which offer online subscriptions to training videos of every type imaginable. YouTube is also a great source for instructional videos if you know what to search for.

If you are content in being a proficient VirtualBox user that knows more than your friends, then just keep on practicing what you have learned. Don't be afraid to poke around with some of the settings and tools that you normally don't use and see if you can figure out what they do without having to research it since learning by doing is the most effective method to gain new skills.

Thanks for reading **VirtualBox Made Easy**. You can also check out the other books in the Made Easy series for additional computer related information and training. You can get more information on my other books on my Computers Made Easy Book Series website.

https://www.madeeasybookseries.com/

What's Next?

You should also check out my computer tips website, as well as follow it on Facebook to find more information on all kinds of computer topics.

www.onlinecomputertips.com
https://www.facebook.com/OnlineComputerTips/

About the Author

James Bernstein has been working with various companies in the IT field for over 20 years, managing technologies such as SAN and NAS storage, VMware, backups, Windows Servers, Active Directory, DNS, DHCP, Networking, Microsoft Office, Photoshop, Premiere, Exchange, and more.

He has obtained certifications from Microsoft, VMware, CompTIA, ShoreTel, and SNIA, and continues to strive to learn new technologies to further his knowledge on a variety of subjects.

He is also the founder of the website onlinecomputertips.com, which offers its readers valuable information on topics such as Windows, networking, hardware, software, and troubleshooting. James writes much of the content himself and adds new content on a regular basis. The site was started in 2005 and is still going strong today.

www.ingramcontent.com/pod-product-compliance
Lightning Source LLC
Chambersburg PA
CBHW081429220526
45466CB00008B/2317